Out of the Ashes

Out of the Ashes

Destruction and Reconstruction of

East Timor

James J. Fox and Dionisio Babo Soares (Editors)

THE AUSTRALIAN NATIONAL UNIVERSITY

E PRESS

ANU

E PRESS

Published by the ANU E Press
The Australian National University
Canberra ACT 0200, Australia
Email: anuepress@anu.edu.au
Web: http://epress.anu.edu.au
Previously published by Crawford House Publishing Pty Ltd
Bathurst 2795 New South Wales, Australia

National Library of Australia Cataloguing-in-Publication entry

Out of the Ashes: Destruction and Reconstruction of East Timor

New ed.
ISBN 0 9751229 1 6
ISBN 0 9751229 0 8 (Online document)

1. East Timor – Politics and government. I. Fox, James J.,
1940– . II. Soares, Dionisio Babo.

320.95986

Typeset inhouse in Garamond
Cover design by Brendon McKinley

Contents

Foreword

Out of the Ashes: Destruction and Reconstruction of East Timor marks the beginning of what, I hope, will be a continuing assessment of East Timor's development as it enters the 21st century as the world's newest democracy. Like a phoenix, Timor Loro Sa'e will rise from its ashes to take its place in the community of nations.

The book provides an introduction to the culture and society of East Timor, discusses the political, diplomatic and military background to events in 1999 and then looks at the initial phase of the reconstruction. Looking to the future is now as important as assessing what has occurred in the past.

The 18 contributors to this volume represent a wide range of views. Several contributors were participants in the events that they describe and assess. I am particularly pleased that Fernando de Araujo has provided an account of the CNRT campaign for independence in which he was actively involved. Ian Martin, who headed the UNAMET mission for the popular consultation, provides his first reflections on the momentous events of 1999. Catharina Williams describes her experience as an electoral officer in the Suai area.

It is gratifying that among this international group of commentators, East Timorese contributors figure so prominently. Their contributions to this volume give some glimpse of the current dialogue that is now under way within East Timor. Increasingly East Timorese will be expected to contribute to international discussions.

I congratulate the editors, James J. Fox and Dionisio Babo Soares, for putting together this volume and all of the contributors for their valuable assistance in providing an understanding of East Timor at this crucial moment in the new nation's birth.

Xanana
Dili, 11 May 2000

Preface

As editors of this volume, we have endeavoured to assemble a collection of papers that provides an understanding of East Timorese society and of the momentous political, diplomatic and military events that occurred in 1999 as a result of the international agreement to carry out, under United Nations' supervision, a popular consultation on the future of the territory. In addition to providing this background, we have also endeavoured to provide an assessment of the critical events of August and September and of their implications for the future development of East Timor. Finally, we have extended this discussion of events to focus on the initial plans for reconstruction of East Timor. The volume is thus organised in three sections: Background, Assessment and Reconstruction.

Contributors to the volume have all followed recent events closely and many have been participants in these events. We are particularly pleased to have Ian Martin, who headed the UNAMET mission, offer his 'first reflections' on the popular consultation process. Equally valuable is the first-hand account by Fernando de Araujo of the CNRT campaign. Catharina Williams, a fluent speaker of Tetun, provides a brief account of her personal experiences as a United Nations electoral officer. Januar Achmad describes his involvement as a doctor in providing assistance to East Timorese in West Timor. Others like João Mariano Saldanha and Sarah Cliffe were participants on the World Bank-led Joint Assessment Mission that began reconstruction planning.

In addition to the editors, many contributors to this volume are associated with The Australian National University as faculty, research students or as graduates. Gavin Jones and Terry Hull are faculty members of the Research School of Social Sciences; Harold Crouch and Alan Dupont are faculty members of the Research School of Pacific and Asian Studies; Grayson J. Lloyd and Fiona Crockford are currently completing their PhDs; whereas Januar Achmad, Catharina Williams and Andrew MacIntyre are graduates of the University. It is this ANU network of common interest in, and continuing research on, East Timor and the region that provides the foundation for this volume.

The events of August and September 1999 gained unprecedented international attention for East Timor. The courage and resolution of the East Timorese people in expressing their right to self-determination and the destructive consequences visited upon them for their resolution were the subject of extensive and spectacular media coverage. Inevitably however, after such remarkable coverage, international attention has begun to wane.

Yet the story of East Timor continues. East Timor will be the first new nation to be established in the 21st century. It will have been brought to independence under the guidance of the United Nations in co-operation with the World Bank, the International Monetary Fund and other international organisations. East Timor's development will be a test-case for the capacities of the international community to put into practise its fundamental principles.

A majority of the contributors to this volume have maintained an active involvement in developments in East Timor. This book can therefore be considered as the first chapter in a longer account. It covers the period to the beginning of the year 2000. As editors, we have already begun preparation for the next volume that will carry forward the continuing story of East Timor. We thank all of the contributors to the book and look forward to further collaboration. We would also like to express particular thanks to Norma Chin for her efforts in producing this volume and for her care in providing editorial consistency and to Kay Dancey for her preparation of maps.

Preface to the ANU E Press publication

This volume is the first of an ANU E Press series that is intended to make critical research done at the Australian National University available to a wider readership. The original edition of *Out of the Ashes* was prepared at the ANU in the immediate aftermath of the establishment of the United Nations Mission Transitional Administration in East Timor (UNTAET). At the time there was a particular need for a publication that would provide a context for developments that were underway in 2000.

Fortunately at that time, there were a number of faculty and students at the ANU who had research interests in East Timor. We, as editors of this volume, turned to this group as core contributors. Harold Crouch, Alan Dupont, Terence Hull, and Gavin Jones were the faculty members who responded to our request; while Fiona Crockford and Grayson Lloyd were able to draw on material from their dissertations. Also included in this group were former students, Januar Achmad and Catharina Williams who had been actively involved in developments in Timor. Fernando da Araujo, who now heads the Democratic Party of East Timor, happened to be doing a course at the ANU and we called upon him for a particularly useful contribution.

We were also fortunate in being able to obtain contributions from Ian Martin who had been the Special Representative of the Secretary-General for the East Timor Popular Consultation and the Head of the United Nations Mission in East Timor (UNAMET) and Sarah Cliffe who was Chief of the World Bank Mission in East Timor. Andrew MacIntyre, now Director of the Asia Pacific School of Economics and Governance at the ANU, joined the group as did João Mariana Saldanha, John Haseman and Peter Timmer. Xanana Gusmão, then Head of the National Council of East Timorese Resistance and now President of the Republic of Timor Leste, honoured us with a foreword to the volume.

Our initial goal was to produce a timely and relevant volume.

That the book was in fact published in 2000, that it was quickly sold out and that it required a second printing is evidence that *Out of the Ashes* served a useful purpose.

Out of the Ashes remains a valuable source book on East Timor and on ideas and developments during a critical transition period. This, we feel, justifies its production now as an ANU E Press publication. As editors, we hope that *Out of the Ashes* may now reach an even wider audience and that the interest in East Timor and in the events that led to its independence will continue to be of international concern.

James J. Fox
Dionisio Babo Soares

Contributors

Chapter 1

James J. Fox is Director of the Research School of Pacific and Asian Studies at the Australian National University. He has been doing research on Timor since 1965. In 1999 he was an international observer for the Carter Center during the popular consultation and later was a member of the UN-World Bank Joint Assessment Mission to East Timor. In 2000, he was a member of the King's College team on defence and security. In 2001 and again in 2002, he was part of the Carter Center delegation for the Constituent Assembly and Presidential elections.

Chapter 2

Terence H. Hull holds the John C Caldwell Chair in Population, Health and Development at the Australian National University. He has worked on issues of Indonesian population since 1970. One of his major interests is in the political dimensions of population issues. He has written a number of papers on this topic in collaboration with his partner, Valerie Hull.

Chapter 3

Gavin W. Jones is currently Professor at the Asia Research Institute of the National University of Singapore. He was previously Professor of Demography in the Research School of Social Sciences at the Australian National University. He has written extensively on the demography of Indonesia and South-east Asia. He directed the recently completed Indonesia-Australia Population-Related Research for Development Planning and Development Assistance Project, funded by AusAID. In connection with that project, he made one brief visit to Timor Timur.

Chapter 4

Dionisio Babo Soares is a doctoral student in anthropology in the Research School of Pacific and Asian Studies at the Australian National

University. His research is focused on local political and social developments in East Timor during the transition to independence. He currently works for the Asia Foundation in East Timor.

Chapter 5

Grayson J. Lloyd is a PhD candidate in Pacific and Asian History in the Research School of Pacific and Asian Studies of the Australian National University. His thesis is centred on the interaction between elites, ideology and conceptions of nationalism in the construction of Indonesia's foreign policy during the Soeharto regime.

Chapter 6

Fernando de Araujo is the founder and Secretary-General of RENETIL (*Resistência Nacional dos Estudantes de Timor Leste*). In November 1991, he was charged with 'subversion against the state' and sentenced to prison where he spent six-and-a-half years in Cipinang with Xanana Gusmão and other East Timorese prisoners. During the CNRT campaign for the referendum, he was head of the Section on Social Communication. He is currently a member of Parliament and the Head of the Democratic Party of Timor Leste.

Chapter 7

Catharina Williams (née van Klinken) currently works for the Peace Corp in East Timor. In 1999 she served as a United Nations district electoral officer in the region of Suai. Under the name Catharina van Klinken, she is the author of *A Grammar of the Fehan Dialect of Tetun* (Pacific Linguistics, Research School of Pacific and Asian Studies, Canberra 1999), for which she was awarded a PhD in linguistics at the Australian National University.

Chapter 8

Ian Martin was Special Representative of the Secretary-General for the East Timor Popular Consultation and Head of the United Nations Mission in East Timor (UNAMET). From 1986 to 1992, he was Secretary-General of Amnesty International and has worked for United Nations human rights missions in Haiti and Rwanda, as Special Adviser to the UN High Commissioner for Human Rights, and as Deputy High Representative for Human Rights in Bosnia and Herzegovina. He is presently the Vice President of the International Center for Transitional Justice.

Chapter 9

Harold Crouch is Professor in the Department of Political and Social Change in the Research School of Pacific and Asian Studies at the Australian National University. He taught political science at the University of Indonesia, the National University of Malaysia and the University of the Philippines before joining the Australian National University. In 2000, he founded and served as the first director of the Indonesian office of the International Crisis Group.

Chapter 10

John B. Haseman, Colonel, U.S. Army (retired) served three assignments at the American Embassy in Jakarta, most recently as Defence and Army Attache from 1990 to 1994, during which he made 13 visits to East Timor. He writes on political-military affairs in Indonesia and South-east Asia and consults for government, military and educational institutions.

Chapter 11

Alan Dupont is a Senior Fellow at the Strategic and Defence Studies Centre in the Research School of Pacific and Asian Studies of the Australian National University. He has worked on East Asian security issues for over 25 years in government and academia and was Counsellor at the Australian Embassy from 1991-94. He is concerned with political and strategic developments in Indonesia and South-east Asia and has commented extensively on East Timor for the Australian and international press.

Chapter 12

Januar Achmad holds a medical degree from the University of Gadjah Mada, an MA in medical science from the University of Western Australia and a PhD in demography from the Australian National University. He worked as a public health scientist in the Indonesian Ministry of Health before spending 22 years in Yogyakarta as Director of Yayasan Essential Medica, a non-government organisation active in community development. He organised and led a medical team to assist East Timorese refugees in West Timor. Recently he has been a Visiting Professor at Tamkang University in Taiwan.

Chapter 13

Fiona Crockford is a doctoral student in anthropology at the Australian National University. Her research is focused on East Timorese youth identities in the diaspora.

Chapter 14

Andrew MacIntyre is Director of the Asia Pacific School of Economics and Government at the Australian National University. He was previously Associate Professor in the Graduate School of International Relations and Pacific Studies, University of California, San Diego.

Chapter 15

C. Peter Timmer has retired as Dean and Professor of Development Studies, Graduate School of International Relations and Pacific Studies, University of California, San Diego. He is now Chief Economist for Development Alternatives, Inc. (DAI).

Chapter 16

Sarah Cliffe is currently the Co-ordinator for the Low-Income Countries Under Stress Initiative at the World Bank. She was involved in the organisation of the UN/World Bank Joint Assessment Mission (JAM) to East Timor and served as Deputy Mission Leader and later, as Chief of the World Bank Mission on East Timor.

Chapter 17

João Mariano Saldanha is Executive Director of the East Timor Study Group (ETSG), an independent and non-partisan think tank on public policy issues. He holds a PhD in economics and politics from the Graduate School of International Relations and Pacific Studies, University of California at San Diego.

Chapter 18

Dionisio Babo Soares (already profiled as a contributor of Chapter 4)

Abbreviations and acronyms

ABLAI — *Aku Berjuang Lestarikan Amanat Integrasi* (Struggle for Integration, a militia group)

ABRI — *Angkatan Bersenjata Republik Indonesia* (Armed Forces of the Republic of Indonesia, now TNI)

AIETD — All-inclusive Intra-East Timorese Dialogue

Apodeti — *Associacão Popular Democratica Timorense*

ASEAN — Association of South-East Asian Nations

AusAID — Australian Aid

BAIS — *Badan Intel Strategis* (Indonesian military intelligence)

Besi Merah-Putih — Red and White militia (from Liquiça)

BIA — *Badan Intel ABRI* (army intelligence unit)

BKKBN — Indonesian Family Planning Board

Brimob — mobile police

BRTT — *Barisan Rakyat Timor Timur* (East Timorese integrationist front organisation)

CEB — children ever born

CFA — Central Fiscal Agency

CIDES — Indonesian think-tank associated with ICMI

CivPol — International Civilian Police Force

CNRM — *Conselho Nacional da Resistencia Maubere* (government)

CNRT — *Conselho Nacional da Resistencia Timorense* (National Council of East Timorese Resistance)

CNT — *Convergencia Nacional Timorense* (the National Pact for East Timor)

CPCC — *Comissão de Planeamento e Coordenação da Campanha* (Commission for Campaign Planning and Co-ordination)

CPLP — Community of Portuguese-speaking nations

CS — children surviving

Deplu — Indonesian Department of Foreign Affairs

DHS — Indonesian Demographic and Health Survey

DPKO — Department of Peace-Keeping Operations

DPR — *Dewan Perwakilan Rakyat* (Indonesian People's Representative Council)

ETAN	(Canada-based) East Timor Alert Network
DSMPTT	*Dewan Solidaritas Mahasiswa dan Pelajar Timor Timur* (East Timorese student solidarity organisation)
Falintil	*Forças Armadas de Timor Leste* (East Timor National Liberation Army)
FECLETIL	*Frente Clandestina Estudantil de Timor Leste* (East Timorese student organisation)
FITUN	lit., 'star'
FOKUPERS	*Forum Komunikasi Perempuan* (women's non-governmental organisation)
FPDK	*Forum Persatuan Demokrasi dan Keadilan*
FPI	*Frente Politica Interna*
Fretilin	*Frente Revolusionaria de Timor Leste Independente*
Gadapaksi	*Garda Pemuda Penegak Integrasi* (youth guards upholding integration)
GDP	gross domestic product
GERTAK	*Gerakan Wanita Anti-Kekerasan* (women against violence)
Halilintar	Lightning, a militia group
HRW	Human Rights Watch
ICMI	*Ikatan Cendekiawan Muslim se-Indonesia* (Indonesian Association of Muslim Intellectuals)
ICRC	International Red Cross
IDPs	internally displaced persons
IFIs	international financial institutions
IMF	International Monetary Fund
IMPETTU	*Ikatan Mahasiswa dan Pelajar Timor Timur* (East Timorese student association)
IMR	infant mortality rates
Interfet	UN-sponsored International Force in East Timor
JAM	World Bank-led Joint Assessment Mission (to East Timor)
KAMRA	*Keamanan Rakyat* (civil defence units)
KIPER	Indonesian independent electoral watch for the referendum in East Timor
KKN	*Kuliah Kerja Nyata*
Kodam	*Komando Daerah Militer* (military regional command)
Kodim	*Komando Distrik Militer* (military district command)
Komnas-HAM	Indonesian National Human Rights Commission
Kopassus	*Komando Pasukan Khusus* (Indonesian Army Special Forces command)
Koramil	*Komando Rayon Militer* (military command at the *kecamatan* level)

Korem	*Komando Resort Militer* (Wiradharma Military Resort Command 164)
KOTA	*Klibur Oan Timor Ass'wain* (East Timorese political party)
KPP-HAM	Indonesian Commission for the Investigation of Human Rights Violations in East Timor
KPS	Commission on Peace and Stability
LEP	*Liga dos Estudantes Patriotas* (League of Patriotic Students)
LIPI	*Lembaga Ilmu Pengetahuan Indonesia* (Indonesian Institute of Sciences)
Mahidi	Dead or Alive for Integration, a militia group
MAUBERE	Common Timorese name adopted by Fretilin to symbolise its proletarian-political orientation
Menkopolkam	Co-ordinating Minister for Politics and Security
MFA	*Movimento das Forças Armadas* (Armed Forces Movement)
MNF	Multinational Force
MOBUDAN	*Movimento Buka Dalan Foun*
MPR	*Majelis Perwakilan Rakyat* (Indonesian Consultative Assembly)
MSF	*Medicins sans Frontières*
NAM	non-aligned movement
NHRC	National Human Rights Commission (*Komite Nasional Hak Asasi Manusia, Komnasham*)
NCC	National Consultative Council
NEM	*Nilai Ebtanas Murani* (end of school level examination scores)
NGOs	non-governmental organisations
NTT	Nusa Tenggara Timur
NU	Nahdlatul Ulama
OJECTIL	*Organisacão da Juventude Catolica de Timor Leste* (Organisation of Catholic Youth)
OJETIL	*Organisacão de Juventude de Timor Leste* (Organisation of Timorese Youth)
OMT	*Organisação da Mulheres Timorenses* (Organisation of Timorese Women)
OPJLATIL	*Organisacão Popular Juventude Lorico Ass'wain Timor Leste* (East Timorese student youth organisation)
Pam Swakarsa	civilian security forces
PAN	National Mandate Party
Panglima Perang	War Commander
PDI-P	*Partai Demokrasi Indonesia-Perjuangan* (Indonesian Democratic Party in Struggle)
PEPABRI	armed forces' retired officers' association

Perdhaki	Catholic volunteer organisation (from Jakarta)
PKB	*Partai Kebangkitan Bangsa*
PKI	Indonesian Communist Party
PNT	*Partido Nacionalista de Timorense* (Timorese Nationalist Party)
PPA	*Persatuan Pemuda Apodeti*
PPI	*Pasukan Pejuang Integrasi* (Fighters for Integration Force)
PST	*Partido Socialista de Timor* (Socialist Party of Timor)
RDTL	*Republica Democratica de Timor Leste* (Democratic Republic of Timor Leste)
RENETIL	*Resistencia Nacional dos Estudantes de Timor Leste* (East Timorese National Students Resistance)
SARET	Special Autonomous Region of East Timor
SCMM	one of many orders of sisters in East Timor
SOLIDAMOR	*Solidaritas Mahasiswa Untuk Penyelesaian Damai Timor Timur* (student solidarity organisation for a peaceful settlement in East Timor)
STT	*Suara Timor Timur* (Voice of East Timor newspaper)
Supas	Indonesian Intercensal Survey
TAPOL	Indonesian political prisoner
TFR	total fertility rate
TNI	*Tentara Nacional Indonesia* (Indonesian National Army)
Trabalhista	Labour Party of East Timor
TTU	*Timor Tengah Utara* (North Central Timor)
TVRI	Indonesian national television
UDC	*União Democratica Christã*
UDT	*União Democratica Timorense*
UNAMET	United Nations Mission in East Timor
UNDP	United Nations Development Program
UNHCR	United Nations High Commissioner for Refugees
UNICEF	United Nations International Children's Education Fund
UNPKF	United Nations Peace-Keeping Force
UNTAET	United Nations Transitional Administration in East Timor
UNTIM	*Universitas Timor Timur* (University of East Timor)
USAID	United States Aid
WHO	World Health Organisation
Yayasan *HAK*	human rights organisation

Left and below: *United Nations polling posters for the popular consultation*

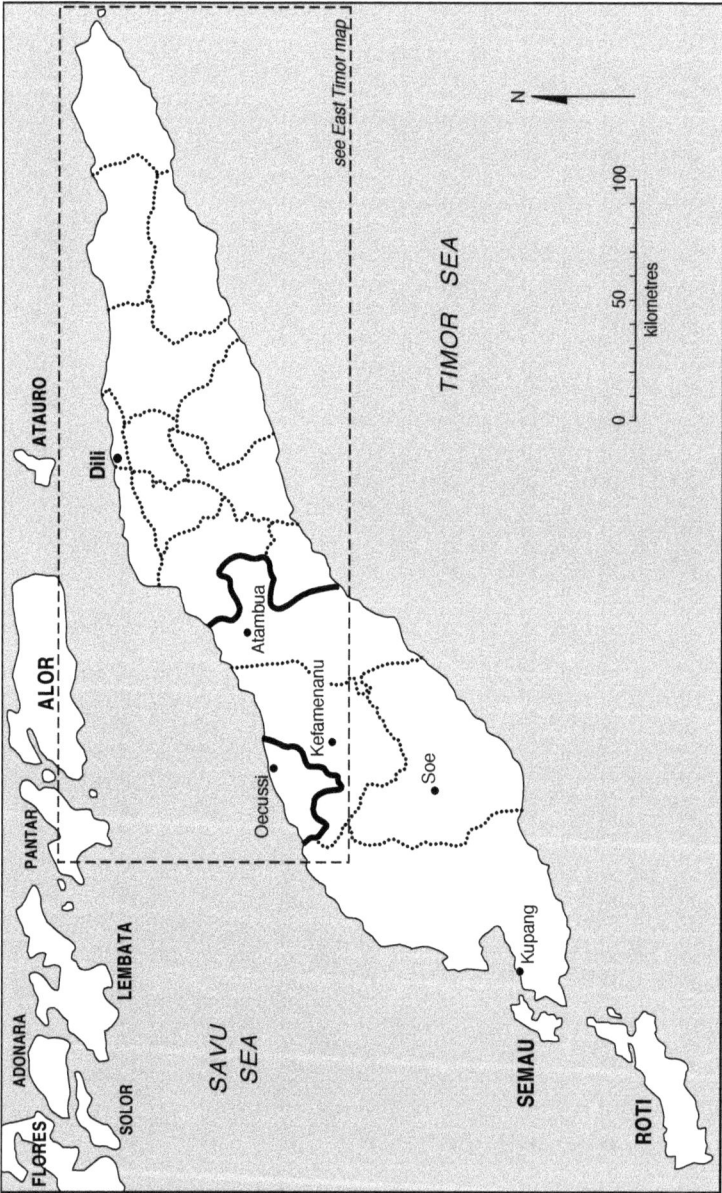

The island of Timor

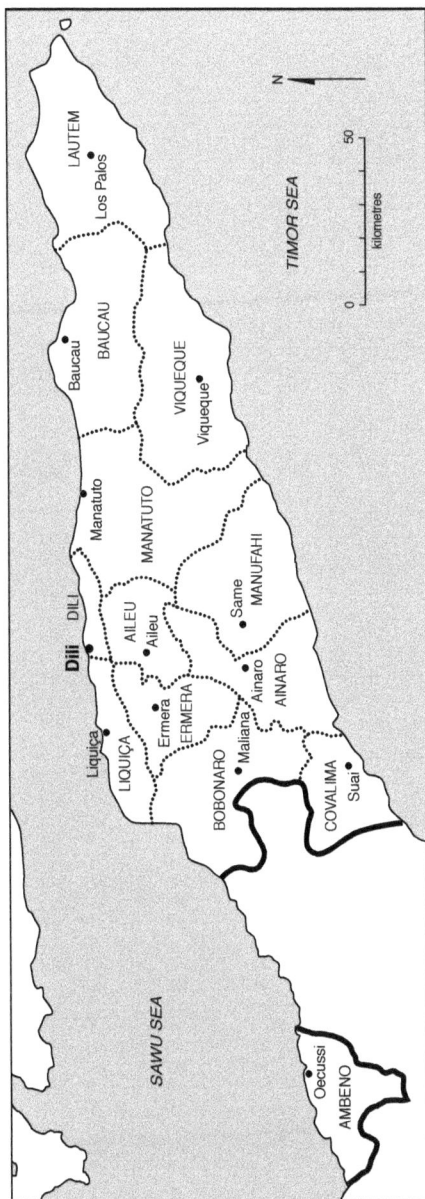

East Timor

1

Tracing the path, recounting the past: historical perspectives on Timor

James J. Fox

The island of Timor, in one of its mythic representations, is described as a half-submerged crocodile, wary and waiting. In another mythic representation, Timor is mother earth, accepting, long-suffering, supportive of all who rely upon her. Geologically, Timor has been described as a 'tectonic chaos'. Linguistically, the island is a babel of languages and dialects. Historically, for centuries, it has been a divided island and a source of continuing dispute. Its local populations have long resisted outside interference and have been fiercely defensive of their different local cultural traditions. From these perspectives, Timor is not one place, but many.

Because of the complexity of its traditions, there have been various attempts to simplify Timor's diversity. Dividing the island's population into East and West is one of the most potent of these simplifications. This division makes little sense in understanding the history of the island, the ethnic composition of its population or the interrelationship of its cultural traditions. Moreover, it leaves the enclave of Oecussi, the historical founding site of Timor's Portuguese traditions, on its own in the West – detached and with little relevance to the rest of East Timor.

To understand East Timor requires a perspective on Timor as a whole. It also requires that careful attention be given to Timor's distinctive cultural traditions. Thus Suai's traditions differ from those of Maliana, Maliana from those of Maubara, Maubara from Manatuto and Manatuto from Los Palos. These traditions form the basis of local resilience and are the source of multiple identities.

This brief introduction will focus on East Timor but will adopt an island-wide perspective, considering, in turn, the physical setting of the island, its linguistic and ethnic diversity and its extraordinary history. This account of Timor's history will consider the foundations of the colonial division of the island and the intermittent negotiations that went on for decades to arrive at an agreement on the borders between the Portuguese and Dutch. It will also consider some of the effects of this colonial presence on the Timorese population.

On Timor, a narrative that recounts the past is described as 'the tracing of a path'. This, then, is one path toward an understanding of the present.[1]

Timor in geological perspective

The island of Timor is itself an extraordinary geological formation which has been formed – and is still being formed – by the forward thrust of the Australian tectonic plate in the direction of the Asian plate. The movement of these massive plates has created and trapped a set of multi-island ridges of which Timor is the most prominent. In the distant geological future, the mountains of Timor, given the enormous pressure that is being brought to bear beneath them, are expected to rise to the heights of the Himalayas.

The dominant soil type on the island is a soft, scaly clay which has been given the Timorese name *Bobonaro*, taken from a region in the centre of the island. This *Bobonaro* clay substratum is overlaid with a jumble of limestone and associated marl derived from the greater Australian land mass and a melange of volcanic materials and scattered outcrops of metamorphic rock piled upon by marine deposits and overlaid yet again by a stratum of raised reefs and corals.

Timor's climate is dominated by brief but intense monsoonal rain – from December through February or March – followed by a prolonged dry season. The south coast of East Timor enjoys a second period of rain which begins, after a short respite from the west monsoon, and extends to July when the dry season begins.

---

[1]   This chapter is, in part, based on a paper, 'The Paradox of Powerlessness: Timor in Historical Perspective' which was originally presented at the Nobel Peace Prize Symposium, *Focus on Timor*, at the University of Oslo (9 December 1996).

Rainwater, trapped in limestone deposits by irregular sheets of clay, often surfaces in a scatter of freshwater springs. Perhaps a third or more of all settlement names on Timor include the word for water – such as *Oe, Wai, We* or *Be* – indicating a source of fresh water.

Timor's clay soils do not support heavy vegetation. They soak up rain and swell in the wet season; dry, crack and fissure in the dry season. Historically, the Timorese population has carried on shifting agriculture on alluvial and limestone terraces or on the mixed, marine-based soils of ridges, slopes and valleys throughout the mountains of the island, or they have developed more intensive agriculture on various alluvial plains, formed by Timor's main rivers, along the coast.

The peopling of Timor: the linguistic evidence

The mix of peoples on Timor is as complex as any other aspect of the island. Prehistorians consider Timor as one of the gateways for the movement of populations to Australia. Given the time-depth of these migrations, the search is on for the equivalent of 'Solo man' in Timor. As yet, however, no human traces of this antiquity have been found in the alluvial riverbeds or caves of Timor.

The first evidence of early agriculture dates back to 3000 BC (Glover 1971). This evidence is generally interpreted as an indication of the initial arrival of early seafaring Austronesian populations into the region. It is from these, and probably from subsequent migrations of Austronesian-language speakers, that the majority of Timor's present languages derive. Glover's research also points to an earlier hunter-gatherer population whose flaked stone tradition he dates to approximately 11 500 BC. Whether this earlier population was assimilated or whether it gave rise to other non-Austronesian-speakers of Timor is still uncertain.

All the languages of Timor belong to one of two major language groupings: the Austronesian language family or the Trans-New Guinea phylum of languages (see Map 1).

The main Austronesian languages of Timor are Uab Meto (the language of the Atoni Pa Meto who are also referred to as Dawan or Vaikenu), Tetun, Mambai, Galoli, Tokudede and Kemak. Other Austronesian languages, about which relatively little is known, are Waima'a (Uaima), Kairui-Midiki, Habu, Idate, Lakalei and Naueti. Some of these languages form contiguous dialect clusters. The Austronesian

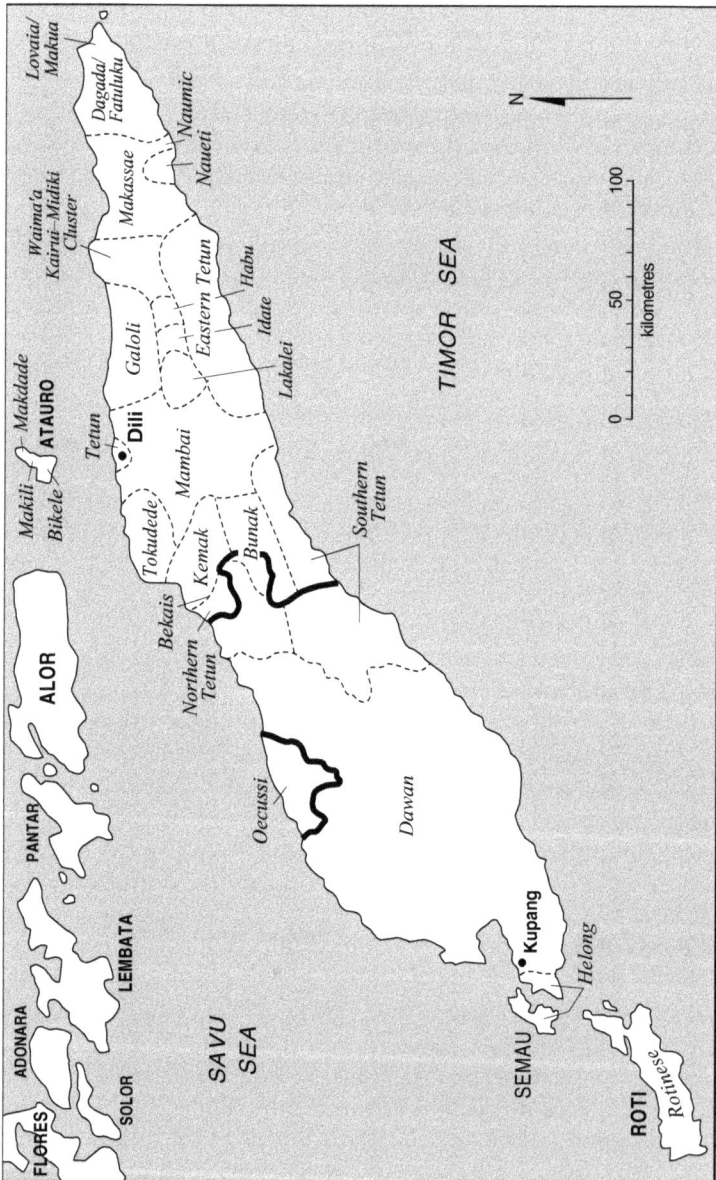

Map 1: *The languages of East Timor*

languages of Timor are closely enough related to one another to form a recognisable subgrouping, which, in turn, shows relationships to the languages on the neighbouring islands of Flores, Solor and Maluku.

The main Trans-New Guinea languages are Bunak, which is spoken on both sides of the border between East and West Timor; Makassae which is spoken in the Baucau district, and Dagada (Fatuluku) which is spoken at the eastern end of the island. There is also another Trans-New Guinea language, Adabe, spoken on the island of Atauro. Even less is known about the subdivisions and dialects of these Trans-New Guinea languages than of East Timor's Austronesian languages. The Trans-New Guinea languages of Timor are related to various languages spoken on the islands of Alor, Pantar and on the tiny island of Kisar. In turn, these languages are related to languages in the Birdhead region (*Vogelkop*) in West Papua. Present linguistic evidence suggests that speakers of these Trans-New Guinea languages arrived on Timor after the initial migration of Austronesian speakers.[2]

What is clear is that these languages, of two very different origins, have borrowed from and influenced one another over a considerable period of time. Thus Bunak shows considerable borrowings from Tetun, whereas the Austronesian languages, such as Kairui/Midiki and Naueti, have been influenced by neighbouring Trans-New Guinea languages.

One striking feature of the socio-linguistics of Timor is the remarkable contrast between the eastern and the western halves of the island. Almeida (1982) lists over 30 different languages and dialects in the East compared with only three languages in the West. The Wurm-Hattori *Language Atlas of the Pacific Area* (Wurm and Hattori 1981) which groups dialects, still identifies at least 17 distinct languages in East Timor compared to three main languages – Dawan, Tetun and Helong – in the West. This sociological difference between East and West is, to a large extent, the result of initial Portuguese historical involvement in the western half of

[2] Professor Stephen Wurm, who was one of the first linguists to recognise the Trans-New Guinea phylum as a major grouping of languages, was a strong supporter of the view that Trans-New Guinea phylum speakers arrived in Timor after Austronesian speakers. In his view, there is evidence in the languages of Timor (and Alor) of linguistic features that developed in the course of the migration of speakers of these languages from the east of New Guinea westward. Other linguists consider that there has been insufficient research on the Trans-New Guinea phylum as a whole and on the Timor-Alor languages in particular to confirm Wurm's bold hypotheses.

Timor, which gave rise to the expansion of the Atoni population. As with much else on Timor, to understand this difference between East and West requires an historical perspective. It is essential therefore to consider the history of Timor over the past 450 years.

Early accounts of Timor

The history of Timor is inextricably tied up with one species of tree, white sandalwood (*Santalum album* L.). This tree once grew, almost as a weed, by root propagation throughout the limestone hills and mountains of Timor. Trade in its precious, fragrant wood may date back centuries before the earliest references. By the fourteenth century, both Chinese and Javanese documents refer to Timor. One such Chinese document reports:

> The island has no other rare product but sandalwood which is abundant and which is bartered for with silver, iron, cups [of porcelain], *hsi-yang ssu pu* [a kind of cloth], and coloured taffetas (Rockhill 1915:257–258).

The first European reference to what had become an extensive trade in Timorese sandalwood can be found in *The Book of Duarte Barbosa* written in 1518:

> In this island there is abundance of white sanders-wood which 'the Moors in India and Persia value greatly, where much of it is used. In Malabar, Narsyngua and Cambaya it is esteemed'. The ships 'of Malaca and Jaoa [Jawa]' which come hither for it bring in exchange axes, hatchets, knives, swords, Cambaya and Paleacate cloths, porcelain, coloured beads, tin, quick-silver, lead and other wares, and take in cargoes of the aforesaid sanders-wood, honey, wax, slaves and also a certain amount of silver (Dames 1921, 2:195–196).

One of the first European vessels to reach Timor was the *Victoria*, a ship of Magellan's fleet. The *Victoria* put in on the north coast of Timor on 26 January 1522. In his account of this visit, Antonio Pigafetta explains:

> All the sandalwood and wax which is traded by the people of Java and Malacca comes from this place, where we found a junk of Lozzon which had come to trade for sandalwood (1969:141).

The Portuguese were the first Europeans attracted to Timor by this sandalwood trade. It took over 50 years after the Portuguese conquest of Malacca in 1511 to establish a presence in the area. Moreover, the

Portuguese chose to establish themselves to the north of Timor, initially, on the island of Solor. It was there, on Solor, that the Dominican preachers gained their first converts.

In 1561-62, the Dominicans built a palisade of lontar palms to protect local Christians but this was burnt down the year after by Muslim raiders, prompting the Dominicans, in 1566, to erect a more permanent stone fortress on Solor. For its first 20 years, the captain of this fort at Solor was nominated by the Dominican Prior in Malacca. Around this fort there developed a mixed, part-Portuguese population of local Christians, many of whom were themselves involved in the sandalwood trade with Timor.[3]

The Dominican fort on Solor had a chequered history. Plundered in a local uprising in 1598, the fort fell, after a long siege, to the Dutch in 1613. According to Dutch sources, their forces were able to take the fort because over 500 of its occupants were, at the time, on a sandalwood-trading expedition to Timor.

Instead of sailing for Malacca, the thousand strong population of the fort, later joined by those from Timor, transferred to Larantuka, a harbour on the eastern end of Flores and from there, established themselves at Lifao on the north-west coast of Timor. With their strongholds on both Flores and Timor, this mixed, part-Portuguese population of local islanders resisted all attempts to dislodge them. This population became known as the *Larantuqueiros* or as the *Tupassi* ('Topasses', purportedly from the word for hat, *topi*, because the Topasses regarded themselves '*Gente de Chapeo*': 'People of the Hat') – or, as was common in all Dutch documents, the 'Black Portuguese' (*Swarte Portugueezen*).[4] In the language of the Atoni Pa Meto population, who had the longest established contact with them on Timor, these Topasses were known as the *Sobe Kase*: 'The Foreign Hats'. (Yet another variant of this designation, among the Rotinese, on the small island at the western tip of Timor, was *Sapeo Nggeo*: 'The Black Hats'.)

These Topasses became the dominant, independent, seafaring, sandalwood-trading power of the region for the next 200 years. They were a multilingual group. Portuguese was their status language which was also used for worship; Malay was their language of trade, and

---

[3]   For an interesting account of the history of this fort, see Barnes (1987).
[4]   C.R. Boxer has written a great deal about the activities of these Topasses. His brief study, *The Topasses of Timor* (1947), which relies on both Dutch and Portuguese sources, is a classic study of its kind.

most Topasses spoke, as their mother-tongue, a local language of
Flores or Timor.

The British buccaneer, William Dampier, visited Lifao in 1699
and has provided a perceptive description of this mixed, multilingual
Topass community:

> These [the Topasses] have no Forts, but depend on their Alliance with
> the Natives: And indeed they are already so mixt, that it is hard to
> distinguish whether they are *Portugueze* or *Indians*. Their Language is
> Portugueze; and the religion they have, is Romish. They seem in Words
> to acknowledge the King of Portugal for their Sovereign; yet they will
> not accept any Officers sent by him. They speak indifferently the Malayan
> and their own native Languages, as well as Portugueze (1703, reprinted
> 1939:171–172).

Neither the Dutch nor the Portuguese who were loyal to the Viceroy
of Goa were able to exert any substantial control over them. On Timor,
there were times when the interests of the Portuguese Viceroy and those
of the leaders of the Black Portuguese coincided. Just as often, however,
the Black Portuguese opposed both the Portuguese Viceroy and the Dutch
East India Company with whom they also carried on trade. However
often the Viceroy's delegates were rejected, Portuguese friars were always
welcomed on Timor and moved freely throughout the island.

The establishment of the Portuguese and Dutch on Timor

While Larantuka remained firmly in Portuguese control, the disputed
fort on Solor, known as Fort Henricus to the Dutch, changed hands
several times during the first half of the seventeenth century. At one
stage, in 1629, the Dutch commander of the fort, Jan de Hornay,
deserted to Larantuka where he married a local girl, converted to
Catholicism and became known thereafter as João de Hornay. (De
Hornay's desertion allowed the Dominicans to retake the fort at Solor
in 1630 and hold it until 1636.)

João de Hornay, through his sons, Antonio and Francisco, gave rise
to one of the dynasties that provided the leadership to the Black
Portuguese community on Timor. The other dynastic founder was
Mateus da Costa, a rival companion in arms of Antonio de Hornay.
Mateus had married a princess of Timor (by one account, the daughter
of the ruler of Amanuban; by another account, the daughter of the

ruler of Ambenu). His son, Domingos, continued the da Costa dynasty on Timor.

These two families fought and feuded, intermarried and succeeded one another, establishing in the process Timorese clans that continue to this day.[5] In the seventeenth century, a wise Viceroy in Goa sent his envoy to Larantuka with identical letters of appointment, one for Antonio de Hornay and the other for Mateus da Costa, instructing him to appoint as his representative whoever he found was in power. (As it happened, this turned out to be Antonio de Hornay but Mateus did not accept this judgment, claiming that his earlier appointment was still valid.)

In 1641, the native ruler of the domain of Ambenu on the northwest coast of Timor (at what is now referred to as Oecussi) was converted to Catholicism by the Dominican friar Antonio de São Jacinto. Prior to this time, the Topasses had traded for sandalwood at several harbours along the coast. Thereafter they made the harbour of Lifao in Oecussi their main trading base, establishing a small settlement there.

In 1642, a Topass captain named Francisco Fernandez, who had been born on Solor, led a band of 90 musketeers across the island of Timor from north to south to strike a blow at the power of the indigenous rulers of the island – the kingdom of Sonba'i in the interior and the kingdom of Wehali on the south coast. Striking at and burning these centres was a demonstration of Topass power and allowed the Topasses to redirect the sandalwood trade through their hands.[6]

From this point, the Topasses steadily extended their influence and control into the main mountainous sandalwood-growing areas of Timor. Their most important stronghold was in the Mutis mountains but their influence extended to the south coast as well.

The Dutch, in turn, repositioned themselves in 1653, by shifting their main garrison from Solor to Timor. On Timor, they took control of and enlarged the fortifications begun by Friar Jacinto in the Bay of Kupang. There they erected a stone fort to which they gave the name *Concordia*. This location gave them the advantage of an all-weather harbour with a fortified settlement which could be supplied from Batavia but it put them at a distance from the main sources of sandalwood on Timor which the Topasses and their local allies controlled.

[5] The da Costa family established itself in the Noimuti region; the de Hornay family in Anas.
[6] For a further discussion of this event and its consequences, see Fox (1982).

To rectify this disadvantage, the Dutch East India Company called upon its most illustrious general, Arnoldus de Vlaming van Oudshoorn, to deal with the Black Portuguese. In 1656, with troops fresh from triumphs on Ambon, de Vlaming marched into the interior of Timor and was completely routed by the Topasses and their allies led by Antonio de Hornay and Mateus da Costa. For a time, after this serious defeat, the Dutch contemplated withdrawing entirely from Timor. For the next 150 years, the Dutch remained confined to Kupang and their influence was limited to a radius of several miles around Concordia.[7]

The Portuguese, who attempted to assert formal rule from Goa, fared no better than the Dutch. The late seventeenth century onward is a catalogue of uprisings against Portuguese authority. Thus, in 1695, Mateus da Costa fomented an uprising in Larantuka to overthrow the first Viceroy-appointed 'Governor and Captain-General of the islands of Solor and Timor', Antonio de Mesquita Pimentel.

In 1701, Antonio Coelho Guerreiro was sent to be governor. He made Lifao the official Portuguese settlement in 1702 and managed to maintain his position for more than two years until he was also expelled and forced to call on the Dutch for his passage back to Goa in 1705. In 1722, Antonio de Albuquerque Coelho was appointed but was besieged in Lifao for three years by the Topasses and their allies led by Francisco de Hornay. His successor also faced fierce opposition and was besieged for long periods of time while the Topasses continued to control the trade in sandalwood from the interior of Timor.

During this period, the Topasses made three unsuccessful attempts – in 1735, 1745 and 1749 – to drive the Dutch from Kupang. Often the Dutch and Portuguese co-operated in their efforts to control the Black Portuguese. Thus, in 1761, the *Opperhoofd* in Kupang, Hans Albert von Pluskow, was murdered by Francisco de Hornay and Antonio da Costa in Lifao where he had gone to attempt to negotiate the reinstatement of the Portuguese governor.

Finally, under siege by the Topasses and with his provisions exhausted, Portuguese Governor Antonio José Telles de Menezes, on the night of 11 August 1769, abandoned Lifao and sailed eastward to establish a new Portuguese settlement at Dili, far from any threat of the Topasses. (It was at this point that Francisco de Hornay offered the Dutch East India

---

[7] For a discussion of the early history of the Kupang area, see Fox (1977); for a more popular account of the history of Kupang itself, see Fox (1981).

Company the possession of Lifao, an offer that was officially considered and declined.)

It is appropriate at this juncture to quote an eighteenth century commentator on Timor, the Scots sea captain, Alexander Hamilton, writing in 1727:

> [The Timoreans] permitted the Portuguese colony of Macao in China, to build a Fort on it, which they called Leiffew, and the Dutch a factory called Coupang, but would never suffer either to interfere with the Government of their country ... they found that the Timoreans would not lose their liberty for fear of the loss of blood ... (1930, II:74).

Only in the nineteenth century – in fact only late in the nineteenth century – through a process of relentless intrusions by military force, were the two colonial powers able to exert their influence on the interior of Timor. Despite continuing contact with Europeans, dating to the early sixteenth century, Timor was never colonised as were other parts of the Indies. For most of the colonial period, control was a matter of pretence and veneer. The Portuguese claimed to have pacified their territory by 1912, the Dutch theirs by 1915.

The division of Timor and the veneer of colonial control

In 1777, the Portuguese in Dili regarded Timor as divided into two provinces: a western province called Servião, inhabited by the Vaiquenos (Dawan or Atoni) and consisting of 16 local kingdoms (*reinos*) and an eastern province called Bellum (or Bellos), inhabited and dominated by the Belu (or Tetun) and comprising no less than 46 small kingdoms. Servião covered much of the area controlled by Topasses. According to the Portuguese, this district had as its supreme ruler or emperor, the Lord Sonba'i. At this time, although then situated in Dili, in the east of the island, the Portuguese had less knowledge of conditions there than in the west. Although the ruler of the Bellos, whom they referred to as the emperor, exerted wide influence, it is doubtful that this ruler exercised hegemony, as the Portuguese implied, over all 46 kingdoms of the eastern half of the island.

The Dutch drew a different picture of this same political situation. In 1756, the Dutch East India Company sent a distinguished envoy by the name of Paravicini to order its relations on Timor. This renowned *Commissaris* returned to Batavia with a contract treaty purporting to have been signed by all of the rulers of Timor in addition to those of the islands of Roti, Savu, Sumba and Solor: 48 signatories on a lengthy document with 30 clauses. Whether, in fact, he obtained the signed agreement of all of these rulers, the contract of Paravicini represented the political geography of native rule more accurately than did Portuguese documents for the same period.

The supreme ruler of Belu and sovereign king of Wywiko Behale [Waiwiku Wehali], whose name is given as Hiacijntoe Corea, is reported to have signed the Contract of Paravicini on behalf of 27 dependent domains, all but four of which can be identified and located on a map to this day. Besides domains on the western side of Timor, this contract included at least 16 dependencies in what is now East Timor.[8]

That these Dutch claims to allegiance involved only a nominal relationship is evidenced by the fact that it was only in 1904 that the Dutch were able to obtain an official audience with the person whom they had designated as the *Keser* or *Keyzer*, having had to make their way to Laran in Wehali with an armed force to meet him. This was the first recorded Dutch meeting with the Tetun ruler of Wehali (Francillon 1980).

Despite doubts over its validity as a formal political document, the Contract of Paravicini asserted Dutch claims to large areas of the island claimed by the Portuguese. By an equally dubious token, through claims to all the territories controlled by the Topasses, the Portuguese were able to claim large areas of western Timor. These overlapping, hardly credible claims to territory on both sides resulted in one of the longest, most drawn-out negotiations in colonial history.

The partitioning of Timor

During the Napoleonic wars, the British occupied the Dutch fort at Kupang and laid claim, for a brief period, to Dutch colonial possessions on Timor. When, in 1816, the British returned colonial authority to the Dutch, the Dutch set out to determine their areas of supposed control in relation to the Portuguese. Almost immediately thereafter there occurred the first of a series of disputes over the borders between the two colonial powers.

The Portuguese claimed a large area of West Timor including the mountainous region of Mutis (thus a territory far larger than the present

---

[8]   The text of this contract can be found in Stapel (1955:87-107).

enclave of Oecussi-Ambenu). The Dutch, in turn, claimed a considerable sweep of territory on both the north and south coasts of what is now East Timor. (The coastal territory of Maubara, for example, was one area of East Timor over which the Dutch both claimed and exercised authority well into the nineteenth century. The Dutch also maintained control over a small but significant enclave, called Maucatar, located near the present town of Suai.) Even more unclear, and thus subject to considerable dispute, was the interior border between the Portuguese and Dutch on Timor.

For a full 100 years, between 1816 and 1916, the Portuguese and Dutch engaged in recurrent territorial disputes that were played out at the local level as diplomatic negotiations continued in Lisbon and The Hague. A settlement of unresolved borders was eventually achieved only through a determination of the Permanent Court of Arbitration in 1914 and officially acknowledged on Timor in 1916.

Just as Dutch Timor was part of the greater Netherlands Indies, so too was Portuguese Timor part of the then Portuguese Indies. In this empire, the Portuguese included Timor as well as territory on the islands of Flores, Solor, Pantar and Alor under the direction of Macau. What little authority the Portuguese could maintain on these islands north of Timor was exerted through local rulers who would hoist the Portuguese flag and visit Dili at appropriate intervals. The lack of almost any Portuguese control on these islands eventually upset the ill-defined political balance that existed between the two colonial powers and forced them to begin negotiations on their mutual boundaries.

In 1838, when the Dutch resident on Timor led an expedition that attacked and burnt the town of Larantuka on Flores as punishment for suspected piracy, this action was represented in Lisbon as a fearsome Dutch attack on Portugal. The Dutch countered with the assertion that if the Portuguese could not control piracy in the territory they claimed, their claim could hardly be considered valid. Yet when a Portuguese ship fired on a perahu from Makassar, also suspected of piracy, this was seen as an attack on Dutch colonial authority.

The Dutch initiated discussions with the Portuguese in 1846 with a view to acquiring Portuguese territories. These discussions were given further impetus in 1848, when the native ruler of Oecussi, who was under Portuguese authority, took part in an armed conflict among various rulers on Alor, over whom the Dutch claimed authority. This prompted the Dutch government to establish an official commission to carry forward negotiations on territory in the Timor region. Although Portugal was initially willing to consider the sale of its territories, a decision was taken in 1851 to decline the Dutch offer of purchase. It was agreed, however, to establish clear boundaries between Dutch and Portuguese areas.

At this time, in 1850, Timor and Solor were made a separate province of the Portuguese Indies, with financial independence from Macau. In the following year, the new governor in Dili, Lima de Lopes, reached an agreement with the Dutch on a major delimitation of colonial boundaries on Timor but faced with an impoverished administration, also agreed to cede – without authorisation from Lisbon – all Portuguese claims to eastern Flores and the nearby islands in return for an immediate payment of 80 000 florin (to be followed by a later payment of another 120 000 florin). The Dutch who had already been prepared to acquire Portuguese territory immediately accepted this offer and made the necessary payment to secure the agreement.

When officials in Lisbon became aware of what had happened, Governor Lima de Lopes was recalled in disgrace, but his agreement could not be rescinded. In the end, a treaty of demarcation and exchange of territory was negotiated in 1854 but only ratified in 1859. Portugal ceded all its historical claims on Flores, Solor, Pantar and Alor to the Dutch. On Timor, the two colonial powers arrived at a demarcation by listing the various traditional states under each other's authority. The Dutch ceded Maubara to the Portuguese. They also recognised Portuguese claims to Oecussi and to the area of Noimuti to the south of Oecussi. The Portuguese, in turn, recognised Dutch authority over the enclave of Maucatar on the south central coast of eastern Timor near Suai (Map 2).

Although this treaty eliminated some indeterminacy of boundaries, it was flawed in two respects. It left two landlocked enclaves – Noimuti and Maucatar – in each other's territory. How was authority to be exercised if access was limited? More uncertain still was the fact that demarcation was based on a division of native states whose mutual boundaries were not determined. The size of the different enclaves and exact boundary between East and West Timor came to rest on a variety of local traditional claims to territory.

Further conventions were needed and were eventually agreed upon in 1893, 1904 and 1913. The 1893 convention was an agreement to achieve a demarcation; the 1904 convention ceded Noimuti to the Dutch and

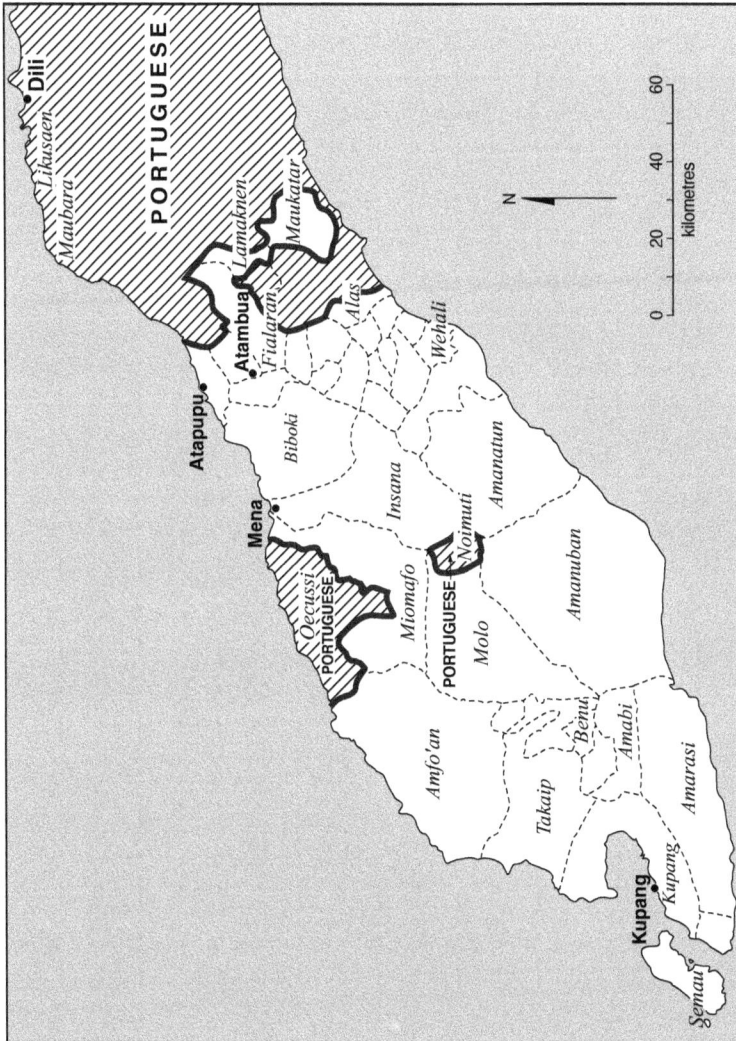

Map 2: Dutch interpretation of Timor's boundaries (1911)

Maucatar to the Portuguese and set forth the boundary between East
and West in terms of specific landmarks; the 1913 convention was an
agreement to submit the dispute over outstanding boundary lines, mainly
for Oecussi, to the Permanent Court of Arbitration. This court issued
its judgment on 25 June 1914, but the final ratification of boundaries was
only concluded in The Hague on 17 August 1916.[9]

There is a particular irony that as negotiations proceeded between
The Hague and Lisbon – all phrased in appropriate diplomatic French
– neither colonial power controlled the territories over which they were
deliberating. At repeated intervals during each dry season, on an almost
annual basis, the Dutch led armed expeditions to wage war in the interior,
particularly against the expansive and powerful domain of Amanuban.

Similarly, the Portuguese mounted no less than 60 armed
expeditions between 1847 and 1913 to subdue the Timorese. In 1860,
even as he was negotiating with the Dutch over 'Portuguese territory
on Timor', the Governor of Dili, Affonso de Castro, described the
situation with remarkable candour: 'Our empire on this island is
nothing but a fiction' (1862:472).

Traditional polities, languages and social identity

From the earliest Chinese sources to the final reports of the colonial
powers, all commentators agree that Timor was comprised of
kingdoms and rulers. Traditional kingdoms dating back to at least the
fourteenth century imply well-established, indeed fundamental, ideas
about order and political relations. Curiously, however, in the long
history of European contact with Timor, virtually no commentator
has credited the Timorese with a political philosophy or has sought
to explore and to treat seriously indigenous ideas of authority.

What is even more remarkable is that the kingdoms of Timor
identified by Antonio Pigafetta on the Magellan voyage in 1522 persisted
through the entire colonial period despite more than 400 years of
turmoil, disruption and upheaval. This, too, would suggest an
extraordinary capacity for local continuity: a capacity to persist, to
endure, and to maintain links with the land.

[9]   These long, drawn-out negotiations leading to the final border treaty are
discussed in detail in Heyman (1895) and Ezerman (1917). The texts of the
various Portuguese-Dutch treaties and conventions plus that of the
Permanent Court of Arbitration can be found in Krieger (1997:1-17).

The Pigafetta reference is particularly revealing in that two of the four kingdoms mentioned in that account of 1522 are Suai and Camanasa, both important sites on the south central coast of East Timor. Suai has become a town, whereas Camanasa, a large village outside of Suai, retains its traditional setting and traditional ruler. Both had large polling stations for the UN ballot.[10]

One of the difficulties, which continually confronted both the Dutch and the Portuguese, was how to conceptualise these native 'polities' to be able to deal with them through their rulers. The Dutch used a variety of titles: king, great prince, kaiser, and regent (*koning, grootvorst, keyzer, regent*) before settling on the use of the general term, *radja*, in the nineteenth century. The Portuguese used the royal designation (*rei*) but also a graded system of military ranks from colonel to lieutenant before they settled on the general term, *liurai* (see de Castro 1862:471).

What was bewildering to European officials were the relations among these various polities. The Contract of Paravicini in 1756, for example, recognised 13 independent rulers, mainly in West Timor, together with the great ruler of Waiwiku-Wehali, who had under his authority two local 'regents' and another 21 named territories, most of which were in East Timor. In addition, the treaty mentions rulers of seven other domains, including Suai, that appear to have been allied to Wehali. Interestingly, the first partitioning treaty between the Dutch and the Portuguese in 1859 was a realignment of many of the same territories nominated in the Contract of Paravicini.

Relations among the local polities of Timor were continually changing. Alliances among these polities shifted, especially as internal relations changed; there was regular, seasonal raiding into each other's territories – some in the form of ritual headhunting; and migration of clan groups in search of land and water was common. The Portuguese and Dutch both contributed to this situation.

In return for diverting the sandalwood trade to Lifao and other ports on the north coast of the island, the Topasses formed close alliances with the local Atoni Pa Meto polities and in several instances became the rulers of these polities. They were the first to introduce

[10] I was an international observer in the Suai area at the time of the ballot and chose to begin my official observations at the Camanasa polling station. That evening, I was introduced to the traditional ruler of Camanasa, who was later reported to have been killed in the mayhem that followed the announcement of the results of the ballot.

muskets to the Timorese and they increased the supply of simple iron tools. The Dutch (rather than the Portuguese) introduced maize to the island and promoted its planting, initially in the area around Kupang (Fox 1977:76). This combination of muskets, iron tools and maize, provided principally to Atoni groups, changed the face of West Timor. With a new highly productive crop, the tools to plant it and the firearms to expand aggressively and open new land in others' territory, the Atoni population, previously subordinate to Tetun rulers who controlled the sandalwood trade, rapidly spread through much of West Timor, assimilating other groups to Atoni modes of livelihood and culture.[11]

The language map of Timor today attests to this Atoni expansion over the last 400 years. Only the remnant Helong speakers, now confined to the western tip of Timor and the island of Semau, give some indication of what West Timor may have been like before the Atoni expansion.

Squeezed between the Topasses and the Dutch, the authority of the once great Atoni ruler, Sonba'i, declined as other Atoni polities rose to prominence. By the nineteenth century, Amanuban had expanded its power over a large area of central west Timor and had developed an effective armed cavalry which was a match for the Dutch forces of the period (see McWilliam 1989).

The role of the Chinese on Timor

It was never just the Topasses, Dutch and Portuguese who influenced developments on Timor. The Chinese, who initiated the earliest trade with Timor for sandalwood, were a major influence as well. Dampier who visited the Topass settlement at Lifao in 1699 noted the presence of 'China-Men, Merchants of Maccao' living among the Topasses. This Chinese connection has long been crucial on Timor and at times has been paramount. As Topass control of trade in the interior of Timor declined, Chinese control increased.

One of the most detailed nineteenth century descriptions of Timor is that of Dr Salomon Müller whose account covers a period from 1828

---

[11] For a more detailed, ecologically oriented examination of the history of Timor and consequences of European involvement, including the introduction of maize and of firearms, on patterns of Timorese livelihood, see Fox (1988). To gain some idea of the local adaptive capacity of Atoni culture, see Fox (1999).

to 1836. Müller, for example, noted the Timorese (especially Atoni) obsession with muskets:

> The trade in flintlock rifles is the most advantageous trade that can be conducted on Timor ... The rifle belongs, above all, to the most important piece of inheritance, to the costliest value that can pass from father to son: indeed a Timorese would often more easily and more happily do without house and livestock, even a wife and child, rather than without such a weapon (1857, 2:234).

Although initially this trade was carried out through the Topasses, by the nineteenth century this important trade was in the hands of the Chinese. Müller described this situation:

> Since the natives do not themselves bring their two foremost products [sandalwood and beeswax] to market, each year, during the dry season, a number of Chinese from Kupang, Atapupu, Batu Gede and other coastal sites travel into the interior on horses laden with specific trade goods to conduct this trade. As these traders go from one district to another, in each domain they first approach the ruler and the *fettors* offering them gifts and requesting permission to trade and be allowed safety and protection in all circumstances (1857, 2:244–245).

Müller marvelled at the fact that despite the considerable value of the goods that these Chinese carried with them into the mountains and of the amount of sandalwood they brought back on horseback, there were no reported incidents of any violation of Chinese safety. This was at a time when both Portuguese and Dutch colonial officials could make only limited journeys into the interior and only under armed protection.

Later in the nineteenth century, as the supply of sandalwood dwindled, coffee was introduced and planted widely in the upland areas of both Dutch and Portuguese Timor. Much of the planting of coffee was done at the initiative of local Chinese who were able to control its trade and export. Although the Portuguese tried repeatedly to channel the export of coffee through Dili, the Chinese preferred to export this crop through the port they controlled at Atapupu.

The emergence of Tetun as a lingua franca in East Timor

Prior to the Atoni expansion, there was an earlier expansion of the Tetun people, probably from what the Tetun regard as their traditional centre of origin on the central south coast. This expansion was both northward and along the south coast. As a consequence of this expansion, there are several distinct forms of Tetun. These are generally described as different dialects, though there are considerable differences among them.

The first of these Tetun dialects is associated with the traditional polities of Waiwiku-Wehali on the southern coastal plain of West Timor where the towns of Besikama and Betun are now located. This dialect, often referred to as 'straight' or 'true Tetun' (*Tetun Terik* or *Tetun Los*), is regarded as the highest and most sophisticated form of Tetun speech. It retains a 'noble register' (*lia na'in*), a special vocabulary, used on formal occasions, for humbling oneself and respecting others. The linguist, Catharina van Klinken, who has studied this dialect intensively refers to it as the 'coastal' (*fehan*) dialect of Tetun (1999). Included in this dialect is the Tetun spoken on the coastal plain of East Timor which is associated with the former polities of Suai and Camanasa. Van Klinken regards the Suai form of Tetun as a subdialect of *Fehan Tetun*. She contrasts both of these subdialects with what she calls the 'mountain' (*foho*) dialect of Tetun, which is spoken to the north, both in the mountains and on the plain, on both sides of the border in West and East Timor. This dialect, for example, is spoken in both Atambua and Batugade.

Yet another dialect of Tetun is spoken in the lowlands further to the east of Suai (see Hicks 1976). This dialect of eastern Tetun (or *Soibada Tetun*) became separated from *Tetun Terik* by the migration of the Mambai-speaking peoples from the mountains onto the coastal plain. In the nineteenth century, the Portuguese in Dili adopted a simplified form of market Tetun as the *lingua franca* for the territory which they controlled. Tetun was adopted only after Portuguese possessions were reduced to just the island of Timor. Prior to this, Malay was the preferred *lingua franca* among the various peoples on Flores, Alor and Timor who acknowledged allegiance to the Portuguese. Thus, for example, until the early 1850s, Malay-speaking volunteers from Sika on Flores, known as the Company of Militia from Sika (*Companhia de Moradores de Sika*) were recruited, on a near annual basis, to do battle for the Portuguese in their local warfare in East Timor.

Writing about the formation of Tetun Dili which is also known as 'market Tetun' (*Tetun Prasa* or *Tetum Praça*), the historian and language scholar, Luis Thomaz, admits that 'the origin of the use of Tetun as a *lingua franca* in East Timor is very obscure' (1981:55). Dili is in an area where one might have expected the Mambai language to have been chosen as a vehicle for communication since the town itself is located within an area originally inhabited by Mambai-speakers.

Promotion of Tetun by the Catholic church toward the end of the nineteenth century was an important factor in the eventual establishment of Tetun as a *lingua franca*. For a period, however, the church seems to have promoted Galoli as much as Tetun (Fox 1997:14). Crucial to the development of Tetun was the establishment of Soibada College in 1898 in an area of the East Tetun dialect. This college was responsible for training all the schoolmasters (*mestre escolas*) who taught throughout Portuguese Timor and provided official staff. The term, *Soibada Tetun*, was coined to refer to this standard of Tetun, which is closely related, but by no means identical with, the vernacular speech of the East Tetun dialect area.

The everyday Tetun of Dili has a simplified syntax and shows strong Portuguese (and, more recently, Indonesian) influences. It could almost be considered a creole derived from vernacular Tetun. Since the Indonesian occupation, the Catholic church has established a form of Tetun, which is sometimes referred to as 'liturgical Tetun', *Tetun Ibadat*. This standard of Tetun, although simplified, resembles *Soibada Tetun*. This liturgical Tetun is widely understood because of its use in churches throughout East Timor but it is not what people speak in ordinary communication. Rather there are a great variety of spoken forms of Tetun ranging from the street language of Dili to the vernaculars of Suai or Viqueque to varieties of learned Tetun by non-Tetun speakers.

Although great attention is given to Tetun, the fact is that the single largest language group in East Timor is that of the Mambai who occupy the mountains of central East Timor, an area that includes the districts of Ermera, Ainaro and Aileu as well as parts of Liquiça, Dili and Manufahi. Although Mambai has various dialects, there is considerable intelligibility among these dialects and a growing sense of identity among the Mambai as a group. On the streets of Dili, among local East Timorese, there is a popular distinction made between talkative Easterners (*firaku*) and more taciturn Westerners (*kaladi*). Based on this distinction, the Mambai are the archetypical *kaladi* (Traube 1980:292,

1986). Formerly, they were also the archetype for the term, *maubere*, which was used politically to designate the Timorese peasant.

Contemporary agriculture and rural identity

Throughout Timor's history, there has always been a contrast between the population of the coasts and the population of the mountains. The more populous north coast, although prone to drought, has the greatest number of rivers that can be harnessed for agricultural production. The mountainous interior of the island has historically been the heartland of the Timorese but its rough, irregular, chaotic terrain has militated against the build-up of populations in large continuous settlements. As a consequence, Timor's mountain population has traditionally lived scattered in small settlements or has concentrated, often seasonally, in specific sites to exploit available resources. Local settlements have shifted periodically to take advantage of ever changing conditions. By contrast, the rainy south coast (with the exception of the alluvial area around Suai) has been the least exploited and least populated area of the island.

Recognising these historical imbalances, the Portuguese government, already in the 1960s, initiated agricultural extension programs to induce a shift of population to the south coast. The Viqueque area to Uato Lari was a major focus of these efforts where the Portuguese, in the late 1960s, were able to introduce high-yielding varieties of rice (Metzner 1977:167).

The Indonesian government renewed these efforts from 1977 onwards, by promoting the use of high-yielding varieties of rice, extending irrigation for rice on both the north and the south coasts, and introducing transmigrants, particularly from Bali, to some of these areas to encourage the transfer of new rice-growing technologies. The promotion of rice over maize (and other dryland crops) but even more, the military obsession with security that forced a significant shift of the population from the mountains, had a profound effect on both agriculture and population distribution. The north coast became even more populous than before the Indonesian occupation while the mountain population decreased. Only in the Viqueque area was there an increase in population and a notable increase in agricultural production. In fact the Viqueque district came to rival the Maliana and Covalima (Suai) districts, particularly in its rice harvests.

Previously a variety of local identities were constructed around particular modes of livelihood. The Atoni, Mambai, Bunak and most of the other mountain populations were seen primarily as subsistence maize cultivators; the Kemak, however, were noted more for their rice planting as were the Tetun, who also distinguished themselves as cultivators of mung beans. Metzner identifies the Makassae of Quelicai as 'skilled and highly esteemed' rice cultivators who pioneered the beginnings of rice cultivation in Uato Lari (1977:283; see also Forman 1980).

Over the past 25 years, many of these particular identities have been eroded by population movement and the greater emphasis placed on rice and other crops. Coffee is now East Timor's most important export crop and most of this coffee is cultivated in Mambai areas. The Mambai have also turned to vegetable growing and have become market–gardeners to the towns of the north coast. The number of water buffalo, once the pride of the Timorese as the mark of wealth and status, have declined throughout the territory. Bali cattle have been introduced to East Timor but until the destruction of livestock in September 1999, these cattle were concentrated mainly in Los Palos in the East and Covalima in the West. The districts of Baucau and Viqueque suffered far less destruction than other parts of East Timor and fewer of their population were forced to West Timor. By contrast, the districts of Los Palos, Maliana and Covalima suffered extensive destruction and widespread deportation. The local populations of these districts will take longer to re-establish themselves and rebuild their way of life.

Conclusion

It is legitimate to ask what patterns of the past are likely to continue in the future. Certainly the resilience of the Timorese, evident throughout their history, is likely to continue in the face of a new wave of outside influences. This resilience has always been tied to different localities and undoubtedly, different localities, linked as they are to various social and linguistic identities – as well as varying modes of livelihood – will continue to play an important role in the development of East Timor.

Dampier's 1699 account of the Topass community portrays a multi-lingual community: Portuguese, Malay and at least one local Timorese language. Translated into the present, this would suggest a combination of Tetun, Indonesian and Portuguese. This simple translation, however, misrepresents the present situation: Tetun and Indonesian are languages understood by a large proportion of East Timorese whereas the use of Portuguese is still limited. Moreover, for most East Timorese, Tetun is their 'second' Timorese language. Indonesian, whether or not it continues to be taught in schools, will – as in the past – remain the language of inter-island communication. The teaching of Portuguese will inevitably conflict with the need of the East Timorese to learn English to communicate internationally. Whatever solution is worked out over time, the people of East Timor are likely to remain a multilingual population.

In their various philosophies of life, Timorese distinguish between spiritual authority and political power. As a result of its defence of the people against oppression, spiritual authority is now clearly vested in the Catholic church. This authority provides the basis for the development of a common purpose and a cohesive civil society. Political power, on the other hand, may fragment, as has repeatedly happened in the past. The history of Timor is replete with all manner of political manoeuvring and this, too, is likely to continue. One need not regard political diversity as necessarily divisive. Diversity can also be a source of strength. In co-operation with UNTAET, over the next year or two, the East Timorese must now fashion formal structures to channel their political activities. This task will be crucial to the creation of the new nation of East Timor.

References

Almeida, Maria Emilia de Castro e, 1982. *Estudio serologico dos grupos etnolinguisticos de Timor-Dili*. Lisboa: Institute de Investicacão.

Ataupah, Hendrik, 1992. Ekologi, Persebaran Penduduk, dan Pengelompokan Orang Meto di Timor Barat. Unpublished PhD thesis, Universitas Indonesia.

Barnes, R.H., 1987. Avarice and iniquity at the Solor fort. *Bijdragen tot de Taal-, Land- en Volkenkunde* 143:208-236.

Berthe, Louis, 1972. *Bei Gua: Itinéraire des Ancêtres*. Paris: Edition du CNRS.

Boxer, C.R., 1947. *The Topasses of Timor*. Amsterdam: Koninklijke Vereeniging Indisch Instituut, Mededeling No. 73, Afdeling Volkenkunde No. 24.

Castro, Affonso de, 1862. Résumé historique de l'établissement Portugais à Timor, des us et coutumes de ses habitants. *Tijdschrift voor Indische Taal-, Land- en Volkenkunde* 11:465-506.

Cunningham, Clark, 1962. People of the dry land. Unpublished D.Phil. thesis, Oxford University.

Dames, M.L. (ed.), 1921. *The Book of Duarte Barbosa.* London: The Hakluyt Society.

Dampier, W., 1703. *A Voyage to New Holland in the Year 1699.* (Reprinted in 1939: The Argonaut Press, London.)

Ezerman, H.E.K., 1917. Timor en onze politieke verhouding tot Portugal sedert het herstel van het Nederlandsch gezag in Oost-Indië. *Koloniaal Tijdschrift* 6(2):865-896; 1047-1078; 1209-1232.

Forman, Shepard, 1980. Descent, alliance, and exchange ideology among the Makassae of East Timor. In James J. Fox (ed.), *The Flow of Life: Essays on Eastern Indonesia,* pp.152-177. Cambridge, MA: Harvard University Press.

Fox, James J., 1977. *Harvest of the Palm: Ecological Change in Eastern Indonesia.* Cambridge, MA: Harvard University Press.

—— (ed.), 1980. *The Flow of Life: Essays on Eastern Indonesia.* Cambridge, MA: Harvard University Press.

——, 1981. Sailing to Kupang. *Hemisphere* 25(6):374-377.

——, 1982. The Great Lord rests at the centre. *Canberra Anthropology* 5(2):22-33.

——, 1988. Historical consequences of changing patterns of livelihood on Timor. In D. Wade-Marshall and P. Loveday (eds), *Contemporary Issues in Development,* Vol. 1, pp.259-279. Canberra: Research School of Pacific Studies, The Australian National University.

——, 1997. The historical position of Tetun among the languages of the Timor area. Paper prepared for the Tetun Language Conference, Darwin, 13-15 August.

——, 1999. Precedence in practice among the Atoni Pa Meto of Timor. In Lorraine V. Aragon and Susan D. Russell (eds), *Structuralism's Transformations: Order and Revision in Indonesian and Malaysian Societies,* pp.1-36. Tempe: Arizona State University.

Francillon, G., 1967. Some matriarchic aspects of the social structure of the Southern Tetun of Middle Timor. Unpublished PhD thesis, The Australian National University.

——, 1980. Incursion on Wehali. In J.J. Fox (ed.), *The Flow of Life: Essays on Eastern Indonesia,* pp.248-265. Cambridge, MA: Harvard University Press.

Friedberg, C., 1978. *Comment fut tranchée la liane céleste.* Langues et civilisations à tradition orale 25. Paris: SELAF.

Glover, I.C., 1971. Prehistoric research in Timor. In D.J. Mulvaney and J. Golson (eds), *Aboriginal Man and Environment in Australia,* pp.158-181. Canberra: The Australian National University.

Hamilton, Alexander, 1727. *A New Account of the East Indies.* (Reprinted in 1930: The Argonaut Press, London.)

Hamilton, William, 1979. *Tectonics of the Indonesian Region.* Geological Survey Professional Paper 1078. Washington: United States Government Printing Office.

Heyman, Albertus, 1895. *De Timor-Tractaten (1859 en 1893).* Proefschrift. Rijks-

Universiteit te Leiden. Leiden: S.C. van Doesburgh.

Hicks, David, 1976. *Tetun Ghosts and Kin.* Palo Alto: Mayfield Publications.

Klinken, Catharina Lumien van, 1999. *A Grammar of the Fehan Dialect of Tetun: An Austronesian Language of West Timor.* Pacific Linguistics C-155. Canberra: Research School of Pacific and Asian Studies, The Australian National University.

Krieger, Heike (ed.), 1997. *East Timor and the International Community: Basic Documents.* Cambridge International Documents Series, Vol. 10. Cambridge: Cambridge University Press.

McWilliam, Andrew, 1989. Narrating the gate and the path: place and precedence in southwest Timor. Unpublished PhD thesis, The Australian National University.

Metzner, Joachim K., 1977. *Man and Environment in Eastern Timor.* Development Studies Centre Monograph No. 8. The Australian National University.

Müller, Salomon, 1857. *Reizen en Onderzoekingen in den Indischen Archipel, gedaan op last der Nederlandsche Indische Regering tusschen de jaren 1828 en 1836.* 2 Vols. Amsterdam: Frederik Müller.

Ormeling, F.J., 1955. *The Timor Problem.* Djakarta: J.B. Wolters.

Parera, A.M., 1971. Sedjarah Politik Pemerintahan Asli: Sejarah Radja-Radja di Timor. Stenciled Manuscript, 188pp. Fakultas Keguruan, Universitas Nusa Cendana, Kupang.

Pélissier, René, 1996. *Timor en Guerre: Le Crocodile et Les Portuguais (1847-1913).* Paris: Pélissier.

Pigafetta, A., 1969. *Magellan's Voyage.* (Translated and edited by R.A. Skelton.) New Haven: Yale University Press.

Renard-Clamagirand, B., 1982. *Marobo: Une société ema de Timor.* Langues et Civilisation de L'Asie du Sud-Est et du Monde Insulindien 12. Paris: SELAF.

Rockhill, W.W., 1915. Notes on relations and trade of China with the eastern archipelago and the coasts of the Indian Ocean during the fourteenth century. *T'oung Pao* 16:236-271.

Schulte Nordholt, H.G., 1971. *The Political System of the Atoni of Timor.* Verhandelingen van het Koninklijk Instituut voor Taal-, Land- en Volkenkunde No. 60. The Hague: Martinus Nijhoff.

Sherlock, Kevin, 1980. *A Bibliography of Timor.* Canberra: Research School of Pacific Studies, The Australian National University.

Stapel, F.W. (ed.), 1955. *Corpus diplomaticum Neerlando-Indicum*, Vol. 6. The Hague: Martinus Nijhoff.

Therik, Gerson Tom, 1995. Wehali, the four corner land: the cosmology and traditions of a Timorese ritual centre. Unpublished PhD thesis, Department of Anthropology, Research School of Pacific and Asian Studies, The Australian National University.

Thomaz, Luis Filipe F.R., 1981. The formation of Tetum-Praça, vehicular language of East Timor. In N. Phillips and Khaidir Anwar (eds), *Papers on Indonesian Languages and Literatures*, pp.54-83. Paris: Association Archipel.

Traube, Elizabeth G., 1980. Mambai rituals of black and white. In James J. Fox (ed.), *The Flow of Life: Essays on Eastern Indonesia*, pp.290-314. Cambridge, MA: Harvard University Press.

———, 1986. *Cosmology and Social Life: Ritual Exchange Among the Mambai of East Timor*. Chicago: University of Chicago Press.

Wurm, S.A. and Shiro Hattori (eds), 1981. *Language Atlas of the Pacific Area*. Pacific Linguistics C-66. Canberra: Department of Linguistics, Research School of Pacific Studies, The Australian National University.

2

From province to nation: the demographic revolution of a people

Terence H. Hull

Estimating populations of a changing polity

When the history of East Timor comes to be written, the transition of the region from a colony to a province of Indonesia, and finally to an independent nation will stand out as a major political and social transformation in South-east Asia. However, historians will encounter serious difficulties as they attempt to describe the social and personal changes of the people of East Timor because the political manifestations of change carry with them important but confusing redefinition of who the Timorese are, where they live, and the size and structure of the population. In this chapter some aspects of demographic change are reviewed to identify how important problems of definition arise, and how they might be interpreted by those with responsibilities of caring for and responding to the citizens of the new nation of East Timor.

The story to be told here is one that poses many difficult conundrums. While we know something of the demographic changes that shaped the populations of East Timor between 1975 and 1999, we know too little to be definitive in the statement of numbers. In particular it is difficult to say with total precision how many Timorese were living in the former colony of *Timor Portugues* at the time of Indonesia's takeover in 1975 because the statistical collections were often limited in their scope, and lacking in methodological rigour. Nor can we say definitively how many died from violence, hunger, or illness in the turmoil that followed. Such records as may have been kept are unreliable, often unpublished, and in any case are subject to controversy.

TABLE 1: *Population estimates and projections for the colony, province and nation of East Timor, 1920-2000*

Year	Males	Females	Total	Implied intercensal growth rates
Colonial estimates for Timor Portuguese				
1920	215 916	181 959	397 875	
1930	249 257	222 964	472 221	1.71
1946	217 354	185 878	403 232	-0.98
1950	232 018	210 360	442 378	2.31
1960	267 783	249 293	517 079	1.56
1970	316 446	293 031	609 477	1.64
1973	340 128	306 207	646 155	1.95
Province of Timor Timur estimates				
1980	283 280	272 070	555 350	-0.93
1990	386 761	360 796	747 557	2.97
Nation of Timor Loro Sa'e estimates and projections				
1995	426 879	412 840	839 719	2.33
1999	a	a	539 719	-
2000 Low			689 719	-3.94
2000 High			764 719	-1.87
2005[b]	520 900	512 200	1 033 100	8.08

Notes: a It is not possible to estimate the sex ratios of the refugees and remaining population without more detailed data from the Indonesian government.

       b Projection for 2005 from the BPS (1998) provincial projections for Indonesia.

Sources: Colonial figures: Ranck (1977:62), reprinted by Kevin Sherlock in a collection of population data in 1981. Provincial figures from Indonesian Central Bureau of Statistics. National estimates and projections based on the latest Indonesian figures, and speculation about likely population changes post-independence.

The top section of Table 1 shows the growth of the colonial population from 1920 through 1973 according to the most reliable official figures available. The population growth was not remarkably fast between 1930 and 1960, being under half a per cent per annum on average over the three decades. This was due in part to the large and lasting impact of depression and war on numbers during the period. However, by the 1970s the growth rate was picking up substantially, and in the years prior to the withdrawal of the Portuguese was reaching an annual average growth of two per cent per year. If sustained this would have led to demographic doubling in 35 years.

Such doubling did not come to pass because of the impact of the conflicts that began in 1974 and continued in waves thereafter. Many people were lost to the population. The validity of the numerical estimates of population loss became a major focus of debate in the 1980s (see Arndt 1979). Attempts were made to estimate deaths of Timorese from the demographic figures published before and after 1975. One calculation compared an unofficial count in 1974 of 688 769 with an Indonesian Army count in 1978 of 329 271 to raise the question 'where are the missing 359 498 people?' The difficulty in validating such calculations lies in the fact that neither the Portuguese nor the Indonesian enumerations were of sufficiently high quality to simply apply demographic calculations to estimate the number of people missing. The most detailed work on this issue was done by Patsy Thatcher at Monash University in the early 1980s. After tracking down as many of the diaspora as she could identify in various international records, and making adjustments for Timorese living in other provinces of Indonesia, and Indonesians moving into Timor, Thatcher projected the 'might-have-been population' for 1980 of 718 095. This is the population that might have been living in Timor had the 1960-70 growth rate continued uninterrupted by revolution and invasion. Such a calculation indicates as many as 162 745 missing Timorese in 1980. Subtracting the approximate number of 13 000 deaths attributed to the civil war of 1974-75 implies that as many as 150 000 Timorese had left the province, died, or had not been born as a result of the invasion.

Such exercises are of rapidly decreasing value as time passes, and the population responds to other changes in social and economic events. Over the years that *Timor Timur* was the 27th province of Indonesia, many Timorese left their land to live elsewhere, either as part of the large but vaguely defined diaspora in Portugal, Australia, Macau or other nations, or as migrants within the Indonesian nation. Many were seeking education or employment in other provinces. The population of the province came to include a mixture of peoples. This was not new since during colonial times, Portuguese had lived in the colony filling posts in the administration, military, police, schools and the Catholic church, but the scale of non-Timorese mixture into the population changed radically. In 1970 only 1.6 per cent of the population was classified as being non-Timorese. Of these, there were just over 6000 Chinese, around 2000 'mestizos' and 1500 Portuguese. As a province, *Timor Timur* found people coming from Java, Sulawesi, and other islands of Eastern Indonesia to fill many of the posts in the bureaucracy and economy. The new migrants were particularly prominent in expanding the school and health systems and building and managing shops.

Under the Indonesian statistical system it is difficult to estimate the numbers of non-Timorese living in East Timor since the main variables used to identify ethnic background were citizenship, language, and place of birth. The migrants from other provinces of Indonesia were all Indonesian citizens, and many spoke Indonesian at home. Migrants from West Timor often spoke Tetun or other local languages common to East Timor. East Timorese shared such characteristics. Moreover, in the two decades following 1976 many newcomers settling into the province established their families in Timor, so the place of birth of their children was given as *Timor Timur*.

The best way to approach an estimate of the number of true ethnic Timorese living in the province is to divide census and survey populations according to whether the head of household was born in East Timor, or not. This is not a totally accurate way to identify indigenous East Timorese since there may be a number of ethnic Timorese, particularly in the western part of the territory, who were born in the province of East Nusa Tenggara, but have long lived in East Timor. However, for the purposes of rough calculations the method is very robust.

In 1990 there were 684 202 people living in households where the head of household was East Timor born. In contrast there were 63 355 people in households headed by somebody born elsewhere. If this breakdown can be regarded as a measure of non-Timorese presence, then 8.5 per cent of the 1990 population were non-

Timorese, a large change from the Portuguese period.
The populations of Timorese and non-Timorese were very

FIGURE 1: *Population pyramids for East Timor in 1990, according to where the head of household was born*

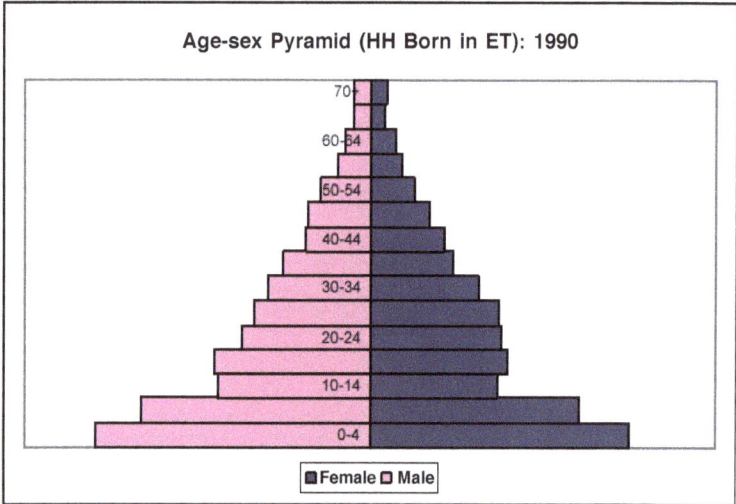

Age-sex Pyramid (HH Born in ET): 1990

| 70+ |
| 60-64 |
| 50-54 |
| 40-44 |
| 30-34 |
| 20-24 |
| 10-14 |
| 0-4 |

■ Female □ Male

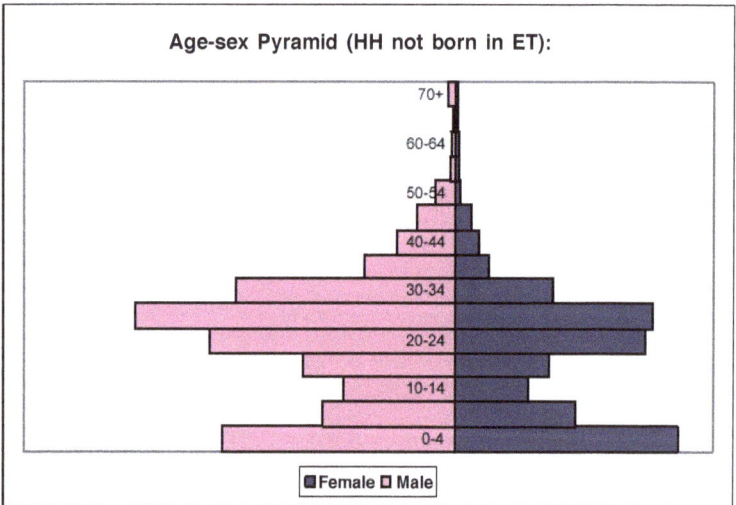

Age-sex Pyramid (HH not born in ET):

| 70+ |
| 60-64 |
| 50-54 |
| 40-44 |
| 30-34 |
| 20-24 |
| 10-14 |
| 0-4 |

■ Female □ Male

different in their structures, as indicated in the two pyramids in Figure 1. In the upper panel the pyramid of the Timorese shows the broad base of a rapidly growing population, but with a serious deficit of 10-30 year olds of both sexes. Such a deficit can be caused by birth deficits in the period between 1960 and 1980, selective out-migration of young people, or the failure to record the young people in the census. Each of these factors is likely to have operated, but it is not possible to say how much. In contrast, the people living in households headed by a non-Timor born person had a very unusual pyramid, indicative of highly selective migration (see lower panel of Figure 1). Males in particular were heavily over-represented in the 20-34 age range. This was the pattern to be expected from a practise of transferring young men to the province to take up military, bureaucratic or other short-term work. The young men were matched by a smaller but still significant number of young women of similar ages indicating a substantial number of young married couples, with the complementary finding of large numbers of very young children (aged from 0-4).

The contrast in the shapes of these two pyramids is moderated when we remember that the number of non-Timorese was small in relation to the total population. Thus when the two groups are combined to form a single pyramid for 1990 the demographic structure to emerge is still a pyramid with a broad base and a significant deficit in the 10-20 year olds.

One useful analysis that can be made is to match the numbers of people living in households headed by East Timor born Heads of Household in 1990 with the same cohorts registered as electors in 1999.

This is done in Table 2. The years of birth taken to define cohorts for comparison are copied from the announcements of the UNTAET Human Rights Unit responsible for compilation of the electoral rolls. The numbers show that people in the cohorts born before 1929 (i.e. age 70 and over in 1999) had a low ratio of voter registration. Some of them had undoubtedly died in the nine years between the census and the election, but others were probably too frail to undertake the difficult registration procedures. Overall, though, from three-quarters to four-fifths of the people aged 10 to 50 at the time of the census survived and registered to vote in 1999. Given the difficult conditions and social disruption in East Timor in 1999 this would seem to be a very creditable rate of registration.

TABLE 2: *Comparison of cohort numbers from the 1999 Voter Registration with the 1990 Population Census*

Year of birth recorded in voter registration	Male		Female		Total		Ratio
	1990	1999	1990	1999	1990	1999	1999/1990
>1909	504	43	444	41	948	84	.088
1910-1919	1 965	451	1 908	283	3 873	734	.190
1920-1929	7 735	3 386	7 269	2 865	15 004	6 251	.417
1930-1939	17 116	10 964	16 347	10 296	33 463	21 260	.635
1940-1949	28 314	21 133	27 938	20 489	56 252	41 622	.740
1950-1959	41 157	33 449	42 115	33 579	83 272	67 028	.805
1960-1969	56 164	48 651	60 867	49 287	117 031	97 938	.837
1970-1980	79 319	66 544	69 906	60 826	149 225	127 370	.854
1981-1982	19 273	6 235	17 096	6 365	36 369	12 600	.346
1983-1999	97 230	NA	91 535	NA	188 765	NA	NA
Total >1983	251 547	190 856	243 890	184 031	495 437	374 887	.757
Total >1999	348 777	NA	335 425	NA	684 202	NA	NA

Sources: The figures for the 1990 Census are based on special tabulations for people living in households headed by a Timor-born resident, according to age groups corresponding to the birth cohorts in column one. Figures for the Voter Registration were provided by the UNTAET Human Rights Unit.

In examining the numbers in Table 2 it is important to remember that the 1990 Census was a sample enumeration subject to potentially large errors in the estimation of numbers of very old people. The data are not robust enough to justify calculations of interenumeration mortality rates because migration and non-sampling errors would heavily affect the estimates, and hence such calculations are not undertaken here.

Fertility and mortality levels

The province of *Timor Timur* was routinely included in the various data collections of the Indonesian Central Board of Statistics, so we have much better information on Timor now than was ever the case in the days of colonial rule. Nonetheless, as is the case of Indonesia as a whole, the vital statistics for East Timor were not based on registration of births and deaths, but rather a series of indirect demographic estimation procedures subject to problems of sampling and reporting errors.

The first reasonably reliable estimate of fertility in *Timor Timur* came out after the 1990 Census, and gave a total fertility rate (TFR) of 5.73 (BPS 1994). This can be interpreted as the number of children women on average would bear if they continued reproducing at the same rate as the reference fertility rates throughout their reproductive lives. The reference fertility rates for this particular measure are based on the experience of women over the period from 1986 to 1989. The TFR was calculated using the 'own-child' method. Using a slightly different calculation method, the BKKBN was able to estimate the TFR for the year 1990, which they found to be 4.86 (BKKBN 1993). These calculations support the notion that fertility was very high in *Timor Timur*, but that it had begun to fall, perhaps due in part to the impact of the family planning program. Such a speculation was reinforced by the results of the 1994 Indonesian Demographic and Health Survey (DHS) that gave a TFR for *Timor Timur* of 4.69 while the 1997 DHS produced a TFR of 4.43. After examining this apparent trend the BPS projected a TFR for Timor in the year 2002 of 3.51, still higher than any other province in Indonesia, but substantially down from the estimates in the 1980s.

The apparently steady decline in fertility is slower than other provinces of Indonesia because the adoption of contraceptive methods has been more recent and slower as well. In 1997 the DHS found that only 27 per cent of women in Timor were using some method of birth control, compared to a nationwide average of 57 per cent and a level of nearly 40 per cent in neighbouring East Nusa Tenggara where the cultural and economic environment is most similar to East Timor. Almost all of the users were receiving the three-monthly contraceptive injection, and a few had the contraceptive implant. Methods such as the pill, IUD, sterilisation, and the various traditional methods all had less than two percentage of women as current users, while there were no recorded users of condoms or vasectomy or withdrawal. Such patterns indicate that when health services are reconstructed some thought will need to be given to the way contraceptive services are provided. There is obvious scope for efforts to broaden the range of options available to include methods such as the pill and IUD, and to deepen the efforts to promote responsible family planning, particularly among men.

TABLE 3: *Average number of children ever born (CEB) and children surviving (CS) by age of mother, 1995*

Age group	Head of household born in East Timor			Head of household born outside East Timor		
	CEB	CS	Proportion surviving	CEB	CS	Proportion surviving
15-19	0.1	0.1	.96	0.0	0.0	1.00
20-24	0.8	0.8	.93	0.4	0.4	1.00
25-29	2.1	1.9	.91	1.4	1.3	.96
30-34	3.6	3.1	.87	2.2	2.1	.98
35-39	4.1	3.5	.86	3.0	2.9	.98
40-44	4.3	3.5	.80	4.3	4.0	.94
45-49	4.3	3.3	.78	4.9	4.7	.96

Mortality estimates have shown similar trends. The 1990 Census produced an estimate of infant mortality for the year 1986 of 85 per 1000 live births. Using a different estimation method the figure for 1994 was 46 per 1000. Perhaps as a sign of concern over the possible errors of these estimates, the BPS projections assumed much higher levels of infant death, with figures of 90 per 1000 for 1997 and 73 per 1000 for 2002. It needs to be stressed that the variety of estimates in the BPS publications is not an indication of political manipulation of data, but rather the real difficulty of ascertaining mortality levels for small populations when using indirect demographic methods of estimation.

The difficulties of producing demographic rates to describe the situation of East Timor can be overcome to some extent by referring instead to three measures of family structure that can easily be tabulated from censuses and surveys. These are the average number of children ever born to women (tabulated in five-year age groups), the average number of these children surviving to the time of the enumeration, and the calculation of the proportion surviving. Table 3 sets out these measures for women in households headed by Timor born and non-Timor born people in 1995. What is clear from the figures is that the Timorese have only slightly larger families, both ever-born and surviving, than the non-Timorese in the age groups under 40, but this is in a situation where the proportion of children surviving is consistently lower.

If these figures were converted into infant mortality rates (IMR) they would indicate that the Timorese had an IMR of 78, while the non-Timorese had a rate of 29 per 1000 live births on average over the decade preceding the 1995 survey.

Restoring and projecting the population of Timor Loro Sa'e

While fertility and mortality are the most important determinants in the growth of most national populations, over the foreseeable future the greatest factor setting population numbers in East Timor will be migration. The events of 1999 have already shown the power of migration in changing the demographic landscape. From as early as January 1999 when President Habibie announced that Indonesia would co-operate with a referendum on the future of East Timor, there were reports of departures by teachers, traders and government functionaries returning to other provinces of Indonesia. Concern about the escalating violence and the outcome of the referendum encouraged them to pack up their belongings, and prepare to evacuate. A trickle, then a flow, culminated in a flood of people moving out as the aftermath of the referendum unleashed forces of violence, anxiety and anger. Movements of this type are virtually impossible to monitor, with the result that it is difficult to estimate the numbers of people who remained in East Timor. However, by October various Indonesian and United Nations officials were estimating the number of Timorese refugees in West Timor to be in the order of 250 000 people, or 30 per cent of the 1995 population. Assuming that virtually all the members of households headed by non-Timor born people (something over 50 000) also left, gives the rough estimate of the population of Timor Loro Sa'e of 539 719 in late 1999 (see Table 1). This is a population approximately equal to the level of the late 1970s.

However this low population number changed rapidly as people who moved out of East Timor in September 1999 began to make decisions about their futures. According to UNHCR (in *Jakarta Post*, 5 October 1999) 60 per cent of the 250 000 East Timor refugees in Nusa Tenggara Timor wanted to return to their homeland. If this had been effected immediately then by 1 January 2000, the young nation would have had a population of 689 719. At the same time some Indonesian leaders estimated that the number wishing to return was more like 10 per cent, implying a potential restoration of only

25 000 people. This assumption has been invalidated by the fact that 150 000 people had returned home by the middle of January 2000, leaving 100 000 refugees in West Timor, some of whom were still intending to return if peace and security could be assured. The assumption of some independence leaders was that the number of people who wanted to return was more realistically given as 90 per cent of all those who had fled or been transported out in September. Depending on the desires of refugees and the options available to them, the population in 2000 could reach as much as 764 719 Timorese, plus the number of foreigners recruited to work with peace-keeping and development assistance activities. The best guess for 2000 lies between the conservative assumption of a 60 per cent rate of immediate return of refugees, and a somewhat larger return that is still in process. The former still implies an annual -3.9 per cent per annum decline of population compared to the 1995 estimates while the decline for the latter is just -1.87 per cent.

The actual population will depend on many factors, including the co-operation of the Indonesian government in allowing easy access of cross-border traffic, the scale of humanitarian relief efforts, and the numbers of peace-keeping and aid personnel recruited to the task. Obviously any attempt to deal with the highest priorities of development – that is the education of children and the provision of health services for all – will require the recruitment of large numbers of teachers and health workers to fill the gaps left by departing Indonesian professionals. It was estimated that 11 000 teachers, including 7500 primary teachers, left the province before the referendum. Some of these were ethnic Timorese and they may intend to return once the situation stabilises. However, most teachers and university lecturers were from other provinces of Indonesia, and it is hard to imagine them returning to East Timor in the near future, if ever. Estimates of the number of personnel to be recruited are only possible once the basic structures are decided upon. But before the teachers must come the curriculum, and before that must come the issue of a national language. When the schools and universities open, though, there will be a need for between 10 000 and 15 000 teachers and lecturers.

While it is tempting to suggest that doctors and nurses can be recruited in advance of the establishment of a health service, it would soon become clear that delivery of health implies a reliance on systems of logistics, structures of referral, and systems of priority that do not come easily. If East Timor is not to be totally dependent on the random benefits of ongoing charities, government will need to create a health service that balances the needs of primary, domiciliary, and specialist care in a sustainable fashion. Throughout the time of Indonesian rule there were difficulties recruiting skilled people to fill these roles. In 1992 there were just on 190 doctors and dentists in the province including seven specialists. Most direct services to patients were provided by 660 nurses and 200 midwives. Many of the latter groups are probably still in East Timor, but few of the doctors remain or are likely to return. With 10 hospitals, 70 clinics and 250 sub-clinics running before 1999, the need for medical personnel is clear, but equally there is a need to recruit staff who have both the skills (including linguistic skills) and the dedication to serve the people.

If skilled professionals can be recruited to serve the new nation, and if an open and stable relationship can be formed with a democratised Indonesia, the potential for rapid population growth is certainly embedded in the current demographic structure. In Table 1 the projection for the year 2005 is based on the most simple assumption of 'no population loss' in comparison with what trends were showing at the end of the 1990s (BPS 1998:117-120). Had fertility and mortality continued to fall in the 1990s, and had net migration intake of two per 1000 people per year (the experience of the five years from 1990-95) been maintained, then the population could be expected to pass the 1 million mark in the year 2004. The disruptions of 1999 will probably push that landmark off a few more years, but the young age structure of Timorese means that rapid population growth will be the immediate result of any return to stable political conditions. The 'baby boom' embedded in the age structure will be a major challenge to the planners of health and educational services, and a substantial encumbrance to young women who want to participate fully in the task of rebuilding their nation.

Timor Loro Sa'e could recover many of the Timorese who moved out of the province in 1999. An independent nation could draw home some of the diaspora and attract people from the region (including West Timor) who want to participate in the development of a new country. If so, the projection for 2005 in Table 1 could be the edge of a blueprint to the future population. But if less enticing scenarios unfold, the population of Timorese in 2005 could, like the population today, be the story of demographic divisions with a scattered and growing diaspora. It is against the stark contrast of such futures that the project of building Timor Loro Sa'e is set.

Acknowledgments

Thanks to Karen Ewens, Rajesh Chauhan and Freda Mason for assistance with the demographic calculations undertaken in this chapter.

References

Arndt, H.W., 1979. 'Timor: vendetta against Indonesia', *Quadrant*, December, 13-17.

Timor Timur Dalam Angka, 1993. Dili: BAPPEDA and Kantor Statistik.

BKKBN, 1993. *Perkiraan Tingkat Kelahiran di Indonesia, Tahun 1980 dan 1990: Penerapan Metode Kelahiran Anak Terakhir (Last Live Birth)*. Jakarta: Badan Koordinasi Keluarga Berencana Nasional.

BPS, 1994. *Tren Fertilitas, Mortalitas dan Migrasi*. Jakarta: Biro Pusat Statistik.

BPS, 1998. *Proyeksi Penduduk Indonesia per Propinsi 1995-2005: Supas 95 Seri S 7*. Jakarta: Biro Pusat Statistik.

BPS, BKKBN, DEPKES and DHS, 1998. *Survei Demografi dan Kesehatan Indonesia, 1997: Laporan Pendahuluan*. Jakarta.

Rogers, Peter, 1981. 'The Timor debate goes on: a formal Indonesian population figure for the former Portuguese province fails to settle the death question', *Far Eastern Economic Review*, February 6, 16-18.

Saldanha, João Mariano de Sousa, 1994. *The Political Economy of East Timor Development*. Jakarta: Pustaka Sinar Harapan.

3

East Timor: education and human resource development

Gavin W. Jones

The educational situation at the time of Indonesian invasion

The Portuguese colonialists did very little to educate the population of East Timor. Until almost the very end of their 450 years of colonisation, education was established solely to meet the demand for colonial administrative officials. The Portuguese left the country with an embryonic education system, and a predominantly illiterate population. The literacy rate at the end of Portuguese rule is estimated to have been only 10 per cent (Saldanha 1994:60). Since literacy rates for the adult population as a whole reflect the educational situation prevailing decades before the present, the adult literacy rate for East Timor in 1990 (33 per cent, compared with 79 per cent in Indonesia excluding Eastern Indonesia) also reflects the very limited efforts of the Portuguese to provide education.

The Portuguese left educational activities largely in the hands of the Catholic church, which established a number of schools (*colegio*). The colonial administration began to give more attention to education following a revolt in 1959. The number of elementary school students rose from 4 898 in that year to 27 299 a decade later, and a further sharp rise was recorded to 57 579 in 1971-72 (Saldanha 1994:Tables 2.3, 2.4). The latter figure must be viewed with some suspicion, however, because the figure the year before was only 32 397. Pupil-teacher ratios were very high, rising from the mid-30s in the early

1960s to over 50 from 1968-69 onwards, a figure so high that it has serious implications for the quality of education. Teachers were very hard to find, because few Timorese had more than a primary school education, and recruitment of teachers from Portugal or from the more advanced colonies met with the obstacles of lack of funds and lack of enthusiasm on the part of the teachers to go to East Timor.

The first secondary school was only opened in 1952. Enrolments remained extremely small, with numbers fluctuating in the range from 200 to 800 students during the course of the 1960s. There was no provision of education at the tertiary level.

Educational developments since 1975

The greatest source of pride for Indonesia since its annexation of East Timor in 1975 has been its provision of basic education. The number of schools has multiplied, and every village had a primary school by about 1985.[1] Table 1 shows the trend in the number of schools, teachers and pupils at the primary education level, and Table 2 shows the trends for high school and tertiary education. The number of primary school pupils in the first two or three years of Indonesian rule appears to have been lower than in the final years of Portuguese rule, presumably reflecting the difficulties the Indonesians experienced in imposing order and initiating a new system of education. But the numbers were building up quickly by the beginning of the 1980s.

In the case of both primary and secondary education, there were impressive increases in number of schools and of student numbers through the 1980s, but decreases in student numbers beginning in the late 1980s in the case of primary education and after the school year 1990-91 in the case of lower and upper secondary education. These decreases, occurring in the face of continuing increases in the numbers of children in the relevant age groups, imply significant declines in school enrolment ratios in the early 1990s.

---

[1]   This is a rough estimate. There are 442 villages (*desa*) in East Timor. By 1985 there were 497 primary schools in the province. Even allowing for the fact that many of these primary schools were in the towns such as Dili and Baucau, the figures suggest that in 1985 or shortly thereafter, there would have been a primary school in every village.

TABLE 1: *East Timor – Trends in primary school education, 1976-93*

School year	No. of schools	No. of teachers	No. of new pupils ('000)	Total no. of pupils	Pupils per school
1976-77	47	499	10.5	13.5	287
1977-78	107	614	18.8	23.0	215
1978-79	202	959	22.4	41.5	205
1979-80	208	1 610	13.3	59.1	284
1980-81	293	1 515	21.7	68.7	234
1981-82	339	1 821	52.1	77.6	229
1982-83	376	2 226	38.0	90.4	241
1983-84	400	2 446	38.6	99.4	249
1984-85	410	2 614	31.7	100.6	245
1985-86	497	2 910	31.3	111.2	224
1986-87	540	3 359	31.4	126.7	235
1987-88	559	3 723	27.2	129.6	232
1988-89	565	4 894	27.9	105.1	186
1989-90	574	4 739	20.9	100.4	175
1990-91	559	4 574	28.9	95.9	171
1991-92	590	4 653	21.1	104.4	177
1992-93	654	5 260	24.1	110.6	169
1993-94	652	6 656	27.4	128.0	196

*Source: Timor Timur Dalam Angka (*1993:Table 4.1.3).

The 1990 Population Census and the 1995 Intercensal Survey (*Supas*) are the most up-to-date and complete sources of data on the educational composition of the population of East Timor. Tabulations from these sources with regard to literacy, school enrolment, and educational attainment are available in Jones and Raharjo (1995:Chapter 8) and Tandjung and Sutomo (1998). They indicate a rapid improvement over time in all these measures, but a continuing lag compared with other provinces of Indonesia. For example, in 1995, 33.1 per cent of the adult population of East Timor (aged 15+) had completed primary school or proceeded further in their education, compared with 65.2 per cent in Indonesia. In East Timor, 19.9 per cent had completed junior secondary school or more, compared with 33.1 per cent in Indonesia. But these figures partly reflect the limited provision of education during the Portuguese period. The rise in educational attainment between the cohorts educated mainly in the 1960s and 1970s and the cohorts educated mainly in the 1980s and 1990s was very sharp. A relevant comparison

TABLE 2: *East Timor – Trends in secondary and tertiary education, 1976-93*

School year	No. of lower secondary schools	No. of lower secondary students	No. of upper secondary schools	No. of upper secondary students	No. enrolled in tertiary education
1976-77	2	315	-	-	-
1977-78	9	926	-	-	-
1978-79	14	1 041	-	-	-
1979-80	15	1 248	-	64	-
1980-81	19	2 474	1	225	-
1981-82	23	4 272	1	454	-
1982-83	28	5 453	2	977	-
1983-84	35	8 247	2	1 541	-
1984-85	43	9 836	2	2 770	-
1985-86	57	11 735	7	5 310	443
1986-87	71	22 905	17	7 599	675
1987-88	81	26 787	19	10 889	799
1988-89	90	28 342	22	10 088	969
1989-90	90	28 964	31	14 574	1 210
1990-91	94	31 482	35	19 634	1 383
1991-92	97	24 261	38	17 177	2 037
1992-93	101	21 972	42	17 947	2 199
1993-94	103	21 779	43	18 303	2 658

Source: *Timor Timur Dalam Angka* (1993:Tables 4.1.4, 4.1.6, 4.1.7, 4.1.23, 4.1.55).

is with the neighbouring province of East Nusa Tenggara (NTT). According to data in the 1995 SUPAS, East Timor was ahead of NTT in the proportion of the 20-29 year age group who had completed at least lower secondary school (35.5 per cent in East Timor; 30.6 per cent in NTT). But East Timor lagged far behind NTT in the same statistic for the age group 40-59: 6.1 per cent for East Timor; 12.7 per cent for NTT. This age group passed through the school-going years during Portuguese rule in East Timor.

Neither the numbers in school shown in Tables 1 and 2 nor the figures on educational attainment just cited differentiate between native East Timorese and the children of non-East Timorese (for example the children of transmigrants, government servants and the military). Since virtually all non-East Timorese fled prior to or following the 1999 referendum into East Timor's future, and few are likely to return to East Timor after independence, the relevant information in relation to East Timor's prospects for future development concerns the

TABLE 3: *East Timor – Proportion of population illiterate, by age group and birth-place of head of household, 1990*

Age group	Head born in East Timor		Head born elsewhere	
	Males	Females	Males	Females
15-19	21.6	31.2	5.2	5.7
20-24	35.0	56.6	2.3	6.2
25-29	53.2	74.6	2.0	9.1
30-34	62.5	83.9	3.2	5.0
35-39	72.0	88.5	4.2	19.6
40-44	82.2	93.7	8.1	12.1
45-49	84.2	93.6	0.0	26.7
50-54	85.9	93.6	8.8	40.7
55-59	89.4	94.8	14.9	51.0
60-64	89.4	96.6	37.6	60.8
65-69	88.8	94.5	22.2	35.5
All ages 15-69	57.3	73.0	3.5	9.2
Number	193 467	193 219	26 829	15 602

Source: Computed from data tapes, 1990 Population Census.

schooling of the native East Timorese. It has been possible to extract such data from the 1990 Population Census and the 1995 SUPAS by tabulating the educational data according to whether the head of household was born in East Timor or not. Tables 3 and 4 compare the educational attainment, enrolment ratios and literacy for those living in such households and those living in households where the head was not born in East Timor.

Table 3 shows the proportions illiterate in 1990 in households where the head was born in East Timor and in other households. The differences are striking. Among the East Timorese population, illiteracy is extremely high in all age groups aged 40 and over, particularly among women. It only falls below 50 per cent in the 15-24 year age group. By contrast, illiteracy among non-native East Timorese is much lower; for males, percentages illiterate fall to single digit figures at all ages below 55-59, and for females at all ages below 35-39.

Educational attainment reflects the same kinds of extreme differences between native East Timorese and non-Timorese. Table 4 shows the 1995 data on educational attainment of persons living in households where the head of household was born in East Timor. The most striking fact is that even in the age group 15-19, which grew up under Indonesian administration, slightly less than half of both males and females had completed primary education. The equivalent figure for the non-native East Timorese (not shown in the table) was 95 per cent for both sexes. The proportion with senior secondary education or above was very low for the East Timorese, though it has been increasing rapidly over time. At ages 25-29 this proportion reached 23 per cent for males, though it was less than nine per cent for females. In striking contrast, more than half of all adult males, and almost half of all adult females, living in households where the head was not born in East Timor had senior high school education and above.

Tertiary education

It is essential to have a core of well-educated people in any country to provide leadership, professional services in education, medicine and other fields, and to fill the senior positions in the public service. There were very few well-educated East Timorese at the time of incorporation into Indonesia, as no institutions of higher education had been developed under Portuguese rule. During the Indonesian period, higher education institutions were developed. The University of East Timor (UNTIM) was established in 1992, financed not by the central government but by the provincial government, with assistance from Catholic foundations. It was affiliated with the University of Gadjah Mada. By 1992 it offered only four courses: agricultural sciences, English, social and political science, and pedagogy. The quality of the education offered at this university was very questionable (Beazley 1999:52) and its students numbered only in the hundreds. In 1995, there were 436 students registered at the Open University in Dili, and there was also a polytechnic with a capacity of 100 students.

Thousands of East Timorese students have also gone to study in Indonesian universities or abroad, most of them on government scholarships. Many of them were reported to drop out, and on their return often had to wait for months or years for a job. As a result, many sought jobs outside East Timor (Beazley 1999:52-53). There is certainly no evidence from Table 4 that many of them had returned to East Timor: fewer than 500 persons living in households where the head was born in East Timor had completed tertiary education.

TABLE 4: *Proportion of persons according to educational attainment, ages 15-69, 1995 (head of household born in East Timor)*

Age group	Male					Female				
	None or some primary	Complete primary	Lower secondary	Upper secondary	Tertiary	None or some primary	Complete primary	Lower secondary	Upper secondary	Tertiary
15-19	52.9	32.1	13.8	1.3	0.0	52.4	32.1	13.5	2.0	0.0
20-24	44.6	21.8	18.9	14.2	0.5	58.4	17.7	13.4	10.4	0.1
25-29	48.6	15.2	12.4	23.1	0.7	70.1	13.0	7.9	8.6	0.4
30-34	67.5	13.5	4.6	13.0	1.4	86.3	7.2	2.8	3.3	0.5
35-39	77.6	11.6	4.9	5.3	0.5	91.5	5.0	1.9	1.6	0.0
40-44	80.1	12.6	3.7	3.2	0.4	93.2	3.5	1.3	1.7	0.2
45-49	92.6	4.6	1.4	1.2	0.2	98.2	1.6	0.0	0.2	0.0
50-54	94.7	3.9	1.4	0.0	0.0	98.2	0.9	0.7	0.2	0.0
55-59	94.9	4.4	0.7	0.0	0.0	98.1	1.6	0.3	0.0	0.0
60-64	97.5	1.3	0.8	0.4	0.0	99.5	0.5	0.0	0.0	0.0
65-69	98.5	1.5	0.0	0.0	0.0	99.4	0.0	0.6	0.0	0.0
Total	68.6	14.7	8.0	8.2	0.4	79.4	10.8	5.7	3.9	0.2
Number	142 017	30 467	16 625	16 878	931	164 772	22 503	11 794	8 052	334

Source: Computed from data tapes, 1995 Intercensal Population Survey.

TABLE 5: *Proportion able to speak Bahasa Indonesia, persons living in households where the head was born in East Timor*

Age group	Male	Female
15-19	85.0	77.4
20-24	78.3	59.3
25-29	64.6	43.2
30-34	57.5	31.7
35-39	46.8	27.1
40-44	34.7	16.8
45-49	30.5	15.4
50-54	25.0	12.3
55-59	20.5	8.9
60-64	16.0	9.1
65-69	20.0	8.7
All ages	56.4	39.4

Source: Computed from data tapes, 1990 Population Census.

Language

Language is a key issue for the future of East Timor. It has to be resolved whether the national language will be Tetun, Portuguese, Indonesian or English. Each have their particular claims to value. One important issue is the proportion of the population that can speak each of these languages. In the case of Bahasa Indonesia, data are available from the 1990 Population Census. Table 5 presents these data, for the East Timorese whose head of household was born in East Timor. Clearly, there is a strong generational difference in the ability to speak Bahasa Indonesia. The younger cohorts, most of whom were taught in school in the Indonesian language, have high proportions able to speak Bahasa Indonesia, but this proportion drops off sharply to only 35 per cent for males and 17 per cent for females at age 40-44, and even lower at older ages.

The structure of employment

The East Timorese are heavily concentrated in primary industry (agriculture, fishing, animal husbandry, etc.). Table 6 shows the striking differences between their occupational structure and that of non-East Timorese in 1990. Non-East Timorese were heavily concentrated in clerical, professional and sales occupations, with about 10 per cent

TABLE 6: *East Timor – Proportion of workers in broad educational categories, by birthplace of head of household, 1990*

Broad occupational category	Head born in East Timor		Head not born in East Timor	
	Male	Female	Male	Female
Professional	1.5	1.2	13.9	24.1
Administration and managerial	0.1	0.0	0.8	0.3
Clerical	6.0	1.7	43.0	23.8
Sales	2.9	4.7	11.9	28.7
Service workers	2.5	0.9	6.8	8.3
Agriculture	81.1	80.8	8.7	11.7
Production workers	5.9	10.7	14.9	3.1
Total	100.0	100.0	100.0	100.0

Source: Computed from data tapes, 1990 Population Census.

in agriculture, presumably most of them transmigrants. This occupational structure reflects the concentration of non-East Timorese in government service (including teaching, nursing, and many clerical occupations), and in trading and marketing activities. An extraordinarily low proportion of East Timorese workers were in professional, clerical and sales occupations, presumably reflecting their low levels of education, a bias in favour of outsiders in some government service activities, and the domination of markets and retail trade by inmigrants such as the Buginese and Makassarese from South Sulawesi.

Issues – looking ahead

Shortage of teachers and quality of education: A high proportion of teachers in East Timor shortly before the referendum of August 1999 were non-East Timorese. A 1999 report stated that East Timorese constituted less than 12 per cent of teachers in the province (427 out of 3698). The other teachers came principally from Java (1205) and NTT (1353) (Beazley 1999:49). Another report stated that only two per cent of junior and senior high school teachers (67 out of 3362 teachers) were East Timorese (*Kompas* 8/3/1999). The rapid development of education clearly required recruitment of teachers from outside the region, but there were complaints that these teachers did not understand the local population, did not speak a local language, and lacked cultural sensitivity.

Many children say that Indonesian teachers are unsympathetic to them, that they have to pay a 'fee' to attend school, and even a bribe to go up in class. Teachers themselves complain about the children having short concentration spans, coming late to class, not wearing uniform, being disobedient and undisciplined, being only interested in talking about East Timorese independence, and of walking out of class ... The conclusion which the teachers and officials often come to is that East Timorese students do not want to learn (Beazley 1999:49).

Frustrations of school pupils were undoubtedly related to dissatisfaction with continuing Indonesian rule, as well as to the shortage of jobs for those with education, to be discussed below. The lack of discipline reached serious levels in some schools, with teachers facing threats of violence from students if they were not given the grades they wanted or were not promoted. In some cases teachers feared for their lives (Tirtosudarmo and Handayani 1993:485-486). The same kinds of concerns were widely expressed in 1998 and 1999 (*Kompas* 8/3/1999, 9/3/1999). In this situation, quality of education was the loser, and the NEM (*Nilai Ebtanas Murani*: end of school level examination scores) scores for East Timor certainly indicated a poorer performance by students there than elsewhere in Indonesia.

Looking ahead, the supply of school teachers is clearly a major concern. Few East Timorese are qualified to teach above the primary school level, and it is unrealistic to expect that more than a handful of the non-Timorese teachers would be interested in returning after independence (except, perhaps, some of the quite large numbers of former teachers from West Timor). Special recruitment of teachers from abroad is likely to be needed, via development assistance agencies and non-government organisation (NGO) groups, including the Catholic church. One aspect of the problem concerns the language of instruction. The choice between Tetun, Indonesian, Portuguese or English as a national language has yet to be settled, and similarly for the language (or languages) of instruction in schools.

Shortage of jobs for the high school educated: The Indonesian authorities in East Timor always had trouble coming to terms with the fact that it was the young people, born since Indonesian occupation of East Timor and given educational opportunities, who were the most vocal critics of the regime. There were many reasons for this, of course, but one source of deep frustration was the lack of job opportunities for the better-educated (Mubyarto and Soetrisno 1991:55; Saldanha 1994:259). This was partly the result of a perceived preference for non-Timorese in civil service positions. If so, it will cease to be a factor under an independent government. Nevertheless, as noted by one observer in 1989, 'there are almost 25 000 high school students in the province, but the government can employ at most only 50 new civil servants each year' (Soesastro 1989:219). The most basic issue is the heavily agricultural nature of the East Timor economy, and the small modern sector. The need to rebuild a structure of government administration, as well as the need to rebuild infrastructure after the destruction wreaked in the post-ballot violence will provide considerable employment, provided that enough foreign aid is provided. Once the basic infrastructure has been repaired, and a new government formed, there will be a need for teachers, doctors, nurses, other professionals and clerical workers. This should provide opportunities for the better-educated Timorese for some time to come – again, with the proviso that funds to employ them must come from somewhere.

After some years, assuming that educational enrolments can be raised again to the levels reached in the later stages of the Indonesian administration, the problem of limited job opportunities will re-assert itself. Unless the East Timor economy is able to develop more strongly in areas such as manufacturing or tourism, it will fail to provide many job opportunities for the better-educated. And as citizens of a small, independent country, educated East Timorese will no longer have the option of looking for work elsewhere in Indonesia.[2]

References

BAPPEDA, 1993. *Timor Timur Dalam Angka.* Kerjasama BAPPEDA Tk. 1 dan Kantor Statistik Propinsi Timor Timur.
Beazley, Harriot, 1999. *East Timor: Background Briefing for Project Identification Mission (PIM).* Canberra: Australian Agency for International Development.

[2] Under the Indonesian administration, not only could East Timorese spontaneously look for jobs outside the province, but the Yayasan Tiara of the Department of Manpower had a systematic program of sending East Timorese to other parts of Indonesia to work (Saldanha 1994:264).

Jones, Gavin W. and Yulfita Raharjo, 1995. *People, Land and Sea: Development Challenges in Eastern Indonesia.* Canberra: Demography Program, The Australian National University.

Mubyarto and Soetrisno, 1991. *East Timor: The Impact of Integration, An Indonesian Socioanthropological Study.* Yogyakarta: Gadjah Mada University Research Center.

Saldanha, João Mariano de Sousa, 1994. *The Political Economy of East Timor Development.* Jakarta: Pustaka Sinar Harapan.

Soesastro, M. Hadi, 1989. 'East Timor: questions of economic viability', in Hal Hill (ed.), *Unity and Diversity: Regional Economic Development in Indonesia Since 1970.* Singapore: Oxford University Press.

Tandjung, Ichwan Ridwan and Haryoto Sutomo, 1998. *Updated Tables for People, Land and Sea: Development Challenges in Eastern Indonesia.* Center for Population and Manpower Studies, Indonesian Institute of Sciences (PPT-LIPI) and Demography Program, Research School of Social Sciences, The Australian National University.

Tim P3PK UGM, 1990. *Masyarakat Desa Timor Timur: Laporan Penelitian Sosio-Antropologis.* Yogyakarta: Universitas Gadjah Mada.

Tirtosudarmo, Riwanto and Titik Handayani, 1993. 'Pembangunan dan penduduk usia muda: kesenjangan pendidikan dan kesempatan kerja di Timor Timur', *Analisis CSIS*, Tahun XXII(6):476-497.

Newspaper reports

'Derita guru pendatang di Timtim: di bawah Bayang-bayang teror dan kekerasan', *Kompas*, 8/3/1999.

'Guru berdemonstrasi, mendesak pindah dari Timtim', *Kompas*, 9/9/1999.

4

Political developments leading to the referendum

Dionisio Babo Soares

B.J. Habibie was appointed President of Indonesia after student demonstrations ousted the former President, Soeharto, from power in 1998. On 27 January 1999, Habibie agreed to hold a 'consultation'[1] with the East Timorese where they would be asked to choose between wide ranging autonomy within Indonesia and independence. The consultation or referendum was conducted by the United Nations under its mission in East Timor, UNAMET (United Nations Assistance Mission in East Timor) and saw a 99 per cent turn out on the ballot day. 94 388 East Timorese representing 21.5 per cent of voters supported the proposal for wide-ranging autonomy within Indonesia while 344 580 East Timorese representing 78.5 per cent of voters rejected it. The army-led pro-Indonesian militia, who were already responsible for earlier violence in the territory rampaged throughout East Timor, burning houses, killing hundreds of people and forcing the evacuation of a large number of East Timorese into West Timor.

This chapter deals primarily with the political developments before the referendum. It is divided into various parts. The first part highlights

---

[1] 'Consultation' was the preferred term and the one insisted upon by Indonesia to use instead of the term 'referendum' throughout the process. Although Indonesia gave little reason to show the difference between these words, many do not see the difference between the two when it comes to implementation. The word 'referendum', instead of 'consultation', will be used throughout this chapter.

political developments in the 1970s and analyses how past and current events have shaped East Timor's political climate. The second part describes events which took place prior to and after the historic announcement of 27 January 1999. The third part explores political developments after the 5 May Agreement between Indonesia and Portugal as well as developments leading to the ballot day, 30 August 1999. The fourth part examines the development in the aftermath of the ballot announcement and underlines necessary measures to prevent further bloodshed in the future.

The dynamics within the resistance

In the aftermath of the 1974 *Flowers Revolution* in Portugal, five political parties emerged in East Timor: *União Democratica Timorense* (UDT), *Frente Revolusionaria de Timor Leste Independente* (Fretilin), *Associacão Popular Democratica Timorense* (Apodeti), *Klibur Oan Timor Ass'wain* (KOTA) and Trabalhista, the Labour Party. The three major parties – UDT, Fretilin and Apodeti – were quick to declare their political visions and other small parties, KOTA and Trabalhista, whose political visions were unclear, sought to form coalitions with each of the three major parties. UDT advocated a period of continuing affiliation with Portugal as a means toward achieving full independence, Fretilin supported immediate independence, and Apodeti sought a transitional autonomy within Indonesia before independence (Singh 1998).[2]

In August 1974, UDT launched a surprise coup aimed at quelling the other four political parties and controlling the territory. Fretilin reacted quickly to this event by launching a counter-attack and successfully overthrew the remaining Portuguese government in the territory. The leaders of UDT[3] and some members of its army, after resisting briefly, withdrew into West Timor, part of the Indonesian province of Nusa Tenggara Timur. The evacuation included approximately 40 000 refugees, most of whom were unaware of

---

2   Apodeti's political platform (political manifesto) states that East Timor would need a period of transition with Indonesia, not integration, before having its own independence.

3   UDT leaders were Francisco Lopes da Cruz, Indonesia's former roving ambassador for East Timor, João and Mario Carrascalão and Domingos Oliveira.

political circumstances in Dili, the capital of East Timor. The leaders of KOTA and Trabalhista were also evacuated to West Timor, while the president of Apodeti, Mr José Osorio Soares, was later captured and killed by Fretilin forces (Dunn 1996; Singh 1998).

The evacuation into West Timor and subsequent takeover of East Timor by Fretilin forces sparked further political chaos in East Timor. Subsequently, the Portuguese government in Timor including its governor, Lemos Pires, withdrew from Dili in August 1975. Fretilin declared the independence of East Timor on 28 November 1975. The Indonesian military responded quickly to this 'power vacuum'[4] by launching an invasion of East Timor on 7 December 1975, and annexation followed six months later. Fretilin forces retreated into the mountains and began the 24-year-long guerilla war against the Indonesian army (Dunn 1996).

In 1979, after three years of brutal war, Fretilin's president and leader of the armed forces, Nicolau Lobato was killed. Xanana Gusmão who replaced Lobato took a new approach in Fretilin's campaign for independence. He abandoned the conventional tactics used by his predecessor and converted the party into a guerilla force, employing hit and run tactics and successfully penetrating the Indonesian army's intelligence circles, thus setting up regular contacts with sections of the Indonesian army for information and weapons transactions.[5] This new approach, coupled with the people's determination, helped the resistance to survive Indonesian military campaigns until 1986. In the early 1980s, Xanana successfully forced the Indonesian military to accept a ceasefire, but the ceasefire was later violated by the Indonesian army, causing a breakdown in further military negotiations. Colonel Purwanto upheld the ceasefire in the

---

4   After the Portuguese abandoned East Timor, Indonesia believed that there was a power vacuum in the territory. It responded quickly to this event with a military invasion several months later despite the fact that Fretilin was the '*de facto*' administration in the province (see various publications by the Indonesian Information Ministry 1980-90).

5   In 1996, I interviewed a university student in his mid-20s who admitted that in the 1980s he was working as a negotiator for 'weapon transactions' between the resistance and Indonesian officials. He admitted that the army official, with whom he had a well-planned and regular contact, agreed to accept around Rp 4 000 000 or US$1 750 (the exchange rate was Rp 2,285 = US$1) for four rifles and a box of ammunition.

early 1980s in Lariguto on behalf of the Indonesian army. When General L.B. Moerdani replaced General Mohammad Yusuf as the Indonesian Minister of Defence, he dismissed the 'ceasefire agreement' and continued the war.

In the early 1980s some political parties successfully formed an umbrella body known as *Convergencia Nacional Timorense*, the National Pact for East Timor. This body, which consisted of all but Apodeti, failed to survive the differences over national interest that prevailed among its leaders at the time. The fact that Fretilin continued to assert its presence on the ground as *de facto* administration made other parties feel uneasy, particularly when it came to the issue of 'who represents the resistance'. UDT viewed Fretilin as using the body to legitimate itself as the only voice of the resistance.[6] KOTA and Trabalhista[7] also sought to disengage themselves from the pact quietly.

From 1975 to 1986, the resistance remained divided and no measures were taken to form a single body. In 1987, Xanana Gusmão and José Ramos Horta, the spokesperson for the resistance, quit Fretilin and formed CNRM (*Conselho Nacional da Resistencia Maubere*). UDT, however, continued to reject the legitimacy of this body, claiming it was another metamorphosis of Fretilin. The heart of these disputes centred on the term MAUBERE. Literally, *maubere* refers to a common name found among the Mambae people, the largest ethnic group in East Timor (see Traube 1986). During the Portuguese colonial period, *maubere* was generally used to distinguish the native East Timorese from the upper class, educated Portuguese and, to a certain degree, the *mestizos*, the half caste group. 'Maubere' was often employed as a synonym for the illiterate, uneducated and, to some degree, uncivilised (see Traube 1986).

Fretilin, being a proletariat-based political party,[8] identified itself with

---

[6]   Pers. comm. with a refugee from East Timor in Portugal, October 1998.

[7]   The party, 'Trabalhista', seems to have disappeared from the political scene in East Timor by the late 1970s.

[8]   Being a proletariat-oriented political party does not necessarily make its ideology identical with Marxism, as was widely assumed among liberal democracies. Nevertheless, there is a still unanswered question on the issue of 'communism' and whether the Fretilin of the 1970s did identify itself with Marxist ideology. 'Communism' was an issue used by Indonesia in the late 1970s during its military campaign in East Timor to discredit Fretilin, at the height of the Cold War between the US and the former USSR.

the term *maubere*. It indeed attracted many supporters among the common people who saw themselves as victims of colonialism. On the other hand, parties such as UDT, which advocated continued affiliation with Portugal, and KOTA, the feudal-oriented political party, rejected the term *maubere*. The same argument was used when these political parties rejected Xanana and Ramos Horta's CNRM whose aims were to:

• unify factions within the resistance, which had remained divided until that time;
• set up a body that represented this umbrella organisation as the voice of the resistance abroad;
• represent the resistance as comprising not just Fretilin but other political parties that included pro-integration supporters who later joined the resistance;
• develop the three main aspects of the resistance: the diplomatic front, the underground movement and the military arm (Falintil).

The resistance became more united when in 1997, in Peniche, Portugal, all factions agreed to change CNRM into CNRT (*Conselho Nacional da Resistencia Timorense*). Preparation for a new government was the main agenda of CNRT as developments in support of East Timor reached their height in the 1990s. The Santa Cruz massacre in 1991, the Nobel Peace Prize in 1996 to Bishop Ximenes Belo and Ramos Horta, the renewed debate on East Timor in the UN, and support from solidarity groups around the world helped bring the cause of East Timor onto the world stage.

Democratic changes in Indonesia had started to unfold and public awareness of East Timor had increased. East Timor, long a 'pebble inside the shoe' of Indonesian international diplomacy, had come to influence Indonesian politics both domestically and internationally, and Indonesian leaders had to put extra effort into minimising the harm to Indonesia's international credibility. The departure of former dictator Soeharto opened new prospects for a political solution to be found to the question of East Timor. President Habibie paved the way for a popular consultation in 1999.

Falintil's role in the resistance

Forças Armadas de Timor Leste (Falintil) is the armed wing of CNRT. Formerly, Falintil was the armed wing of Fretilin, which had fought Indonesia from 1975 until 1985. On 20 August 1987 when Xanana Gusmão restructured the resistance movement, Falintil was changed from the armed wing of one political party into a national army. Falintil constituted one of the three major elements of the resistance organisation throughout the years of struggle against Indonesia. The other two were the clandestine movement led by several leaders[9] and the diplomatic front represented by Mr José Ramos Horta. Xanana Gusmão assumed the leadership of the resistance movement and served as the commander of Falintil.

When Xanana was captured in 1992 by the Indonesian forces, the leadership of Falintil was handed over to José Antonio da Costa who was known as Ma'Huno (*nom de guerra*). Only two months later, Ma'Huno was also captured by the Indonesian army. He was replaced by commander Nino Konis Santana. When Konis Santana came to the leadership of Falintil, the structure of the resistance was maintained allowing Xanana to continue to play a leadership role from his prison in Jakarta. Nino Konis Santana died in 1998 and was replaced by Taur Matan Ruak who assumed the role of local commander of Falintil until the popular consultation was held in August 1999. Under Taur Matan Ruak, Falintil was structured as follows:

- Kay Rala Xanana Gusmão as the Supreme Commander;
- Taur Matan Ruak as the Vice Commander of Falintil and Commander of Region II (Baucau, Manatuto and Dili);
- Lere Anan Timor as the commander of Region I with authority over Los Palos and Viqueque;
- Falur Rate Laek as commander of Region III with authority over Same, Ainaro and Suai;
- Ular, commander of Region IV with authority over Liquiça, Ermera, Bobonaro, Suai and the enclave of Ambenu.

Newly emerged political organisations

During the 1990s various political organisations were formed in East Timor. Most of these organisations operated under the banner of resisting Indonesia's presence in the territory. Students studying in Indonesia set up the first wave of such organisations. The first was

---

[9] Being an underground organisation and to avoid enemy detection, the names of these leaders were not disclosed to the public.

RENETIL (*Resistencia Nacional dos Estudantes de Timor Leste*),[10] the largest East Timorese students underground organisation. Other groups followed, such as *Frente Clandestina Estudantil de Timor Leste* (FECLETIL) and *Liga dos Estudantes Patriotas* (LEP).

The second wave took place in East Timor. The most important of these groups were *Organisacão da Juventude Catolica de Timor Leste* (OJECTIL) which later became *Organisacão da Juventude de Timor Leste* (OJETIL), FITUN (lit., 'star') and OPJLATIL (*Organisacão Popular Juventude Lorico Ass'wain Timor Leste*). Another group which called itself *Republica Democratica de Timor Leste* (RDTL), surfaced in East Timor politics in the mid-1990s, taking Fretilin's declaration of independence on 28 November 1975 as its political platform. This group believed that there was no need for a referendum since East Timor was already an independent state, invaded by Indonesia in 1975. It insisted on the Indonesian army withdrawing from the territory, and East Timor being returned to its status as an independent state.

Other groups came later and affiliated themselves with the resistance movement, such as MOBUDAN (*Movimento Buka Dalan Foun*), a movement yet to announce its political platform, and PPA (*Persatuan Pemuda Apodeti*), a group comprised of the children of the former Apodeti party members. However, the activities of such organisations were hardly seen in public until the referendum day.

Interestingly, most of these organisations did not convert themselves into political parties nor did they identify themselves with the existing political parties of the resistance. Only FECLETIL, in the late 1990s, declared itself as *Partido Socialista de Timor* (PST) and became a new contender in East Timor politics. One of its leaders, Avelino Coelho, known as Salar Kosi, was trapped in the Austrian embassy in Jakarta for more than a year when seeking political asylum there. He was not allowed to leave, according to Ali Alatas, because of the alleged crimes he had committed. Earlier, a new political party was formed in Portugal, a breakaway from UDT, called UDC (*União Democratica Christã*). A former leader of the independence movement turned integrationist,

---

[10]   This organisation was led by Fernando de Araujo who is known as Lasama. He was a student in the Linguistics Department of the University of Udayana Bali in Denpasar (1985-91) but was captured in 1991 and imprisoned in Cipinang prison in Jakarta for his political activities. He was released in 1998, seven years after his arrest.

Abilio Araujo, formed another new party in Dili just a week prior to the referendum: *Partido Nacionalista Timorense* (PNT).

Developments prior to and after 27 January 1999

Soon after his appointment as the President of Indonesia, B.J. Habibie sought to introduce political reform in his country. One of his most active campaigns was to resolve the issue of East Timor and improve Indonesia's image abroad. In his first ever interview with foreign media (CNN) after his appointment, Habibie surprised many by announcing a policy shift on East Timor, promising to grant a broad autonomy package to the province.[11] Nevertheless, this sudden announcement was received with caution by the sympathisers and proponents of East Timor independence. Xanana, as the leader of CNRT welcomed the decision but argued that President Habibie did not go far enough. He challenged Habibie to put his words in action.[12] Like other resistance leaders, he expected this shift of policy in Indonesia would mark the beginning of a lasting solution on the question of East Timor.

Since 1988, Xanana had begun to receive regular visits from representatives of various nations around the world. When he was moved to a house a year later, Xanana continued to receive regular visits by high profile leaders from friendly nations such as the US representative for Asia and the Pacific, Stanley Roth, and former President Nelson Mandela from South Africa. These visits made Xanana a particularly high profile prisoner.

Such developments, coupled with the changing environment in Indonesian politics, helped place the East Timor case at the centre of the Indonesian political debate. Leaders of newly emerging political parties such as Amin Rais (PAN, the National Mandate Party) and Abdurrahman Wahid (PKB), who was later elected President, while proposing their own agenda, called for a referendum in the territory. As the race to improve Indonesia's political image was at its height, President Habibie and Foreign Minister Ali Alatas proposed a referendum package before a cabinet meeting, in October 1998. Habibie and Alatas' proposal surprised the commander of the armed forces,

---

[11] The interview was conducted in June 1999 in Jakarta.
[12] *Kompas*, July 1999.

General Wiranto, who insisted that 'ABRI (now TNI), the Indonesian armed forces, was not prepared to face a sudden policy change'.[13]

Although there was no ensuing action by the military to prevent further division over the East Timor issue within the cabinet, the period between October 1998 and January 1999 witnessed two major changes as far as the military operation in East Timor was concerned. One was the reorganisation of the existing three semi-paramilitary groups: Tim Alfa in Los Palos and Saka and Makikit in Baucau became 'Civil Defence Units' (Keamanan Rakyat: KAMRA). Los Palos and Baucau are located in the eastern region of East Timor. The second change was the establishment of two new paramilitary groups in central and western Timor, Mahidi (Dead or Alive for Integration) and Halilintar (Lightning) in Maliana.[14] Cancio Carvalho, the leader of the Mahidi militias stated in an interview with Australia's ABC in April 1999 that his group was set up in December 1998.

Coincidentally, in December 1998, the Australian Prime Minister, John Howard, sent a letter to President Habibie asking him to reverse Indonesia's policy on East Timor, a policy that former Australian Foreign Minister, Gareth Evans, once dubbed 'irreversible'. When President Habibie announced that his government would allow the East Timorese to choose between autonomy within Indonesia and independence in January 1999, Mahidi responded immediately by killing several people in the village of Cassa, Ainaro district and in the sub-district of Zumalai. The victims included a pregnant woman and two teenage boys. In the same interview with the ABC, Carvalho acknowledged the killings and justified his actions by arguing that the pregnant woman was the wife of a Falintil (East Timorese Liberation Army) fighter.

Reaction to Habibie's proposal also came from different parts of the world. While the international community welcomed it as

[13] Pers. comm. with an East Timorese resistance leader in Darwin, 27 September 1999.
[14] Such paramilitary groups were led by the following personalities: Tim Alfa was commanded by the mayor (*bupati*) of Los Palos, Edmundo Conceicão; Saka (Baucau) and Makikit (Viqueque) were commanded by a Timorese-born sergeant who was a member of TNI, Joanico Belo; Mahidi was commanded by the son of a traditional landlord in Cassa, Ainaro; and Halilintar was commanded by João Tavares, the commander of pro-integration forces, who is now in West Timor.

an unprecedented democratic gesture that showed the President's willingness to distance himself from Soeharto's past wrongdoings, Habibie's proposal was received with mixed reactions in Indonesia and East Timor. Megawati Sukarnoputri, the leader of the PDI-P (Indonesian Democratic Party in Struggle) rejected the proposal arguing that the President did not have the mandate to reverse Soeharto's decision of incorporating the territory into Indonesia.[15] The same reaction came from sections within Indonesian society, particularly from Muslim leaders. They argued that Habibie's lack of consideration in tackling the issue of East Timor might not help but only exacerbate the situation. It was widely perceived among the Muslim circles in Java that the East Timorese, the majority of whom are Catholics, would vote for independence, thus laying the foundation for renewed secessionist movements in Indonesia. Likewise, some members of ABRI showed their discontentment with Habibie, claiming the President's announcement could create a 'domino effect', thereby setting a precedent for other provinces such as Aceh and Irian Jaya to follow suit.

In East Timor, the pro-independence group welcomed Habibie's statement with doubt. On the one hand, José Ramos Horta, the spokesperson for the CNRT, argued that despite being happy with the announcement, much remained to be seen since Indonesia had never kept its promises with regard to East Timor in the past. On the other hand, the CNRT leaders responded quickly to Jakarta's change of heart by reorganising its campaign across the territory. In Dili, the students at the University of East Timor (Universitas Timor Timur, known as UNTIM) took the initiative to 'socialise' Habibie's proposal. These students went to remote villages all over the territory to campaign for independence.[16]

In the meantime, the pro-integration group which, despairing over Habibie's announcement, and with much to lose if the United Nations proceeded with a referendum in the territory, felt threatened.

---

[15] She later reversed her statement arguing that she would accept the results, whatever the people chose.

[16] Three prominent students who helped organise this activity were Antero Benedito da Silva, Aderito and Francisco da Costa, who set up an organization called DSMPTT (*Dewan Solidaritas Mahasiswa dan Pelajar Timor Timur*), an acronym for The Solidarity Board of Students of East Timor.

With the help of the Indonesian army, the group set up the second wave of militia groups to add to the strength of groups like Mahidi and Halilintar:

• Aitarak (Thorn) led by Eurico Guterres in Dili;
• Naga Merah (Red Dragon) led by Miguel Soares Babo in Ermera;
• Darah Merah (Red Blood) led by Lafahek Saburai in Ermera;
• Besi Merah Putih (Red and White Iron) led by Manuel de Sousa in Liquiça;
• Laksaur (Eagle) led by Olivio 'Moruk' Mendonça;
• ABLAI (Struggle for Integration) was set up in Same led by Nazario Cortereal;
• Dadurus Merah Putih in Bobonaro (leader unknown) plus
• Hametin (Bobonaro) (leader unknown);
• Sera (Sera Malik) (leader unknown);
• Rajawali (leader unknown);
• Jati Merah Putih (Real Red and White) in Los Palos (leader unknown);
• Mahadomi in Manatuto led by Vital Doutel Sarmento and Aquino Caldas;
• Pana (Liquiça) (leader unknown);
• Sakunar led by Simão Lopes in Oecussi.

The violence carried out by such militia groups took place simultaneously several weeks after Habibie's offer of a referendum and resulted in the killings of a number of pro-independence supporters. Mr Rui Lopez, the former *bupati* of Covalima, claimed in a television interview (*SBS*, September 1999) from his hiding place in Macau that there were 443 people killed in his area alone prior to the referendum. Mr Lopez himself was a militia leader who defected after disagreeing with the military's overall plan to eliminate both the independence supporters and the clergy in East Timor.

Some defectors from the militia[17] and accounts from eye witnesses confirmed that:

> It is rare for the military to appear in the front line during militia operations. Their tactics are pushing the militias who use the traditional arms such as

[17] Mr Rui Lopez and Mr Tomas Aquino Goncalves defected to safety in Macau and have given accounts of military and militia planning.

machetes, *parang* and sword to attack a defenceless population. They normally
stand behind the militia to protect them in the case of counter-attack but
also normally engage in shooting using automatic weapons.[18]

There were two attempts initiated by the Catholic church to
reconcile the two opposing factions, pro- and anti-independence
groups. The first, known as Dare I, took place soon after the January
announcement in an old seminary on the outskirts of Dili. The
meeting brought together a number of both pro- and anti-
independence leaders and aimed at forging close links, starting a
dialogue and eventually, halting all violence between the two sides.
Indeed, the meeting, which took place over two days, resulted in
both sides issuing a statement pledging their commitment to a non-
violent campaign. In practise, militia activity continued unabated.

The climax of events surrounding militia activities was the
5 April massacre in Liquiça, a district located 45 km to the west of the
capital, Dili. Militia, backed by the military, shot and hacked to death
more than 40 defenceless civilians who were gathering in a churchyard
(*Sydney Morning Herald*, 6 April 1999).[19] Interestingly, while accounts by
church clergy and other witnesses confirmed that the military was behind
the attack, no action was taken to launch an inquiry or to investigate the
killings. The TNI persisted with its claim that the deaths resulted from
a clash between pro-independence and pro-integration groups.

By June 1999, UNAMET with its international CIVPOL (Civil Police)
had set up a local presence throughout the territory. Yet they failed to
bring peace to the territory. As the tense situation continued, violence by
the militia was directed not only at civilians, but also toward NGOs,
humanitarian agencies and human rights activists. Consequently, the call
for a Multinational Force (MNF) gained much publicity. In an attempt to
safeguard the 'fragile' 5 May Accord, Jakarta rejected any call for a MNF
to be deployed in East Timor and maintained that its army could handle
security in the territory.

It was understood that the violence perpetrated by the militia and

---

[18] Interviews with four UNAMET local staff working in Suai namely, Eusebio
da Costa, Artur Lopez, Alipio Baltazar and Simão Barreto in Darwin, 2-4
October 1999.

[19] Reference can also be made to other major newspapers in Australia (6 April
1999) such as *The Age*, *The Australian*, *The Canberra Times* and others.

members of the Indonesian armed forces (TNI) aimed to achieve the following objectives:

- To lure Falintil to respond to provocation and thereby legitimate the argument that there was an internal conflict in East Timor;
- To use this conflict as the basis for the TNI to intervene and prevent the push for the presence of an international force in East Timor;
- To picture East Timor as an area of conflict and therefore insist that any international supervised referendum would be doomed to failure.

Fortunately, such provocations failed to draw Falintil into the conflict and hence provide justification for the claim that a conflict was taking place in East Timor. In the meantime, international pressure on Habibie to implement his promises grew even stronger.

In another development, the Indonesian government also set up its own team to oversee the referendum and to guarantee that the 5 May Agreement was implemented accordingly. One of the team's members was General Zacky Anwar Makarim, the former head of BIA (Indonesia's Army Intelligence Unit) who had worked previously in East Timor in the 1980s. General Zacky Anwar was known for his organised terrorist-style attacks[20] on the leaders of the pro-independence movement in the territory and is believed to have been involved in the killings in Aceh and Irian Jaya prior to accepting his post in East Timor.[21] Major-General Syafrie Syamsuddin, a TNI officer who had just completed his work in Aceh province, joined Anwar just prior to the ballot. According to an eyewitness, Francisco Kalbuadi, General Syamsuddin was seen at the scene of the militia's attack on Bishop Belo's house where more than 25 people were killed, just days after the ballot result was announced, an accusation flatly denied by General Syamsuddin (*Sydney Morning Herald*, 11/10/99).

Developments after 5 May 1999

Despite continuing violence, Indonesia and Portugal, under the auspices of the UN, reached an agreement on 5 May 1999 to give the UN a mandate to consult the people of East Timor, whether to accept or

---

[20] The most notorious of these was the Ninja-style attacks conducted in the mid-1980s and early 1990s.
[21] See reports compiled by *TAPOL* and *Amnesty International* from June to September 1999.

reject Indonesia's offer of autonomy. Based on that agreement the Secretary-General (SG), Kofi Annan, after consulting the Security Council, set up a special mission for East Timor (UNAMET) in the same month. The mission initially planned to conduct the ballot on 8 August 1999. Increasing army-backed militia activity forced the UN to postpone the ballot on two separate occasions.

While negotiations were taking place in New York, sporadic violence continued on the ground. In a public display before the eyes of the Jakarta appointed governor, Abilio José Osorio Soares, the leader of the Aitarak militia, Eurico Guterres, pledged to hunt and kill the opponents of integration. His words were followed by action hours later with the murder of several people including the son of a pro-independence leader, Manuel Carrascalão. Torture, terror and abduction, as widely reported by foreign media, were carried out systematically. Targets were chosen carefully. They included CNRT leaders, students, people working for NGOs (non-governmental organisations) and those considered to have some influence in the society.

David Jenkins, a veteran Asia correspondent, argued that the method adopted by the Indonesian army followed the tactics of the US Phoenix program in the Vietnam war, which killed tens of thousands of peasants and much of the indigenous South Vietnamese leadership. This tactic had been used previously by the Contras in Nicaragua. Jenkins said that the state terrorists were 'not simply going after the most radical pro-independence people, but … the moderates, the people who have influence in their community' (*The Guardian* [UK], Tuesday, 02/10/99).

Indeed, well before the referendum, the commander of the Indonesian military in Dili, Colonel Tono Suratman, in an interview for Australian ABC television in June 1999, warned of what was to come:

> If the pro-independents do win … all will be destroyed. It will be worse than 23 years ago. An army document of early May, when the international agreement on the referendum was reached ordered that massacres should be carried out from village to village after the announcement of the ballot if the pro-independence supporters win. The Independence movement should be eliminated from its leadership down to its roots (*The Guardian* [UK], Tuesday, 02/10/99).

In a theatrical show, the Indonesian armed forces commander, General Wiranto, flew from Jakarta to Dili and staged a reconciliation meeting between the leaders of pro- and anti-independence groups.

Again, just hours after Wiranto left Dili, the anti-independence militias returned to the streets and started beating, torturing and even killing people who they claimed to be pro-independence sympathisers. Meetings between the two Timorese factions took place several times in Jakarta. Domingos Soares, the leader of FPDK (*Forum Persatuan Demokrasi dan Keadilan*), the anti-independence faction together with the head of the Third Way Movement, Abilio Araujo met Xanana Gusmão in Jakarta to discuss the reconciliation process (*Lusa Broadcasting Corporation*, 30/08/99). Other subsequent meetings also took place between leaders of pro- and anti-independence groups both inside and outside East Timor. However, none of these meetings bore the fruit of true reconciliation. A workshop held by the Australian National University in Canberra in late April 1999, despite bringing together leaders from the two different factions in East Timor in an amicable atmosphere, failed to produce a framework for reconciliation.

The Catholic church sponsored a second reconciliation meeting, Dare II, between the two opposing factions in Jakarta. It too failed to yield a fruitful outcome that could have served as the ground for a peaceful settlement of the conflict. Meanwhile, efforts to undermine and to cancel the ballot continued unabated. The threat against UNAMET officials was obvious. The head of the Aitarak militia, Eurico Guterres, made several threats to David Wimhurst, the UNAMET spokesperson in East Timor, saying 'he does not want to see Mr Wimhurst in East Timor' in the future.[22]

As a result of militia and Indonesian army activities, thousands of people left their homes and took refuge in churches and places considered to be 'safe'. According to John Martinkus of *AAP*, by 30 July 1999, more than 50 000 people were classified as internally displaced people (IDP) throughout the territory. The number went higher in the lead up to the ballot day.

As a result, the UN postponed the ballot from 8-22 August 1999, and later postponed it again until 30 August 1999. Registration began on 12 August and ended a week later amidst continuing violence by the militia. The UN, according to the Portuguese *Diario das Noticias* (20/08/99), had asked the Indonesian government to apprehend the militia and bring the members of the military, who were actively

---

[22] Television interview with Eurico Guterres during the Dare II meeting in Jakarta.

supporting them, to justice. Pressure to quell militia violence was also put forward by the governments of the US, Britain, the Republic of Ireland, Brazil, Portugal and some South-east Asian countries (*Diario das Noticias*, August 1999).

Increasing pressure also forced General Wiranto to recall several of his commanders in East Timor just days before the referendum. These were Colonel Tono Suratman who was the commander of the TNI in the territory, Letkol Siagiam, the commander of Korem in Maliana and General Zacky Anwar Makarim the liaison officer for Indonesia's team of observers in the referendum (*The Canberra Times*, August 1999).

In the weeks leading up to the ballot, a group of Indonesian ministers including Ali Alatas (Foreign Affairs Minister), General Wiranto (Commander of the Armed Forces) and Faisal Tanjung (the Minister for Politics and Security Affairs) twice visited East Timor. Their aim was to observe the situation as well as persuade the militia to stop their campaign of terror.

However, the military and General Wiranto in particular, seemed to be ambiguous in responding to events in East Timor, particularly in the period leading to the referendum. As a member of Habibie's cabinet, Wiranto did not intend to undermine both Habibie's determination to hold the ballot based on the accord signed between Indonesia, the United Nations and Portugal on 5 May 1999. Yet he continued to remain silent over militia atrocities in East Timor. He seemed unable to resist the push from some members of the military who did not want to see East Timor gain independence. In many cases the army was involved in militia attacks on a defenceless population.

It was understood that military involvement in militia atrocities could undermine its image and halt efforts to rebuild its credibility before the international community. Therefore, whenever international pressure was mounted, TNI would intervene as if it continued to maintain a neutral role between the militia and the resistance body.

Throughout these developments, the armed pro-Indonesian militia continued their campaign of violence. Thus, for example, Yayasan HAK, a local human rights body, confirmed that on 19 August, the militia attacked a crowd of pro-independence supporters outside a church compound in the town of Suai leaving several injured (*AFP*, 19/08/99).

The pro-Indonesian side also started their autonomy campaign even before the official campaign period was launched. Banners encouraging voters to vote for autonomy were displayed around the territory; awareness campaigns promoting the autonomy package took place in different parts of the territory and distribution of pamphlets carrying autonomy messages were common. As a response to the pro-Indonesian campaign, the CNRT chose to undertake a muted campaign. According to the Indonesian news daily, *Kompas*, during the month of June and July more than 1000 East Timorese university students dispersed to remote villages to make the population aware of the option for independence.

During the months of May and June, several students from the University of East Timor, who were doing their practical work in Suai, were beaten unconscious and two of them were abducted and later found dead. On 19 August, in a gesture to appease mounting criticism of the Indonesian military, the leader of the Aitarak militia made a symbolic hand-over of weapons saying that it was to ease the tension and pave the way towards a peaceful referendum (*Reuters*, 19/08/99).

On 15 August 1999, the CNRT raised its flag for the very first time in Dili, marking the first day of its political campaign in East Timor and the official opening of its first office in Dili. It took only two days for the new office to witness several shots fired by the militia, who renewed their campaign of violence.

On 20 August 1999, more than 10 000 people attended a ceremony commemorating 24 years of Falintil in Waimori, a location designed by UNAMET as one of the four cantonment areas for the Falintil. Similar ceremonies took place in the other three Falintil cantonment areas in Los Palos, Ermera and Bobonaro (*AFP*, 20/08/99).

Although militia violence appeared unstoppable, the church still tried to bring peace to the East Timorese. On 29 August, one day before the ballot, Bishop Carlos Ximenes Belo and the parish priest of Suai, Father Hilario Madeira,[23] successfully sponsored a peace settlement between the militia and the CNRT. In a mass attended by more than 800 people, the leaders of the two opposing parties, pro-

---

[23] Father Hilario Madeira was shot dead together with two other priests, Father Francisco Soares and Father Tarcisius Dewanto, and a large number of refugees who were seeking protection in the church of Suai on 7 September 1999. According to eyewitnesses, the shooting took place in front of the church and was conducted in a joint operation between the militia and the Indonesian army (interview with four UNAMET local staff working in Suai: namely, Eusebio da Costa, Artur Lopez, Alipio Baltazar and Simão Barreto in Darwin, 2-4 October 1999).

and anti-independence, embraced each other and vowed to commit themselves to peaceful means of settling their differences. The militia leader Vasco da Cruz[24] was among those who handed over their weapons to the bishop who, in turn, gave them to Indonesian police. Later, according to several first-hand accounts, Vasco da Cruz and several members of his Mahidi militia were disarmed by other militia members for agreeing to attend the church-sponsored peace.[25]

Closing remarks

This chapter has described briefly the political developments in East Timor on the eve of the referendum on 30 August when the East Timorese voted overwhelmingly for independence. The period between September and October 1999 saw several major political developments in the territory.

The first was the Indonesian army and militia rampage throughout the territory, during what ought to be known as 'Black September', resulting in large-scale destruction and killing in the territory. Thus, after the ballot was announced on 4 September 1999, the militia, backed by the Indonesian army, started their rampage throughout the territory, burning houses and forcing the evacuation of people from their homes. More than 250 000 people fled to West Timor and hundreds, if not thousands, of independence supporters were subsequently abducted and killed by the same militia.[26] The Indonesian military helped transport the refugees into West Timor and other, yet to be known parts of Indonesia. Amnesty International accused the military of orchestrating the mass exodus of people and forcing them to leave East Timor at gunpoint. The International Crisis Group for East Timor refers to the militia rampage as a 'scorched earth policy' planned carefully by both the militia and the Indonesian army.

The second development was the introduction of an Australian-led multinational peace-keeping force and the withdrawal of the

---

[24] Mr Vasco da Cruz was the leader of the Mahidi militia branch who oversaw the sub-district of Zumalai in the district of Covalima.
[25] Interview with four UNAMET local staff working in Suai before and after the referendum (Darwin, 2-4 October 1999).
[26] International Crisis Group, East Timor Briefing, Darwin, 6 October 1999.

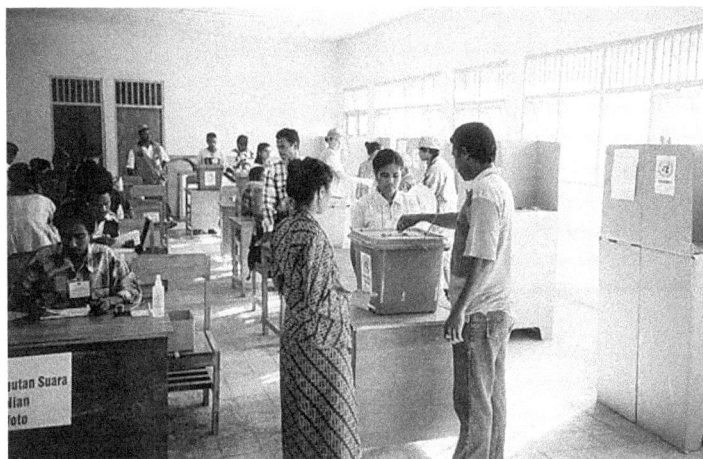

UN polling station at Camanasa, in Covalima, 30 August 1999

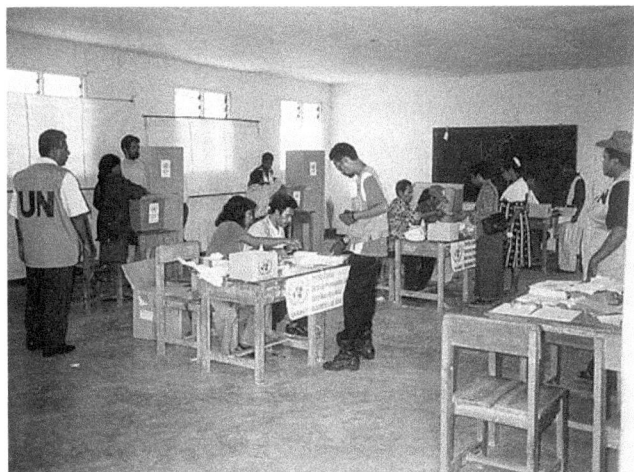

UN polling station it Covalima, 30 August 1999

CNRT rally in Dili, 27 August 1999

*East Timorese waiting to vote outside the UN polling stations at
Camanasa, 30 August 1999*

Indonesian army (TNI) from East Timor. This was followed by the return of the United Nations Mission for East Timor (UNAMET) and other international humanitarian groups as well as non-governmental organisations (NGOs). Subsequently, the United Nations Transitional Administration in East Timor (UNTAET), headed by Sergio Vieira de Mello, was established to administer East Timor in its transition to independence.

On 19 October 1999, the Indonesian Parliament (MPR) endorsed the ballot result, opening the way for East Timor to become a new nation. A new chapter in East Timor's political history had begun.

References

Dunn, James, 1996. *Timor: A People Betrayed*. Sydney: ABC Books.

Singh, Bilveer, 1998. *Self-determination: Problems and Prospects in East Timor*. Singapore: Geo-Strategic Analyses.

Traube, Elizabeth G., 1986. *Cosmology and Social Life: Ritual Exchange Among the Mambai of East Timor*. Chicago: University of Chicago Press.

5

The diplomacy on East Timor: Indonesia, the United Nations and the international community

Grayson J. Lloyd

The diplomatic history of the East Timor issue means that the future, notwithstanding the momentous nature of recent breakthroughs, will present conundrums to test the most skilled diplomat. Since July 1983, the diplomatic approach to the East Timor issue has focused on the UN-sponsored tripartite dialogue between Portugal and Indonesia. While the tripartite dialogue process was complex, it was the principal construct that led to the current diplomatic resolution. Of course this process has not operated in isolation. International and organisational pressure of various kinds across the economic, political and cultural realms contributed, as did various acts of defiance initiated by figures such as Bishop Carlos Belo, Xanana Gusmão and José Ramos Horta. With the downfall of the Soeharto-led New Order regime in Indonesia, the East Timorese community, aided by international and United Nations diplomatic and economic pressure, was presented, on 30 August 1999, with the first opportunity to determine its future since the vote for integration in 1976.[1]

---

[1] On 31/5/1976 the newly-formed 37-member Popular Representative Assembly met and endorsed a petition to be sent to the Indonesian President, Soeharto, for the territory to be integrated into the Republic of Indonesia (the figure is stated as 44 in a cable sent to the Chairman of the Special Committee on Decolonisation by the provisional government of East Timor, dated 7/6/76). The petition was presented to Soeharto on 7 June, and followed by the mission sent to East Timor to make an 'on-the-spot' assessment of the wishes of the East Timorese. For further information consult James Dunn (1983:298-299).

Sensing the mood for change, and compelled by pressing domestic concerns, President Habibie, on 9 June 1998, declared that he was considering offering special status and wide-ranging autonomy to East Timor, albeit with East Timor remaining a part of Indonesia. Since that point the role of the UN and the Secretary-General in particular, as well as the international community, has been crucial. Habibie's willingness to compromise sparked a process that had been stalled for numerous reasons, typified by the cynical 'pebble in the shoe' comment by Ali Alatas. The Indonesian President's decision in late January 1999 to offer independence as an option if autonomy was rejected set the stage for a tumultuous year.

This chapter is divided broadly into four sections. The first deals briefly with Indonesia's interest in and invasion of East Timor and the nature of the issue in the international sphere prior to the emergence of the Habibie administration. Secondly, examination is centred on the rather cumbrous and complicated diplomatic process between Habibie's initial statement, and the ballot in East Timor on 30 August 1999. Thirdly, analysis is presented of events from the ballot until the present day. Finally, I will summarise some prospects and problems likely to be faced by an independent East Timor in the community of nations in the years ahead.

Indonesia and the beginning of the East Timor issue

After many months of internal destabilisation in East Timor orchestrated, in part, by Ali Moertopo and Benny Moerdani, Indonesia invaded East Timor on 7 December 1975.[2] President Soeharto was manoeuvred by the Indonesian armed forces (TNI)[3] into a position such that annexation and integration of East Timor became the only possible outcome. The temporary union and then breakdown of the Fretilin-UDT alliance in August 1975, and subsequent brief three-week civil war, combined with Fretilin's unilateral declaration of independence on 28 November provided the catalyst and

[2] This was the same team that organized the OPSUS operation during the campaign to crush Malaysia (*ganjang Malaysia*) during the 1963-65 period, and which secured the 1969 'free vote' in West Irian.
[3] The acronym TNI (*Tentara Nasional Indonesia*, Indonesian National Army) is the recent terminological replacement for ABRI and will be used throughout this chapter.

rationalisation for the Indonesian invasion. The decision by the Indonesian government to invade East Timor was based principally on security fears, concerns over territorial unity and an obsession with anti-communism. Fretilin was portrayed as a Marxist-inspired and infiltrated organisation. Memories of the campaign against the Indonesian Communist Party (PKI) conducted at the start of the New Order figured prominently in the Indonesian mind-set at the popular and elite levels. The collapse of the Caetano administration in Lisbon, Portugal, in 1974, at the hands of the Armed Forces Movement (MFA – *Movimento das Forças Armadas*) exacerbated fears among the Indonesian military of the potential for future instability in East Timor. The commencement of the Indonesian invasion, known as Operation Komodo (*Operasi Komodo*), necessitated the resurrection of Indonesia's international status at the UN and within other fora such as the non-aligned movement (NAM). This restoration process consisted of realigning its foreign policy objectives, silencing opposition within East Timor and conditioning the international community to the irreversibility of its occupation.

On the East Timor issue Indonesia's diplomatic rhetoric seldom matched its pragmatic *realpolitik*. In a 1974 letter, Adam Malik, the New Order's first foreign minister, admitted to José Ramos Horta that Indonesia had no territorial designs on East Timor and assured Mr Ramos Horta of his country's respect for the sovereignty of an independent East Timor:

> The Independence of every country is the right of every nation, with no exception for the people of [East] Timor ... whoever will govern in Timor in the future after independence can be assured that the government of Indonesia will always strive to maintain good relations, friendship and cooperation for the benefit of both countries.[4]

Indeed at the talks held between Portugal and Indonesia in Rome in early November 1975, there was no indication that Indonesia's official diplomatic position had altered in any way. Yet, scarcely five weeks later, nine days after the unilateral declaration of Independence by Fretilin

[4]   Adam Malik's letter to José Ramos Horta (representing the ASDT) came at the conclusion of the Jakarta talks with Adam Malik and Ali Moertopo in 1974. A brief description of the contents and significance of the Malik letter is contained in James Dunn (1983:66). The selected quotation was taken from a speech given by José Ramos Horta (1996) to the Royal Institute of International Affairs.

on 28 November 1975, Indonesia officially invaded East Timor.[5] This invasion followed closely a letter from Indonesia's permanent representative to the UN to the organisation's Secretary-General dated 4 December 1975. In it Indonesia reiterated its support for the decolonisation policy of the Portuguese government. But it also contained an indication that Indonesia would not be prepared to sit back and, in the view prevalent among the Indonesian administration at that time, watch East Timor disintegrate.[6] It also pointed to a lack of communication between Deplu (Department of Foreign Affairs) and the Indonesian Armed Forces (*Tentara Negara Indonesia* – TNI) – a problem that would lead to future confusion in the policy-making process. Moreover, it indicated the state of play in the power relationship between TNI and Deplu and the secondary role of the latter in the decision-making process.

The integration of East Timor by the Indonesian government was not recognised by the United Nations which considered Portugal to be the administering power. The first action taken by the United Nations was General Assembly resolution 3485 on 12 December 1975. This called for respect of the inalienable right of the people of Portuguese Timor to self-determination and independence, and for the Indonesian government to '... desist from further violation of the territorial integrity of Portuguese Timor and to withdraw without delay its armed forces from the territory ...'[7] The General Assembly resolution was followed ten days later by a Security Council resolution calling for Indonesia to 'withdraw without delay all its forces from the territory'.[8] However, the Indonesian government, believing that it had been asked to intervene to rescue the situation in East Timor ignored the resolution.[9]

---

[5]   I say officially, because there is evidence to suggest that Indonesian-sponsored forces had for a number of months been present in East Timor fomenting unrest.
[6]   'Statement of the Government of Indonesia on the Current Developments in Portuguese Timor, 4 December 1975', letter dated 4 December 1975 from the Permanent Representative of Indonesia addressed to the Secretary-General, A/C.4/808, 4 December 1975. Cited in Heike Krieger (ed.) (1997:41-42).
[7]   UNGA Resolution 3485 (XXX), 12 December 1975.
[8]   UNSC Resolution S/RES/384, 22 December 1975.
[9]   Based on this Security Council resolution the UN Secretary-General sent a representative to East Timor for an on-the-spot assessment. The subsequent report was discussed in April 1976. Notwithstanding Indonesia's assurances the Security Council remained dissatisfied and once again called for the withdrawal of Indonesian forces.

The General Assembly moved a further seven resolutions on the East Timor issue in the period 1976-82. Despite a narrowing of the margin between those supporting and those opposing the resolution, Indonesia did not manage to remove the East Timor issue from the General Assembly's agenda, nor change the UN's standpoint and recognition of Portugal as the administering power. Beginning in 1983 with the first formal talks, the Secretary-General presided over private negotiations between Portugal and Indonesia, known as the tripartite dialogue.[10] While attention on the East Timor issue within the international community wavered throughout the 1980s, Indonesia met opposition particularly from ex-Portuguese colonial territories as it attempted to gain leadership of the Non-aligned Movement (NAM). Nonetheless there was a growing feeling in Jakarta that the Indonesian government's position on East Timor would eventually prevail.

The Dili massacre on 12 November 1991 changed this presumption irrevocably. This reignited the cause of East Timorese resistance to Indonesian occupation and reawakened world attention. The more the UN and the world community understood what was happening in East Timor – and the Dili massacre served to refresh many memories – the more impetus was given to the armed and civil resistance. The capture of Xanana Gusmão in 1992, although initially celebrated in military circles in Jakarta, also markedly increased pressure on Indonesia by providing a focal point for East Timorese and their supporters who favoured independence. Pressure also increased as a result of the rapid process of globalisation which challenged old norms and modes of thinking. The start of the democratisation process in Indonesia, the onset of the Asian financial crisis, and the collapse of the Soeharto regime, all contributed to a rise in tensions and expectations.

Progress under the Habibie administration

Notwithstanding UN Secretary-General Kofi Annan's dynamism on the issue of East Timor, a relaxation of Indonesia's hard-line position on the issue was a remote possibility under the Soeharto regime. President Soeharto throughout 1975 was clearly concerned about the potential international economic ramifications of an invasion of East

---

10   The issue has not been subject to a specific resolution since 1982.

Timor. However, his belief in the centrality of territorial integrity and 'domino theory' philosophy of communism made significant concessions unlikely once East Timor had been incorporated into the unitary Indonesian state. This ostensibly personal response was reviewed when Jusuf Habibie acceded to the presidency on 21 May 1998.

Assessed from a pragmatic standpoint, President Habibie probably had little choice but to offer something by way of a concession to the international community. The monetary crisis in South-east Asia was impacting heavily on Indonesia, and arguably the autonomy concession was, in a sense, a trade-off for much needed IMF restructuring loans. Indonesia could ill afford the irritation sparked by the East Timor issue, either domestically or externally. This was particularly the case given the panoply of economic, political and ethnic problems threatening disinte-gration of the nation state. Whether by choice or compulsion Habibie's actions contributed significantly to the direction and modalities of the East Timor issue. A body of opinion developed within civilian and among some retired military figures in Jakarta, principally, arguing that Indonesia was better off rid of East Timor.[11] Naturally such opinion confronted nationalist views insisting on the territorial integrity and sovereignty of the Indonesian unitary state. Proponents of such views pointed to the possibility of the detachment of East Timor triggering the disintegration of the Republic. A number of Western analysts and observers expressed concern that the loss of East Timor could precipitate the loss of other regions in Indonesia, raising fears about a 'Balkanisation' of the Republic. The argument for jettisoning East Timor not surprisingly also met fierce resistance in the TNI.

The diplomatic process after June 1998

President Habibie's statement on 9 June 1998 offering wide-ranging autonomy for East Timor was an important breakthrough. On

[11] The genesis of this argument lies, in part, in the views (rarely expressed publicly) of Deplu officers (some of whom are still active) and other 'internationally-minded' individuals who assessed the situation objectively and strategically and concluded that Indonesia's long-term foreign policy objectives were being hindered by ongoing involvement in East Timor. Some argued that the loss of East Timor would not cause 'Balkanisation' to occur, but would actually allow the government to focus more on other regions of concern.

18 June 1998, Ali Alatas formally confirmed the details of this offer to
the UN Secretary-General, Kofi Annan, and to Portugal. Indonesia
saw its proposal as a complete, internationally acceptable and realistic
solution to the impasse.[12] Portugal received the proposal as a step in the
right direction but rejected it as an ultimate solution. However, while
some within the Indonesian government were keen to resolve the issue
based on this proposal, it was clear that the international community
viewed it as merely the first step in a lengthy process. As a measure of
goodwill, on 24 July, President Habibie announced a program of troop
withdrawals from the territory. The Indonesian government genuinely
expected that its response would satisfy the people of East Timor. The
free speech campaign conducted in rallies by East Timorese youths
from July to September 1998 undermined this assumption, and
reinforced to the UN and the Indonesian government their rejection
of autonomy and endorsement of an UN-supervised referendum.

Officially the Indonesian government's reasons for not agreeing to a
referendum resided in two factors. Firstly, it believed that such a process
would only lead to the opening up of old wounds and the likely reoccurrence of civil war and the creation of a pro- and anti-integration
divide in East Timor. Secondly, it argued that it should not be submitted
to a referendum because the East Timorese people had already opted
for integration in 1976.[13] The first statement probably represented genuine
concern, although it did so by perpetuating the mythology surrounding
the civil war in July-August 1975. The second sought to legitimate a
spurious selection process which occurred in 1976 and upon which

---

[12] 'Keterangan Pers Menlu Ali Alatas Kepada Wartawan Nasional Setelah
Pertemuan Dengan Abilio Araujo', Di Deplu, Jakarta, 23/6/98.
[13] Transcription of Questions and Answers Between the Press and the Minister
for Foreign Affairs, H.E. Mr Ali Alatas, MPR/DPR Building, Jakarta, 29/6/98.
A more complete, although unofficial, explication of the Deplu mind-set on
East Timor was presented by Dino Patti Djalal, Head of the Decolonisation
Section, Directorate for International Organisation, Deplu, in a paper delivered
in his private capacity. See Dino Patti Djalal. 'Sebuah Pandangan Mengenai
Penyelesaian Politik Yang Damai, Langgeng Dan Manusiawi Terhadap Masalah
Timor Timur', paper presented at a seminar entitled 'Menuju Penyelesaian Damai
Timor Timur Pasca Soeharto', organised by SOLIDAMOR (*Solidaritas Mahasiswa
Untuk Penyelesaian Damai Timor Timur*), Jakarta, 14/7/98. Dino Patti Djalal was
spokesman for the Indonesian government's task force monitoring the
UNAMET presence and the lead-up to the 30 August ballot in East Timor.

Indonesia has based its occupation of East Timor. Against such a back-ground the process advanced gradually for the next six months before the dramatic policy bouleversement of January 1999.

International pressure mounted on Indonesia to continue the pace of reform on the East Timor issue.[14] In late June 1998, the ambassadors from the United Kingdom, Austria and The Netherlands visited East Timor and concluded that lasting resolution of the issue required a firm commitment to direct consultation of the wishes of the people of East Timor. The Senate and Congress in the United States of America again became proactively involved on the issue. In July, a Senate resolution called for an internationally-supervised referendum on East Timor. In October, Congress supported a ban on the use of US-supplied weapons in the territory.[15] Within this international environment the next round of the tripartite dialogue series under the auspices of the United Nations took place in New York on 4-5 August at the ministerial level. President Habibie reiterated his 'special autonomy' proposal before the Secretary-General and preliminary agreement was reached between Indonesia and Portugal on the agreement. The ministers agreed to hold in-depth discussions on Indonesia's proposals for special status and hoped that dialogue at the senior officials' level could encourage resolution on the issue before the end of the year.

Agreement was also reached on the need for the closer involvement of East Timorese, both inside and outside East Timor, in reaching a solution.[16] But the senior officials' meeting in early October was marred by UN concerns over rising tensions in East Timor, and the occurrence of armed clashes and large-scale protests in the territory. On 31 October 1998, the fourth All-inclusive Intra-East Timorese Dialogue (AIETD) opened in Krumbach, Austria. This was clearly the most important meeting in this series initiated in June 1995 in Burg Schlaining, given both the autonomy proposal offered by the Indonesian government and the pivotal stage of UN-sponsored negotiations.

Doubt was cast over the sincerity of the Indonesian approach to the negotiating table by persistent allegations that rather than withdrawing its forces, Indonesia had been secretly marshalling them and attacking

14 This fact was recognized by Xanana Gusmão in 'Xanana Gusmão writes from a Jakarta prison cell', *The Washington Post*, 21/10/98.
15 'Indonesia: East Timor Outlook', *Oxford Analytica Daily Brief*, 10/9/98.
16 'Foreign Ministers of Indonesia and Portugal Conclude Two-Day Meeting on East Timor Question', UN Press Release, 5 August 1998, SG/SM/6666.

Falintil forces. Leaked military documents indicated that troop numbers had not been cut in East Timor, contrary to the government's claim.[17] In November 1998 the Australian foreign minister, Alexander Downer, reinforced the UN position by stating that resolution of the East Timor issue must involve the leaders of East Timor. But the Australian government was not in favour of a referendum on independence in East Timor. Shortly thereafter, however, key figures in the Australian government realised that they had to adjust their thinking on the issue. In December, the National Security Commission of the Australian Cabinet met to consider the security, economic and political issues relevant to East Timor and the possibility of Indonesian disengagement and Australian intervention. From this meeting emerged the idea that Prime Minister John Howard would write to the Indonesian President.

In his letter dated 19 December and delivered to President Habibie on 21 December by ambassador John McCarthy, Australian Prime Minister Howard drew together several themes.[18] These were the necessity of the continuation of reform and the possibility of granting independence to East Timor. He illustrated his point with reference to the Matignon accords. This agreement provided for a referendum for the people of New Caledonia and, it was suggested, could function as a model for East Timor. A referendum would proceed after a sustained period of development both of local political institutions and confidence-building measures. However, as one analyst noted, President Habibie's rejection of the letter was not unexpected given the implicit correlation drawn between French colonialism and Indonesia's occupation of East Timor.[19] Moreover, it was clear that the Howard letter caught the Habibie administration off-guard.

It was apparent that the Indonesian government was struggling

---

[17] James Cotton (ed.), *East Timor and Australia: AIIA Contributions to the Policy Debate* (Canberra: ADSC and AIIA, 1999), p.12.

[18] Ibid., p.13. Former Indonesian Foreign Minister Ali Alatas reported that President Habibie's initial reaction to the Howard letter was one of anger and annoyance that Australia had taken upon itself to become involved in something that, in the Indonesian view, was clearly not its problem. See Ali Alatas, 'Ali Alatas looks Back on 11 Years of Indonesia's Foreign Policy', *The Jakarta Post*, 2/11/99. Alatas's comment can be taken at face value. However, it is also important to remember that Ali Alatas was not at the special Cabinet meeting that decided to offer independence to East Timor via a ballot.

[19] Cotton, op.cit., p.13

at this point to develop a cohesive and internationally (as well as domestically) acceptable position on the East Timor issue. The reasons for this struggle were threefold. Firstly, because of the large human and resource investment in East Timor, and the diversity of opinions within the Indonesian government, the East Timor issue assumed a great significance for key decision-makers and government officials. Secondly, longstanding fissures inspired by the East Timor issue resurfaced among the elite. Hankam (Department of Defence and Security), TNI (Armed Forces), Deplu (Department of Foreign Affairs) and senior foreign policy adviser in the presidential office, Dr Dewi Fortuna Anwar, competed to varying degrees for the running on the issue. Gradually, outside of its purely functional diplomatic obligations, Deplu, led by Ali Alatas, was virtually marginalised from any meaningful participation in the decision-making process surrounding the East Timor issue. Thirdly, the Indonesian government appeared unprepared for the scope and determination of the UN-led international response to this phase of the issue. This is, perhaps, partially explainable by a discernible and increasing sense of frustration with the issue and the corresponding desire among some elements in the Indonesian government to bring closure to the case. This lack of cohesion at the elite level was exacerbated as diplomatic negotiations intensified from early February onwards.

The new year ushered in some surprising developments. The first came on 12 January 1999, when Australian Foreign Minister Alexander Downer announced a major change in Australia's policy on East Timor. It was now the government's position that the East Timorese should be allowed to vote in an act of self-determination to decide whether to become independent of Indonesia after a period of autonomy. On 27 January the Indonesian government stunned the international community with a message delivered by the foreign minister. In it he referred to the possibility of complete independence for East Timor if autonomy proved unpopular and impractical. Thus, in addition to the proposal of special status with wide-ranging autonomy, the details of which were at that time still being negotiated, Foreign Minister Alatas would meet with the Secretary-General of the UN on 7-8 February to outline the possibility of independence as an alternative solution. President Habibie's decision was influenced by the fact that he was in the midst of formulating a national budget, and he thus needed to reinstate a sense of normality across a range of sectors. Interestingly, Alatas declared that the issue had been discussed several days earlier at a defence and security cabinet meeting, although it is believed the foreign minister was not a participant in that discussion.[20] Moreover, it was suggested that Ali Alatas was not in favour of such a proposal at that time.[21]

Pace gathered quickly on the issue, especially when President Habibie declared that whatever the result of the consultation process in East Timor (not a referendum) Indonesia wished to be free of the Timor problem by the year 2000. In a series of interviews Foreign Minister Ali Alatas was keen to clarify the government's position and the statement

[20] According to a report from the KITLV news composition service dated 28/10/99, presidential foreign affairs adviser Dewi Fortuna Anwar revealed that the foreign minister Ali Alatas had not attended the restricted ministerial council at which the President's proposal had been submitted. It is reported that all ministers present, including General Wiranto, agreed with the President's decision although Wiranto insisted that the armed forces had not made a mistake when they invaded East Timor in 1975. Habibie's military adviser, General Sintong Panjaitan, merely pointed out that it had been 'the President's personal decision'. http://iias.leidenuniv.nl/cgi-bin/Daily Report.py?Day= 19991029, Ref: FA10-1999/10/21 'Operasi Sapu Jagad — Indonesian Military's Plan to Disrupt Independence', p.65. It was reported elsewhere that Habibie, clearly aware of the opposition, had declared to his close aides that 'It [the East Timor issue] will roll like a snowball and no one can stop it', *Jakarta Post*, 16/2/99.

[21] There are two distinct points here: whether Alatas was consulted and what he advised if he was. In an interview reflecting on his tenure as foreign minister, Ali Alatas offered the following comment in response to a suggestion that he was initially against the idea: 'Well, I have advised, among other things, OK we can solve it, but isn't it premature? But after that in a very democratic manner we discussed that in the cabinet and it became a cabinet issue', 'Ali Alatas Looks Back on 11 Years of Indonesia's Foreign Policy', *The Jakarta Post*, 2/11/99. In an interview much closer to the time of the decision he declared: 'We thought it was time to give our perception of what an alternative could be. And this is how it started. It didn't start with the President telling me or any one of us. He's not that type. He always said: "What can we do with all these kinds of things? Please give me an advise [sic] ..." He proposes the questions. So we went and discussed it thoroughly in the Polkam.' Excerpts of the interview between the Minister of Foreign Affairs with Mr Frank Ching, Foreign Editor, *Far Eastern Economic Review*, on the Question of East Timor, Jakarta, 2 February 1999. Although it is not entirely clear, it is probable that Minister Alatas was talking about a Polkam meeting arranged to discuss in greater detail aspects of the President's plan announced at the initial restricted ministerial council.

of 27 January. The preferred option of the Indonesian government was the one enunciated in June 1998: special status for East Timor with wide-ranging autonomy. It was clear that the Indonesian government was working on the basis that this option would be adopted by the people of East Timor.[22] Ali Alatas reiterated this view at a press conference at the conclusion of the Fourth Indonesia-Australia Ministerial Forum in Bali. Acknowledging that Indonesia had made mistakes in East Timor, he insisted that wide-ranging autonomy was the principal option for the Indonesian government and moreover the best solution for all concerned and the region.[23] The apparent success of this meeting was important for the Australian government, which had been forced to reassess its position based on a deteriorating security situation and the possibility of prolonged chaos in East Timor as a result of a rapid Indonesian departure, and also for the UN diplomatic process.

In hindsight the likelihood of Indonesia simply washing its hands of East Timor and withdrawing was remote. Certainly the mood was evident in some quarters in Indonesia to dispense with the problem quickly. However, even with this opinion circulating within elite circles, such a move was not seriously contemplated before the verdict from the East Timorese people had been received. The TNI certainly had no desire to hasten its departure from East Timor. This was chiefly because departure would denote the failure of its mission in East Timor and, in a sense, the abandoning of the memories of those soldiers killed in the territory.[24] It would also mean the potential loss of a rich seam of wealth for certain elite members of the TNI. In the ministerial council that endorsed Habibie's proposal, it is possible that Wiranto and Habibie formed some kind of agreement. Even if

[22] In support of the application of such an autonomy proposal Foreign Minister Alatas cited examples of autonomy in the Basque region in Spain, in Bougainville, and in the Azores and Madeira. See excerpts of 'Interview Between the Minister for Foreign Affairs with Journalists from Portugal on the Question of East Timor', Jakarta, 2/2/99.
[23] This was an interesting reversion to the rationalisation used at the time of the Indonesian invasion in 1975 emphasising the pre-eminence of regional interests. 'Transcript Questions and Answers Minister Ali Alatas and Foreign Journalists at the Fourth Indonesia-Australia Ministerial Forum and the Australia-Indonesia Development Area (AIDA) at Nusa Dua, Bali, 22-25 Februari 1999'.
[24] It should be remembered that the TNI may have lost as many as 10 000-12 000 troops in East Timor.

an agreement was not made, it is arguable that the military believed that it would be able to influence the result in East Timor.

It is difficult to fathom the exact nature of Habibie's relationship with the military in relation to the Indonesian government's formal (and informal) position on East Timor. Relations between them were complicated by the fact that Habibie was viewed as an interim leader who lacked widespread and genuine support within the military. Habibie's decision was a calculated risk, cognisant as he was of the degree of opposition felt within the military, and among 'nationalist' elements within society represented at the popular level by the views of Megawati Sukarnoputri. It is also highly possible that President Habibie made the decision without thorough consultation with the military, thus placing the onus squarely on the TNI to develop mechanisms to salvage a bargaining position through whatever means possible.

Concern was rising over the potential for, and occurrence of, violence in East Timor, and the support, training and funding of armed militia groups by the Indonesian military, particularly the special forces Kopassus unit.[25] The involvement of militia groups in assorted acts of violence and intimidation in East Timor complicated the sensitive diplomatic negotiations occurring at the UN, and for a while cast doubt over the entire process of achieving a ballot result. It was widely suspected by many well-informed observers that the creation of this instability, and subsequent doubt over the outcome of the process, was precisely the point of such activities.

Pressure quickly mounted internationally for some form of intervention in East Timor to curtail the activities of the militia groups. These groups were particularly virulent in the western region of East Timor, but by the 5 May Agreement such groups were active in almost every district in East Timor.[26] A spate of militia attacks in February indicated an escalation in the degree and intensity of militia activities and coincided with the early phases of the TNI's reaction to Habibie's initiative for East Timor. A meeting of pro-integration leaders with President Habibie in Jakarta in February gave them an unwarranted and, in terms of the diplomatic process, unhelpful legitimacy. In April, General Wiranto was

[25] 'Transcript: Press Conference Minister Ali Alatas and US State Secretary, Madeleine Albright at the Department of Foreign Affairs', Jakarta 4/3/99. In the Alatas-Albright press conference the notion of Indonesian forces training militia groups was explored, and subsequently refuted by the Indonesian foreign minister.
[26] See John Zubrzycki, 'Observer Mission Into Fear', *The Australian*, 25/5/99.

directed by the President to travel to Dili to deal with the problem. However, the resulting 21 April peace agreement signed by Xanana Gusmão and pro-independence and pro-integration representatives failed to bring an end to the violence chiefly, but not exclusively, because it did not provide for the disarming of militias, nor did it touch on the issue of support for these groups from the Indonesian military.[27] The situation again boiled over with reports coming through at the end of April and the early part of May of militia groups rounding up East Timorese into refugee camps, and travel restrictions being imposed on foreigners including the ICRC. Caught off balance by the rapid collapse of civil order in East Timor, the world community vacillated on the question of intervention and repeated pleas for the Indonesian government to restore peace and security to the territory.[28]

Mechanically the diplomatic process proceeded apace amidst increasing practical and humanitarian hurdles. On 12 March 1999, at the conclusion of another round of tripartite negotiations, the Secretary-General of the United Nations announced that all parties had agreed that a 'method of direct ballot will be used to ask the people of East Timor whether they accept or reject' a proposal for autonomy.[29] On 8 March Foreign Minister Alatas presented a paper to President Habibie and the inner cabinet concerning the text of the autonomy package produced as a result of the tripartite discussion held on 7-8 February. The cabinet and the President decided that modifications were required and for this task a ministerial-level team co-ordinated by the Menkopolkam (Co-ordinating Minister for Politics and Security), Feisal Tanjung, was formed.[30]

[27] Don Greenlees, 'Timorese Rush to Sign Pact', *The Australian*, 22/4/99.
[28] The world community was to revisit the question of uncontrolled violence in East Timor and the apparent condoning of such activities by the Indonesian government in the immediate post-ballot period in the first half of September. Short of invasion, which was not an option in any sane analysis, the UN (backed particularly by the US) was compelled to exert what economic and other pressure it could to convince the Indonesian government to accept an international force in the territory.
[29] United Nations Press Release SG/SM/6922, 12 March 1999.
[30] An excellent overview of the Indonesian government's perception of the issue near the end of March is found in 'Paparan Menteri Luar Negeri R.I. Ali Alatas, Tentang Penyelesaian Masalah Timor Timur Pada Seminar Indonesian Council on World Affairs (ICWA)', Jakarta, 22 Maret 1999.

The intensive phase of the dialogue process on East Timor progressed with the UN at the hub of diplomatic negotiations. Just hours before the start of what was to be a seminal round of negotiations on 8 April, the Indonesian government asked the UN to delay the meeting on autonomy because its blueprint for autonomy was not ready. Talks were rescheduled for 20-21 April, and on 23 April, co-ordinated by Kofi Annan, Indonesia and Portugal agreed on an autonomy deal for East Timor.[31] The substance of this deal was contained in the 5 May Agreement. On another front, Australia's diplomatic involvement in the issue escalated. A phone call from Prime Minister Howard to President Habibie resulted in a meeting of senior leaders in Bali on 27 April. The meeting involved both leaders, Foreign Ministers Alexander Downer and Ali Alatas, and Defence Ministers General Wiranto and John Moore. President Habibie declared that if the autonomy option was rejected, then Indonesia and East Timor would separate in peace. Prime Minister Howard urged that a 'greater measure of stability' be returned to the territory, and that violence must desist. He noted, however, that it would be better for the East Timorese, the Indonesians and the region if the territory remained part of Indonesia under the autonomy package.[32]

The 5 May Agreement and the diplomacy that produced it was widely criticised. Some observers argued that the ballot offering autonomy or independence should have been delayed, not by a matter of weeks which ultimately occurred for security and technical reasons, but by many months to allow for the amelioration of the security situation in East Timor. Had the UN's commitment wavered, however, and the vote been delayed indefinitely, there is no telling what might have happened in East Timor.[33] The agreement eventually signed on 5 May consisted of two parts. The first dealt with the administrative aspects that included the ballot question, voter eligibility, campaign

---

[31] United Nations Portugal-Indonesia Talks, 21-23 April 1999, New York. Transcript of Concluding Press Conference 23/4/99, press release SG/SM/6966.

[32] Tim Dodd, 'Australia Commits to Timor Poll', *Australian Financial Review*, 28/4/99.

[33] The notion that aspects of the agreement favoured Indonesia must be balanced by the realisation that the Indonesian government was in an advantageous negotiating position, notwithstanding the considerable pressure that was being exerted on it through various channels.

duration and the rather controversial area of the security of the ballot. A number of observers took umbrage with Section G of the modalities applying to the vote charging the Indonesian authorities with ensuring a 'secure environment for a free and fair popular consultation process'.[34] In the context of the apparently unchecked violence in the territory, many saw this as an extraordinary and ironic move.[35]

The second aspect was the proposal on autonomy which, had it been passed, would have established the Special Autonomous Region of East Timor (SARET). Basically the SARET would control political, economic and social policies, but not foreign affairs, defence and fiscal policies. Given these conditions, it appealed to the bulk of the pro-integration supporters.[36] Articles five, six and seven were the key aspects outlining the modalities for a rebuttal and acceptance of autonomy, and emphasising the necessity for the UN to maintain an adequate presence in East Timor during the interim period following the popular

[34] Extracted from Section G of the 'Agreement Regarding the Modalities for the Popular Consultation of the East Timorese Through a Direct Ballot'. A supplementary section, 'East Timor Popular Consultation Agreement Regarding Security', specifies details for the pre-ballot period incorporating the understanding that:

> A secure environment devoid of violence or of other forms of intimidation is a prerequisite for the holding of a free and fair ballot in East Timor. Responsibility to ensure such an environment as well as for the general maintenance of law and order rests with the appropriate Indonesian security authorities. The absolute neutrality of the TNI (Indonesian Armed Forces) and the Indonesian Police is essential in this regard.

> This was mirrored in article three of the agreement proper. See also the Report of the Secretary-General to the United Nations Security Council A/53/951 S/1999/513, 5/5/99.

[35] It was, indeed, a remarkable clause although the UN had little choice but to accept this because the Indonesian government was resolutely opposed to the idea of foreign intervention. Unofficially the hope in the UN was that it could, at least, influence those in the TNI directing the militias to scale down their activities.
[36] The hard-line pro-integrationist Basilio da Araujo from the Forum for Unity, Democracy and Justice (FPDK) declared that he was a reluctant supporter of the ballot and foresaw trouble in the lead-up to the ballot and a likely split between winners and losers afterwards. Tim Dodd, 'Timor Pledges to Accept Ballot', *Australian Financial Review*, 7/5/99.

consultation.[37] Importantly, the 5 May Agreement provided the mandate for the UN to play a significant role in implementing either result of the consultation and to assist in the transition process in East Timor. But as the UN recognised, the agreement would be difficult to implement if the fundamental problems of security remained, thus complicating the process of ensuring a peaceful and free ballot. Nowhere in the 5 May Agreement was provision made for the disarmament of the various forces in the territory.

The signing of the agreement to hold a popular consultation in East Timor impacted little on the frequency and scale of violence in the territory.[38] Indeed Kofi Annan's report (22/5/99) noted that the security situation in East Timor remained 'extremely tense and volatile' and the need for inter-factional reconciliation was great. In this context the 15 May meeting between pro-integration and pro-independence East Timorese factions sponsored by Deplu in Bali could have assumed critical importance. The results, however, proved inconclusive and failed to develop a means of ending the large-scale violence in East Timor.[39] In response to sustained calls by the international community for the release of the Fretilin leader, Xanana Gusmão, the Indonesian government at the end of May reaffirmed its desire to make his release contingent upon an overall solution and not the means of producing this solution.[40]

On 11 June the UN Security Council with Resolution 1246 established

[37] 'Agreement between the Republic of Indonesia and the Portuguese Republic on the Question of East Timor', 5 May 1999. The UNAMET was composed of electoral officers, political advisers, UN security guards and an International Civilian Police Force (CivPol). The legislative mandate for this force came via resolution 1236 of the UN Security Council dated 7/5/99.

[38] Report of the Secretary-General on the Question of East Timor of 22 May 1999 (S/1999/595). UNAMET press statement, 17/5/99.

[39] The Indonesian government initiated, on 18 May, a task force on the implementation of the popular consultation in East Timor to be co-ordinated by the Menkopolkam, Feisal Tanjung. Its primary function was to liaise between the Indonesian government and UNAMET. This existed in addition to a body referred to as *Tim Pengamanan* (Pacification Team) in charge of implementing all that had been agreed regarding East Timor, and an inter-departmental Deplu working group on East Timor. The Pacification Team was also chaired by Feisal Tanjung, and consisted of the Foreign, Interior, Defence, Justice and Information ministers and the head of the State Intelligence Coordinating Body (*Bakin*).

[40] Press Conference of the Minister for Foreign Affairs, Jakarta, 24/5/99.

the United Nations Mission in East Timor (UNAMET) with a mandate to 31 August. The Security Council met again on 29 June to assess the situation on the ground in East Timor and the Secretary-General's report of 22 June. This meeting of the Security Council coincided with the DARE II conference held in Jakarta commencing on 25 June. This conference was significant for the fact that it co-ordinated talks with representatives from all sides in East Timor. It was also noteworthy for the fact that after much negotiation about the issuing of a visa, José Ramos Horta was permitted to enter Indonesia and attend the five-day gathering although he did not travel to East Timor. The resolution also came after the 18 June joint appeal made by CNRT, Falintil and pro-integration factions to halt armed confrontation, disarm and co-operate to ensure security, peace and law and order in East Timor. The main point of the resolution, apart from registering concern at the continuation of violence in the territory, was to acknowledge the three-week delay in the Secretary-General's determination of whether an appropriate security situation existed for the start of the consultation process. The pattern of events continued along these lines punctuated only by a meeting of senior officials of Indonesia and Portugal in New York in mid-July, and the start of voter registration at approximately the same time in East Timor. In a letter to the president of the Security Council dated 28 July, the Secretary-General announced that the date of consultation would be delayed until 30 August 1999.[41] Security Council Resolution 1257, adopted at its 4031st meeting on 3 August, granted the Secretary-General's request for an extension of the UNAMET mandate until 30 September.[42]

On 9 August, the Secretary-General presented another report to the Security Council in which he addressed the question of post-ballot arrangements. He requested that the UNAMET continue through the post-ballot period until the implementation phase of the result. He also reaffirmed that during the interim period, the Indonesian government would continue to be absolutely responsible for the maintenance of law and order in East Timor under the conditions of the 5 May Agreement. The commencement of senior level tripartite talks in Jakarta between the UN, Indonesia and Portugal on 12 August focused on phase two, the

---

[41] United Nations. Letter dated 28 July 1999 from the Secretary-General addressed to the President of the Security Council, S/1999/8830.
[42] United Nations. Resolution 1257 (1999) adopted by the Security Council at its 4031st meeting on 3 August 1999, S/RES/1257.

post-ballot period. These talks slightly preceded the official start of campaigning in East Timor. The Secretary-General's request was authorised by Resolution 1262 of the Security Council at its 4038th meeting. It extended the mandate of UNAMET until the end of November 1999 and again emphasised the responsibility of Indonesia to maintain peace and security in East Timor in the interim phase.

On the eve of the popular consultation, President Habibie addressed the nation. He stressed the benefits of national unity and the commitment of the Indonesian government to finding a solution to the East Timor issue. He urged the East Timorese to take the right path so that the development effort might be continued.[43] The following day, 78.5 per cent of East Timorese voted for independence. The violence which had been temporarily 'turned off' for the popular consultation (and had allowed nearly 99 per cent of registered voters to participate in the ballot) re-ignited the day after the vote and increased dramatically once the result was known on 4 September.

The post-ballot period

In retrospect and based on comments by former Foreign Minister Ali Alatas, it is clear that the Indonesian government was working on a markedly different set of assumptions to the rest of the international community. Based on reports from Indonesian government representatives and from pro-integration people such as Lopes da Cruz in the months preceding the ballot, the Indonesian government felt that its position would prevail on 30 August. Foreign Minister Ali Alatas was sceptical of the information he was receiving from such sources, conscious as he was of the degree of opposition within East Timor to integration with Indonesia.[44] However, he consistently reiterated the government's standpoint, which was that the solution proposed was the best and most realistic on offer and that no-one could pre-judge the decision of the people of East Timor nor the response of the People's Consultative Assembly should this decision be in favour of

---

[43] Pidato Radio dan Televisi Presiden Republik Indonesia Dalam Rangka Menyongsong Pelaksanaan Penentuan Pendapat Rakyat Timor Timur Pada Tanggal 30 Agustus 1999, Jakarta, 29/8/99.

[44] Sentiments cited in 'Ali Alatas Looks Back on 11 Years of Indonesia's Foreign Policy', *The Jakarta Post*, 2/11/99.

independence.[45] The fact that the decision favoured independence produced sincere disbelief and shock among sections of the Indonesian government and military, and placed the onus on the MPR.[46]

The two weeks immediately after the ballot proved as crucial for the future of East Timor as the ballot itself. Pressure increased on the Indonesian government from the UN and the international community to curb the violence and anarchy afflicting the territory. Daily reports emerged of the terror and destruction that was occurring in Dili and across East Timor, and of the intimidation and violence experienced by East Timorese and UNAMET personnel alike. The UN, Australian and the United States' governments in particular worked hard at the political and military levels to hold Indonesia to its commitments to maintain security under the 5 May Agreement. Officially, of course, Indonesia declared that it would adhere to the agreement and that Indonesian forces would be responsible for security and law and order. It was adamant that it would not condone an international peacekeeping force in East Timor and would not consider the idea of peace-enforcement.[47] The first concession came from the Indonesian government on 7 September when it instituted martial law in East Timor. Not surprisingly, the international community greeted this decision with widespread scepticism. Nonetheless, at a point when time was at a premium, this community was prepared to allow several days to assess its impact. In the meantime the release of resistance leader Xanana Gusmão provided a cause for celebration within the pro-independence and international communities. The following day the UN Security Council's mission travelled to Jakarta and Dili and met with Habibie and other senior ministers.

As it became clear that martial law had not improved the security

[45] In an interview where it was put to him that the People's Consultative Assembly may wish for East Timor to stay within Indonesia he replied, '... theoretically there is a chance. But practically I don't think that'. Interview, Minister Ali Alatas and SBS TV Australia, Jakarta 27/5/99.

[46] Ali Alatas admitted in a recent interview that he held grave doubts over the veracity of the reports he was receiving, and felt that there was a great discrepancy between the way people would respond when openly intimidated and how they would vote. 'Ali Alatas Looks Back on 11 Years of Indonesia's Foreign Policy', *The Jakarta Post*, 2/11/99.

[47] See 'Tanya Jawab Pers Menlu Ali Alatas Dan Pangab Wiranto', *Istana Merdeka*, 7/9/99.

situation in East Timor, international diplomatic pressure increased dramatically on Indonesia.[48] The United States of America worked assiduously behind the scenes to exert economic pressure on Indonesia, and President Clinton issued a stark warning to Jakarta to end the violence. The mission's report (S/1999/976) concluded that the violence could not have occurred without the involvement of large elements of the Indonesian military and police. It stated that Indonesian authorities were either unwilling or unable to provide a suitable environment for a peaceful implementation of the 5 May Agreement.

At the critical Security Council meeting commencing on 11 September,[49] prompted by the deteriorating situation in East Timor and necessarily convened before the return of the mission, the Indonesian representative maintained that it was not the policy of the Indonesian government to condone violence or intimidation in East Timor. He also maintained that Indonesia did not '... foresee the need for the introduction of a multinational or peacekeeping force at this stage'.[50] The case for urgent action was cogently argued by the representatives of Portugal and Brazil. Under concerted international pressure, Indonesian President Habibie the next day agreed to the deployment of an international peacekeeping force in East Timor. This was followed by a statement from Ali Alatas after meeting with Kofi Annan and members of the Security Council declaring that Indonesia accepted without condition the UN-mandated force in East Timor.[51] At this stage Indonesian troops and police remained in the territory.

On 14 September broad agreement was reached at the UN Security Council concerning the draft resolution authorising the international security forces to restore law and order in East Timor. The draft put forward by England hinged on Chapter 7 of the UN charter concerning the utilisation of force. The UN force in East Timor would be permitted to exercise all force necessary to

---

[48] Briefing by the Secretary-General at UN headquarters, 10/9/99.

[49] United Nations Security Council Meeting, S/PV.4043.

[50] The agenda that was adopted was based on letters sent by the permanent representatives of Portugal and Brazil on 8 and 9 September respectively. Quoted from the statement by Indonesia's permanent representative to the UN, Mr Makarim Wibisono.

[51] After initial disquiet, the Indonesian government resigned itself to accepting that the UN would determine the form and composition of the contributing states.

implement its mandate – a right won by acclamation. On 15 September, after a marathon fifteen-hour discussion, the UN Security Council ratified the resolution for the formation of a multinational force (Interfet) to be immediately sent to East Timor to restore order and security and end the humanitarian crisis.[52] Several days later, the withdrawal of the first TNI soldiers was evident, and on 20 September the deployment of the multinational force in East Timor under the command of Major-General Peter Cosgrove commenced.[53] On 24 September, Indonesia lifted martial law in East Timor.

In the approach to the next round in the tripartite meeting series on 27 September, the UN Commission on Human Rights embraced a resolution, proposed by Portugal and tabled by Finland, requesting that the Secretary-General establish an international commission of inquiry to investigate human rights violations in East Timor. The resolution passed with a large majority.[54] Indonesia reacted cautiously to the resolution, ultimately reversing its position and opting not to co-operate with the UN Human Rights Commission inquiry, instead insisting that its own National Human Rights Commission (*Komite Nacional Hak Asasi Manusia, Komnasham*) would suffice. In an *aide-memoire* the Indonesian government argued against the holding of the session of the Commission on Human Rights. It was suggested that the post-ballot acts of violence were a result of the pro-autonomy groups' dissatisfaction with what they viewed as the unfair conduct of the popular consultation.[55]

On 28 September discussion at the tripartite meeting in New York centred on the problems of the vacuum of authority, the return of East Timorese refugees and the establishment of a UN transitional administration. It was agreed that ad hoc measures were required to fill the gap created by the early departure of the Indonesian civilian authorities. The critical sense of the situation in East Timor, and his disappointment over the collapse of civil administration in East Timor, were echoed in the Secretary-General's report to the UN General Assembly on

[52] United Nations Security Council, S/RES/1264, 15/9/99.
[53] The force included participation by 14 countries and consisted of approximately 8,000 troops.
[54] The vote was 32 in favour, 12 opposed with six abstentions.
[55] *Aide-memoire* on the special session of the Commission on Human Rights in East Timor, Indonesian mission to the UN, 23 September 1999.

4 October.[56] Meanwhile, East Timorese independence leaders met in
Washington with donor countries to discuss post-independence assistance.
This was an urgent question as the flow of thousands of East Timorese
to Dili, and many other areas, had started.[57] A decision was also required
on the question of the sharing of duties between the UN and the East
Timorese leaders under the transitional administration.[58]

East Timorese diplomacy adapted quickly to the changing
environment. In early October, Xanana Gusmão met with Portugal's
Prime Minister in Lisbon and together they pledged to work to create a
functioning independent state in East Timor. A liaison group was to be
established outlining a technical, financial, and political co-operation plan
for East Timor. Just prior to the commencement of Indonesian
negotiations with the Interfet and UNAMET over the transfer of its
assets, Xanana Gusmão and other East Timorese leaders met in Darwin
ahead of the ratification of the ballot result by the Indonesian MPR. A
range of issues, including the Timor Gap treaty, was discussed in a bid to
develop an official line. The conclusion of the Indonesia-UN talks in
East Timor on 15 October was that Jakarta would grant all of its assets
– excluding state enterprises – to the United Nations. While the MPR
vacillated over formal recognition of East Timor's vote for independence,
the presence of the team in Dili indicated the Indonesian government's
recognition of the loss of East Timor. Ratification by the MPR occurred
on 20 October, repealing its 1978 decree. This was followed some six
days later by a letter from new Indonesian President Abdurrahman Wahid
to the Secretary-General of the UN declaring that the Republic of
Indonesia had ended its government in East Timor. On 20 October,
after a four-day meeting in Darwin, the CNRT announced the composition of a seven-member transition council under the leadership of Xanana
Gusmão to work with the territory's future transitional administration.

On 25 October, the United Nations Transitional Administration
in East Timor (UNTAET) was established by unanimous vote in the

[56] United Nations, 'Report of the Secretary-General on the Situation in East
Timor', S/1999/1024, 4/10/99.
[57] An interagency UN assessment on 27 September estimated that
approximately 500,000 people were displaced by the violence in East Timor.
[58] Press conference on East Timor by Xanana Gusmão and José Ramos Horta,
UN headquarters, 28/9/99. Xanana Gusmão emphasized that the people of
East Timor had voted for independence under the flag of the CNRT, and the
CNRT had 'earned the right to participate actively in the transition'.

UN Security Council with a chiefly political mandate. Led by Brazilian Sergio Vieria de Mello, it is charged with organising and developing the reconstruction of East Timor. The UN Secretary-General had earlier stated that he believed the UNTAET process in East Timor would require two to three years.[59] On the same day Indonesia clashed with Western nations during a Security Council debate on East Timor insisting that reports of human rights violations were unverified and exaggerated. Western delegates urged Indonesia to co-operate with the UN inquiry into human rights, after an earlier version of Resolution 1272 was vetoed by China because it referred to this inquiry.[60] Finally, on 26 October, the Security Council agreed to the establishment of a UN 'blue helmet' force in East Timor which would begin its commission in the new year.[61] This force is to be led by a General from the Philippines with an Australian as deputy. Issues of reconstruction, repatriation and justice have quickly become focal points. The Tokyo donors' conference in mid-December allocated US$520 m to assist in the reconstruction of East Timor over the next three years. One challenge in the future will lie in collecting this money quickly. The Indonesian Commission for the Investigation of Human Rights Abuses in East Timor (KPPHAM), despite much controversy, has proceeded with its summoning of top military leaders for allegedly colluding with the militias in their destructive activities in East Timor. Meanwhile, the issue of repatriating thousands of East Timorese from West Timor continues to provide problems for the Indonesian government, and UNTAET.

Conclusion

The diplomatic process leading to the creation of the independent nation of East Timor has been a protracted and difficult one. The result was testament to the long and bitter struggle launched by thousands of East Timorese. The construction of East Timor's international identity will be a

[59] The initial mandate extends until 31 January 2001.
[60] United Nations Security Council, 4057th meeting, S/RES/1272, 25 October 1999. The wording of the resolution expressed, in part, 'concern at reports indicating that systematic, widespread and flagrant violations of international humanitarian and human rights law have been committed in East Timor'.
[61] UNTAET was authorized under Chapter 7 of the UN charter to take all necessary measures to fulfil its mandate.

gradual process. The ability to conduct diplomatic relations with other countries, and to safeguard national interests via foreign policy, is fundamental to the operation of the international system. This process is more effectively facilitated when based on a harmonious domestic situation and a shared nationalism. As with all newly created states, East Timor will confront the problem of the training and competence of personnel especially in the foreign policy sphere. In this respect, East Timor is likely to face problems similar to those experienced by Indonesia in its immediate post-independence period. It is imperative that East Timor develop a cadre of skilled diplomats of the calibre of José Ramos Horta. The appropriate training of personnel in the art of international diplomacy and the procurement of aid assistance must be a priority. The violence of recent events surprised and horrified many foreign observers and East Timorese alike, and has guaranteed a complex and emotional reconciliation process during the UNTAET phase and beyond. It is essential that this process be facilitated as completely as possible to create a more harmonious domestic environment. Evidence of this achievement at the domestic level will enable East Timor to structure more cohesive and enduring relations at the international level so necessary for its long-term survival.

References

Cotton, James (ed.), 1999. *East Timor and Australia: AIIA Contributions to the Policy Debate*. Canberra: ADSC and AIIA.

Dunn, James, 1983. *Timor: A People Betrayed*, pp.298-299. Milton: The Jacaranda Press.

Horta, José Ramos, 1996. 'East Timor: the struggle for self-determination and its future in Southeast Asia', Royal Institute of International Affairs, Chatham House, London.

Krieger, Heike (ed.), 1997. *East Timor and the International Community*, pp.41-42. Cambridge: Cambridge University Press, Cambridge International Documents Series, Vol. 10.

6

The CNRT campaign for independence

Fernando de Araujo

An historical event, such as the struggle for independence and the birth of a new nation, can be told from many different perspectives. My account is just one perspective and hopefully in the future, other participants and witnesses to this event will contribute other perspectives to enrich our understanding of the history of the struggle for independence in East Timor. The writing of history is always contingent upon the position of the writer, no matter how hard some people convince us of their claim to 'truth' or 'objectivity'. In this case, my position is that of a nationalist in the context of an anti-colonial struggle, who happened to be called upon to play a role not only in the campaign but in the struggle for independence. This is by no means, however, an 'official' account of the CNRT campaign, but rather a personal account in which I write about the important contributions of many people who may be left out, lest their enormous sacrifices and ideals be pushed aside.

Two options: independence or autonomy

After President B.J. Habibie announced the two options of 'Independence' and 'Autonomy under Indonesia', the East Timorese people who for the past 24 years had been struggling with everything they had to regain their independence, which had been taken away from them by the Indonesian military, were suddenly faced with a dilemma. This dilemma emerged because, even before the announcement, the military had already intensified their recruitment of local Timorese to strengthen the ranks of the military and the militias.

Later on it would become evident that Habibie had received false reports from the military claiming that they were in complete control and that they had already done everything they could to convince the people that the best choice for the future of East Timor was the autonomy option. Based upon these military reports and driven by the practical rationalisation that Indonesia's tarnished image abroad must be repaired to expedite the flow of funds from the IMF and World Bank and to revive the Indonesian economy which was crippled by corruption and mismanagement, Habibie with great confidence announced his two options.

The Maubere people welcomed this news with optimism because it represented an acknowledgment of the justness of their long-term struggle to determine their own future. Yet, on the other hand, there was serious concern and suspicion of potential manipulation because of what we had learned from the history and experience of the people of West Papua in 1963, where it is quite clear that an international conspiracy occurred to surrender this territory to Indonesia. During that time, the Jakarta government organised a 'Referendum' appointing 1000 people to represent and vote for the entire population of West Papua. This concern, however, was put aside when the 5 May 1999 Agreement was signed in New York which stipulated that the East Timor Referendum would follow a 'one person, one vote' policy, whereby there would be no opportunity for Indonesia to manipulate the vote.

'One person, one vote' meant that Indonesia lost the opportunity to repeat its fraudulent practice in West Papua. However, the New York agreement still gave other opportunities for Jakarta to control and manipulate matters on the ground. One of the most serious flaws was the relegation of 'security issues' to the Indonesian government. The military then went on to recruit local East Timorese, increased the presence of the military in all regions of East Timor, recruited '*preman*' from Java and West Timor to terrorise, kill and torture ordinary people. Their intention was to produce a climate of fear so that people would choose autonomy as the ultimate solution to the problem of East Timor. Having put in place this climate of fear and terror, they intensified their pro-autonomy campaign, with the argumentation that the Maubere people would die of starvation if they separated from Indonesia; that rejecting autonomy would mean rejecting peace; that there was no way the Indonesian military would ever leave East Timor; that if they rejected autonomy, everything would be annihilated and that the only thing that would be heard would be the chirping of birds: 'choosing autonomy, blood will drip; rejecting autonomy, blood will flow' (*'menerima autonomi darah menetes, menolak autonomi darah mengalir'*).

Against such overwhelming political terror and intimidation, almost all sections of Timor Loro Sa'e society moved to do whatever they possibly could to disseminate information to the people and to strengthen everyone's conviction that independence was close at hand. An initial step by the pro-independence group was to produce a critical analysis of the autonomy proposal presented at the New York meeting on 5 May. In the group's analysis, which was published by the *Sahe Study Club* and distributed in East Timor, the weaknesses of autonomy were critically examined.

Several younger generation activists (*geração foun*)[1] approached Kay Rala Xanana Gusmão hoping that he would give concrete instructions on what needed to be done to prepare for the referendum. Communication occurred through letters, telephone, courier, and through *estafeta* (passing messages from hand to hand). One of the first meetings to discuss the structural division of labour and distribution of information to the East Timorese people occurred at the beginning of March 1999, when Xanana Gusmão as President of CNRT called the leaders of nationalist youth movements in Indonesia and East Timor to Salemba in Jakarta where he was under house arrest. The discussion concerned the tasks that would be assigned to the youth organisations.

Pião Avançado

Following the pattern of mass mobilisation in the past decade where the younger generation (*juventude*) had often been at the front line in demonstrations, the youth organisations agreed to be at the forefront of the campaign for the referendum, despite the fact that there were no guarantees whatsoever of security. During this meeting with the

---

[1]   *Geração foun* or younger generation refers to those who were *not* part of the 1975 leadership generation (now in their fifties and above) and who do not have the same long-standing factionalisms and party conflicts as the older generation. Among other things, intellectual formation under Indonesian colonialism and language facility are also different.

leaders of the youth political organisations, the President of CNRT emphasised that the young people must be the *'Pião Avançado'* (*'Pião'* or pawns advanced as in a chess match to shield the higher ranks). It was the younger generation, not overly confident of victory, who became the motor of this campaign. Xanana emphasised the importance of disseminating information, especially to those who lived in remote areas in the different regions – at the foot of the mountains and hill slopes – because it is they who most deserved our attention. He rearticulated once more the importance of unity among the diverse organisations.

It was also during this meeting on 4 March 1999, at Xanana's place of arrest, that he, along with the leaders of the youth organisations, began to define the shape and model of the campaign. In responding to questions and suggestions from the youth leaders, Xanana Gusmão, who was always too optimistic concerning many things, believed that it was no longer necessary for us to conduct a campaign because the pro-independence campaign had already been going on for 24 years:

> If the autonomy people want to make banners saying that autonomy is the best way to go, we don't need to respond by making banners of the same size saying that independence is the better way to go. Throughout these years, the Maubere people already know their goals, the reasons for their struggle, suffering and death.

This was Xanana Gusmão's response to those who came all the way from Timor Leste and who raised questions about what kind of counter-campaign needed to be mounted against the pro-autonomy group. Throughout East Timor at this time, the autonomy group had already begun their campaign by public exhibitions of force, consolidating all their forces down to the village level and displaying banners in the streets. Stickers with the slogan – *'Hau Hili Autonomia'* ('I choose Autonomy') were posted on almost every street corner.

Listening to these descriptions, Xanana Gusmão merely said that we need not respond 'reactively' to their actions. What needed to be done by the younger generation was to behave with discipline and civility in order to help the process of 'reconciliation' which was currently in progress. 'If the autonomy group wants to distribute money to people to buy their votes, let them do it.' He was quite certain that the people were already politically aware and that they would not sell their rights. He argued that if they (the pro-autonomy group) wanted to mobilise the masses, then we should not be baited to do the same thing. What we had to do was to work hard to create a safe environment so that UNAMET could proceed with its work smoothly. The youth must join with the masses, they must go back to their villages to work with their parents. They must make them aware of the importance of reconciliation and help them in planting their rice fields. This, according to Xanana, was what was crucially needed by the people at this time. The model of the campaign, Xanana proposed, was to be based on 'door-to-door' campaigning. We were to visit each house, sit with the people, and talk about our own experiences. Tell them about our experiences in 1975, about indigenous beliefs and practices, about whatever is interesting in our experience of living in Indonesia. And most importantly, we must make them aware of the virtues of accepting and forgiving each other. It was during this time that Xanana Gusmão gave instructions for students who were enrolled in universities in Java to leave their studies temporarily and to return to the countryside to help in distributing information to the people.

However, even before there were instructions from the President of CNRT, the young people studying in Indonesia had already anticipated what problems might arise and had been preparing themselves for the worst that might happen. They conducted training sessions on how to mobilise and organise the people, how to respond effectively, if for example, Indonesia suddenly withdrew its doctors from Timor Loro Sa'e, and how to fill the vacuum left by migrant teachers who would most surely leave. By this time, it had become increasingly evident that the military wanted to create an unsafe situation so that teachers and doctors would flee.

We specifically wanted to focus on the two fields of health and education because of their strong impact on the lives of the East Timorese people. We were seriously concerned about what needed to be done internally in order to prevent a crisis in obtaining medicines and health services. If the schools were to stop operating and there were no longer doctors to assist the people, then opposition to the pro-independence group could emerge, if they are unable to provide for basic needs – such as food and in helping people in the rural areas with planting and harvesting.

In April 1999, as many as 850 students at universities in Java, Bali, Lombok, Lampung and other provinces decided to leave their studies and return to East Timor to 'distribute information to the people' (an expression used as a substitute for 'campaign' to show the faithfulness of the pro-independence group in following the procedures laid down by UNAMET concerning the referendum.)

The returning students were organised by the Vice Secretary General of RENETIL, who was also the Head of IMPETTU (*Ikatan Mahasiswa dan Pelajar Timor Timur*), Engineer Mariano Sabino Lopes. Several months later, many of these students' parents expressed their anger regarding the discontinuation of their children's schooling.

The students arrived with all kinds of ideas about social programs as a way to open the path to enter villages. An effective strategy – such as going to their own villages to visit their own families – was crucial because the Indonesian military strongly suspected students arriving from outside Timor Loro Sa'e as well as those studying in the University of Timor Timur (UNTIM) and the Polytechnic in Hera. Their movements were put under surveillance and their parents were constantly interrogated about what they talked about at home. As a consequence of this hatred and suspicion of students, two students from UNTIM, who were undertaking KKN (*Kuliah Kerja Nyata*), were murdered in May 1999, in the village of Raimea, in the subdistrict of Zumale, in Kovalima.

During the mobilisation campaign, the students encountered serious difficulties in the different regions, and in many cases were unable to implement their plans because of heightened militia and military terror, including intensified interrogation at checkpoints for identity cards. This was one of the most serious obstacles we faced during the campaign. Due to these difficulties, eventually almost all important activities had to be centred in Dili. However, we continued to hope that the UN would put stronger pressure on Indonesia to abide by the New York agreement of 5 May 1999 and to fulfil its responsibility of guaranteeing safety and security for all parties, so that we would be able to continue our work without endangering our lives.

Presidium Juventude Loriku Ass'wain Timor Loro Sa'e

It was also in April 1999, with the knowledge and approval of CNRT in Dili, that an umbrella organisation called *Presidium Juventude Loriku Ass'wain Timor Loro Sa'e* was formed to unify all youth movements in East Timor. This Presidium was to meet regularly during the campaign to co-ordinate and organise various tasks that needed to be done. Almost all youth organisations joined the Presidium (including Ojetil, Opjelatil, Fuan Domin, Renetil, Uniamorte, Sagrada Familia, Impettu, Fitun, União Juventude Timor Leste, and other youth pro-independence activists). The only exception were the youth groups affiliated with the PNT party (*Partido Nacionalista de Timor*, which was founded and led by Abilio Araujo), such as, for example, RDTL (Republic of Democratic Timor Leste), a group which wants to uphold the proclamation of the Republic of Democratic Timor Leste in 28 November 1975.

The principle of the Presidium umbrella was to be non-partisan, i.e. not affiliated with any of the political parties. The Presidium would therefore put the interests of the people first before that of the divergent parties, in addition to remaining subordinate to and faithful to the CNRT leader, Kay Rala Xanana Gusmão. It was also in April 1999 that violent attacks by the military and militia were intensified: these included the murder of dozens of people in a church in Liquiça, the killing of dozens of people in the house of Manuel Carrascalão, the murder of one of the leaders of CNRT in Dili and attacks in other places, such as Atsabe, Maubara, Zumalae. As a consequence, many people fled their villages to become refugees in Dili and many of the leaders of CNRT also fled, to the extent that only David Ximenes and Leandro Isaac remained in Dili. Leandro Isaac had to seek refuge in the Police office (*Polres*) in Dili while David Ximenes moved from house to house for safety. David Ximenes' political activities could only be conducted at night because it was only when it was dark that he was able to meet with activists and journalists to co-ordinate CNRT activities. His house was burnt down along with the only motorcycle he owned for transport.

From the middle of April to the middle of June, the official activities of CNRT in Timor Loro Sa'e came to a halt. People were confused; some were frustrated and raised questions about where the leadership of CNRT was. It was the youth movement which continued to be organised, trying very hard keep up spirits and to give information to the people. Falintil also worked very hard to organise the people, but faced the same difficulties with the military and militias, especially in the western regions of Suai, Maliana and Oecussi.

Matebian Lian

Due to the impossibility of conducting their tasks in the villages, many students converged in Dili. There they were able to publish three different bulletins – *Unidade, Liberta* and *Loriku Lian*. These bulletins could not be printed because no printing presses in Dili were brave enough to publish them. Their publication was carried out through photocopying. In addition to printed publications they also broadcast a radio program, which was given the name *Matebian Lian. Matebian* means 'spirit' and *lian* means 'voice'. This name was chosen because this particular radio broadcast had no central station but moved from place to place in order to avoid detection by the military. The people could listen to and follow *Matebian Lian* but they did not know from where the voice originated. Because they could only hear it but did not know the exact position of the news emanating from the radio broadcast, it was given this name of *Matebian Lian* ('Spirit Voice'). The news published in the various bulletins and in *Matebian Lian* included updates on the process of 'reconciliation', the announcements made by UNAMET on referendum procedures, and commands given by Xanana Gusmão and the CNRT leadership. Even though he was still under house arrest in Jakarta, Xanana Gusmão tried hard to give direction to the news that was broadcast and published with the goal of facilitating the process of reconciliation which was being initiated by the two bishops (Bacilio Nacimento of Baucau and Carlos Felipe Ximenes Belo of Dili).

In June 1999, Francisco Lopes da Cruz issued a strong threat against the circulation of these bulletins with the accusation that they are insulting the pro-autonomy group and asked the security apparatus to prevent their publication and circulation. A few days' later, there was an order from the military commander (Danrem) in Dili to search for and stop the broadcasts of Radio Matebian Lian, charging that this radio broadcast was instigating anti-autonomy feelings among the people. This order was delivered in a ruthless fashion threatening that the radio program had to be eliminated and its producers brought before him within 24 hours.

The radio continued to broadcast successfully in different regions, including Aileu, Ermera, Maliana, Los Palos, Baucau and Viqueque. After one or two nights in one place, they moved from place to place, sometimes crossing mountains and walking on foot from one subdistrict to another to avoid detection.

Comissão de Planeamento e Coordenação da Campanha (CPCC)

On 27 June 1999, Dare II was held at the Sheraton Hotel in Jakarta, a 'reconciliation' meeting organised by the two bishops, which included leaders from both sides – pro-independence and pro-autonomy. Several CNRT leaders, some of whom had not been allowed to set foot in Indonesia for 24 years were allowed to attend this reconciliation meeting. Those attending included José Ramos Horta, Mari Alkatiri, João Carrascalão, Roque Rodrigues and many others.

After the Dare II meeting in Jakarta concluded, all of the participants gathered at Xanana's place in Salemba, for the CNRT to discuss officially everything that pertained to the upcoming campaign. On 2 July, during a national meeting of the CNRT, the decision was made to form the CPCC (*Comissão de Planeamento e Coordenação da Campanha*) as the official body responsible for the campaign for independence. CPCC formulated programs and co-ordinated all of the elements involved in the struggle, including how to work with UNAMET's electoral section, and producing all materials needed for the campaign. CPCC was responsible to Xanana Gusmão as President of CNRT. On the ground, it was the *Frente Politica Interna* (FPI) in Timor Loro Sa'e who exercised executive duties in implementing programs planned by the CPCC. There were nine departments or sections in the CPCC. After the formation of these sections, Xanana announced the names of those who would be responsible for each section:

1. Social Communications — Fernando de Araujo
2. Logistics (Consumption and Transportation) — João Alves
3. Inter-Regional Relations — Lucas da Costa
4. Political Mobilisation — Mariano Sabino
5. Juridical/Legal Issues — Olandina Caeiro
6. Education and Monitoring — Armindo Maia
7. Training of Cadres for the Campaign — José Reis
8. Information — Agio Pereira
9. Finance — Maria Paixão

Mar Kairos was appointed as overall co-ordinator for CPCC. On the ground, however, the section on juridical issues was eliminated because of several technical problems: among them, the difficulties of investigating violations that were occurring, problems of co-operation from the part of the Indonesian military, and the fact that there was no juridical section within UNAMET itself.

At the time when the CNRT had just formed CPCC, the pro-autonomy group was already well on its way in campaigning all over East Timor. Francisco Lopes went on a tour of the regions, arranging public meetings with the masses and utilising all of the state apparatus he could possibly call upon: from village heads to the governor, from the soldiers appointed to control village heads (Babinsa) to the military commander (Danrem) – all were mobilised to convince the East Timorese people to continue to uphold the red and white Indonesian flag in East Timor.

On 9 July 1999, the CPCC's first meeting in Dili was held to allocate tasks. We began an inventory of all facilities that existed and which we could use for the campaign. The possibilities of using the printing presses, radio stations, television stations or even walkie-talkies (for which it was claimed, we needed a letter of permission (*surat izin*)) were almost nil because the pro-autonomy group had already pressured those who headed these facilities not to give the pro-independence group the chance to use them.

The CNRT flag

Because of the problem of lack of access to communication facilities, during the meeting of 9 July, we decided to conduct the campaign door-to-door and to begin immediately to make people aware of the CNRT flag and the symbols that would be used by both sides. At this time, these symbols were still quite ambiguous because there had not yet been conclusive discussions from the two sides along with UNAMET regarding preferred symbols. However, those of us at the CPCC were quite bold in taking the initiative to go ahead and print thousands of copies of the CNRT flag because during the meetings in Jakarta, the CNRT leadership had already agreed upon the colours and symbolism of the flag, raised on top of a map of East Timor, as the symbol for pro-independence. We calculated that even if the pro-autonomy group were to also use the map of East Timor for their symbol (which they did), they would not be able to claim or appropriate the CNRT flag, unless there was dissension and confusion within the pro-independence group itself about changing the flag.

We saw the issue of the flag as quite crucial when we reflected on the fact that a majority of East Timorese villagers were illiterate, and would probably be attracted by symbols rather than by written materials. Also, the CNRT flag was a new creation and most people didn't even know what it looked like. They were more familiar with the Fretilin and Falintil flags. In the process, people in the pro-independence group became actively involved in looking for the CNRT flag – searching in the web site to copy it. There were those who drew and coloured it by hand, others photocopied it even though it came out as black and white and lost the symbolism of the colours blue, black, white and green.

Within three days, the CNRT flag had been distributed throughout the city of Dili and the door-to-door campaign had begun. The young people involved in the *Presidium Juventude Loriku Ass'wain* began visiting house-to-house to make people aware of the CNRT flag and the pro-independence symbols, and to explain the procedures for registering and voting in the referendum. There were so many people involved in this: non-students, women teachers, ordinary people came to the office of RENETIL asking for banners, flyers and stickers so that they could help distribute them from house-to-house, despite the fact that they were regularly confronted by militia and the military who tried to ensure that they would not be able to distribute this information. In spite of the overwhelming political odds against us, this campaign was successfully realised in the eastern region of East Timor, although the western region was difficult because militia and military activity there was quite intensive.

This informal campaign was carried out following the model of well-disciplined clandestine work, which we had adhered to for more than 10 years. Xanana continually reminded us not to aggravate tensions by demonstrating in the streets or organising mass rallies for this could be used by the pro-autonomy group and the military to provoke clashes which may result in more deaths. He also advised us not to pre-empt the referendum schedule set up by UNAMET.

At the formal level, CPCC leaders attended meetings with UNAMET, in particular the Electoral Affairs Section to discuss the timetable for the campaign, its format, the facilities that would be used, the themes that could be touched upon without violating the rights of the other group, and so on. No word was more misapplied and corrupted than the word 'neutral'. The major NGOs (including Yayasan Hak, FOKUPERS, CARE, Caritas, TimorAid) were supposedly 'neutral'; UNAMET was 'neutral'; all international observers' groups accredited by the UN had to be 'neutral'; the church was 'neutral'. This 'neutral' stance prevented them from openly and publicly supporting the pro-independence campaign, even though individual members of these groups were sympathetic to and actively involved in the struggle for independence.

The politics of reconciliation at the elite level continued to progress even though every day there were reports of violence by the military and militias – shootings, attacks, more refugees displaced from their homes. Several times, our office (the RENETIL office had become the meeting place for the CPCC and contained important computer and other facilities) had to be closed due to threats of an attack by the militias. My family and I were threatened with death, and so was almost everyone we knew who was outspokenly pro-independence. We filed an official report of these threats with UNAMET's Political Affairs Section and with the Dili Police. Everyone involved in the radio, television and newspaper projects had to work in their own homes and come back the following day to discuss their completed work.

In organising this campaign, CNRT received contributions (financial and otherwise) from several solidarity groups. However, the violence that erupted afterwards did not enable the CPCC committee to hold a concluding meeting to find out which groups and people had helped us – only Xanana and Mar Kairos know who the donors were. Each committee was requested to file a report regarding finances and activities; however, by the time I submitted my report to Mar Kairos, the situation had already become so dangerous that everyone was forced to go into hiding.

Organização da Mulheres Timorenses (OMT)

Aside from the students, the other sector of society that was extremely active was the organisation of women's groups. When I think back to the months of June, July, August and September, when the 'campaign' was at its height, it was mostly women who were the most visible and active members of the campaign. And yet in terms of representation in the media they were virtually invisible. There were several women who formed the main 'nerve centres' of political work in East Timor, and who could have literally brought political life to an abrupt halt if they had withdrawn their logistical support and intellectual resources. These women include members of the Organisation of Timorese Women: (OMT: *Organização da Mulheres Timorenses*), GERTAK, FOKUPERS, and individuals such as Lucia Lobato, Maria Paixão, Felicidade Gutteres, Odette Gutteres, Armandina Gusmão, Olandina Caero, Pascoela Barreto, Sister Lourdes (in Dare), Sister Esmeralda (who took leadership of the 1500 or more refugees in the UNAMET compound), Sister Marlene Bautista (a Filipina nun who has worked in East Timor for 10 years). As some observers have noted, women's movements can on their own present a formidable opposition group to any regime that is potentially patriarchal, misogynist and totalitarian.

But perhaps the women who sacrificed the most were the women who suddenly received news one day that their son had died, either drowned, killed by the military, or had disappeared. And the women who waited. The struggle for independence forcibly separated families – sons from their mothers and fathers and brothers and sisters, wives from their husbands and children, lovers from those who might have been their future spouses.

Vox Populi

The Section on Social Communications (CPCC) was successful in publishing a newspaper called *Vox Populi* every two days, after intensive interpersonal lobbying of the only private printing press in Dili which published *Suara Timor Timur* (STT). This was the only daily newspaper circulating in Dili at that time and was owned by the Secretary-General of the pro-autonomy group BRTT (*Barisan Rakyat Timor Timur*) under the leadership of Francisco Lopes da Cruz. Eventually they agreed to print our newspaper because of pressure on the managers of the press from almost all of the journalists and workers (with the courageous lobbying of Hugo Adevito da Costa) within *Suara Timor Timur*.

It was also because of good personal relations with the director of the government-owned Radio Republic Indonesia in Dili that the CPCC was allowed to use radio facilities free of charge to broadcast the pro-independence campaign. This was also true for TVRI where we aired our campaign at least three times. Our radio broadcasters, who were living in Dili at the outbreak of the violence, became prime targets for the militia. These included the highly talented artist and performer Anito Matos as well as Armandina Gusmão and Carmelita Monis. It was extremely difficult for all of us to co-ordinate the taping of the radio programs because of the security problems. It was dangerous for us to still be out collecting news, taping, writing and editing late at night, when the streets were supposed to be empty by 7.00 pm. There were numerous people (not all of whose individual names can be mentioned here), who worked very hard on these projects. They included Virgilio da Silva Gutteres, Maria (Eté) Gracieté, Micha Barreto Soares, Metodio Moniz, Vicente da Costa Pinto, Rigoberto Monteiro, Eusebio Gutteres, Siak or Zeca, Ato', Kim Pai, Juliao M., José Neves, Antonio Conceição, Nuno Rodrigues, Anito Matos, Vitorino Cardoso Santos, Armindo Maia, Jacqueline (Joy) Siapno, Agio Pereira, Ceu Brites, Ines Almeida, Nino Pereira, and Armandina Gusmão.

The other media facilities used by CPCC included *Radio Timor Kmanek*, a well-funded establishment owned by the Catholic church. We signed a contract for 12 days, following the official program schedule laid out by UNAMET. However, we were only able to broadcast until 26 August because by that time, security in Dili already seemed out of control. This was also true for *Vox Populi* and the distribution of pamphlets and other brochures. Many of these documents were left scattered in the office which all of us had to abandon in a hurry. The news which we printed and broadcast was edited by a rigorous editorial team in CPCC to avoid language that might provoke the pro-autonomy group. In retrospect, I am amazed at how we in the pro-independence group tried with great discipline and good faith to follow the UNAMET rules and to help the process of reconciliation, even though there was nothing in the pro-autonomy group that indicated that they were abiding by any rules.

The most problematic were the hundreds of thousands of coloured brochures and flyers which had to be printed in Jakarta and Surabaya because there were no presses in Dili that printed with colour. To prepare and translate them (into Portuguese, Indonesian, English and Tetun) and get them back, we needed at least a week, but there were serious delays because of technical problems. We were constantly worried that there would be sabotage on the part of the military. Ironically, the person in charge of the logistics of all this was an East Timorese (José B.C. Das Neves or Pak Beni) who had an important position in the Indonesian bureaucracy, but who, in private, was quite earnest in supporting our campaign, and using the facilities of his office for our benefit. The CNRT flag had to be produced in Australia and underwent a long journey before arriving in Dili.

After the boxes of materials were unloaded from the ship and planes, the next problem we faced was how to distribute them effectively so that they reached even the most distant regions. At one unloading at the port of Dili, the materials went missing, and we were afraid that they had been detected and confiscated by the military. Several times our volunteer couriers carrying these materials were blocked at checkpoints and arrested and the materials confiscated and destroyed. This happened in Liquiça, Hera and Aileu. We reported these violations to UNAMET staff, but again there was no concrete action against the military and militia members who carried this out. This was one of the most serious flaws with the 5 May Agreement that it did not set out punitive measures against those who violated rules of the agreement and that it gave the responsibility of 'security' to the same apparatus responsible for the brutal acts of violence in East Timor. The official campaign period originally scheduled by UNAMET to run from 14-28 August had to end three days beforehand because of the violence that ensued.

Because of the extreme difficulties faced by all elements of the struggle, the distribution of information only reached up to the regency and sub-district levels. We faced serious obstacles in the villages because the military and militias were intent on isolating village people from the latest information and developments emanating from Dili. This isolation was conducted systematically because the military believed that if they were successful in isolating the villages from information, then at least 60 per cent of the vote would be for pro-autonomy. This tactic gave Foreign Minister Ali Alatas the confidence to announce: 'Now Ramos Horta shall be proven wrong that 99 per cent of East Timorese will choose independence.'

The last days of August

In the last days of August, before the referendum of 30 August, the primary focus of the CPCC was to try our best to ensure that everyone who had registered safely could vote on that day. Even though militia and military violence was on the rise, this was the one and only chance for our people to articulate their political aspirations.

During this time Xanana gave instructions to everyone involved in the struggle on the ground to 'control the masses' and not to be provoked by the military and militia because if this were to happen, more people would be killed. In Jakarta, he continued to establish contacts with the leaders of the pro-autonomy group to negotiate and ensure that there would be no more bloodshed. There were several false promises from Francisco Lopes and Eurico Gutteres that they would give instructions to their various subordinates not to act brutally towards the civilian population. Eurico and Francisco Lopes publicly announced that they themselves would respect the results if the majority of East Timorese chose independence. However, it has now become very clear that while making these duplicitous statements, they were systematically preparing for a scorched earth policy, had already begun accusing UNAMET of not being 'neutral', and were laying out their violent plans not to accept the results of the referendum if it favoured independence.

The pro-independence group strictly abided by Xanana's instructions not to organise public mass rallies. However, because of extraordinary enthusiasm from the people to come out into the streets, the CPCC decided to hold one public campaign rally on 25 August. On that day, the entire city of Dili was a sea of humanity. The roads were filled with people – even toddlers from two to five years old, full of spirit and excitement singing and chanting – *Mate Ka Moris, Ukun Rasik An* – ('Life or Death, Independence') – *Mate Ka Moris, Duni Bapak Sai* – ('Life or Death, Expel the Military'). Grandmothers and elderly people stood by the side of the roads, dancing and instructing everyone to punch a hole in the CNRT flag on top of the East Timor map, which symbolised freedom. It was an extraordinary experience. There was a young boy wearing a funny mask with black glasses and a big nose, a young man who painted his face red with different colours, an estimated 1000 cars and buses packed with human beings, and thousands of people in the streets chanting the convoy along.

On that day there were no provocations toward the military or militia. Sadly a bus carrying dozens of pro-independence supporters overturned and killed two people, and rumours spread that the driver was a pro-autonomy supporter who had intentionally overturned the bus. In spite of this, the rest of the day went quite peacefully until around 4.00 pm when the campaign concluded in front of the CNRT office in *Jalan Lecidere* near the sea.

On 26 August, it was the turn of the pro-autonomy group to conduct its campaign. The pro-autonomy convoy began by insulting people in the streets and throwing stones at houses and people. In Desa Kuluhun, some inhabitants responded to these insults by throwing stones back. What happened next became much more serious than throwing stones and insulting each other. The mobile police (*Brimob*) indiscriminately opened fire with automatic rifles on civilians in the street, killing three people, one of whom was a student member of RENETIL who had been studying in Malang, named Bedinho Gutteres. He was also one of the journalists for *Vox Populi*. Some international and Indonesian journalists who witnessed the event were beaten and intimidated by the police. The corpses could not be buried as they properly should have been. Only the women and children could take the corpses; the men couldn't do so because the military and militia were already swarming at the scene of the crime to prevent people from expressing public grief.

From 26 August onwards, all campaign activities of the pro-independence group came to a stop because it became impossible to carry out our tasks. That night, the CNRT office was attacked; the contents of the office including computers, walkie-talkies, radios and chairs were looted and then the building was burned. The RENETIL office was attacked and the windows smashed, forcing the students to flee in different directions. The same acts of looting and arson were done on other buildings occupied by organisations working for the pro-independence campaign. The following morning, Dili seemed like a dead city; everyone stayed in their houses with nothing to do but wait for 30 August, referendum day.

On that historic day of 30 August, most people came out to cast their vote, but returned soon afterwards to their homes; and, by nightfall the situation was quite tense. There was no shooting on 30 August, voting day. It began the following day. The following day, shooting began everywhere and so did the burning and the fires. It became impossible to meet with other people because it was too dangerous to walk in the streets. Everyone stayed in their houses waiting for the results of the referendum to be announced.

Initially the results were supposed to be announced one week after the vote. However, due to security considerations of possible military tampering with the boxes (at one point UNAMET staff were held hostage), counting began on 1 September. The CPCC members, including myself, were asked to become witnesses to ensure fair counting. Counting went on for three days. However, on 1 September, people were already leaving their houses to seek refuge elsewhere. Several of them went to Dare. Others went to the churches and to Bishop Belo's residence which, they thought, would be safe, but where later on, the military and militias attacked and massacred more than 30 people. Olandina Caeiro had called us that morning inviting us to join them at Bishop Belo's house saying 'We're having a little independence celebration; why not join; everyone is here. If we're going to die, we might as well all be together.' News spread that the military and militias would be conducting house-to-house searches to execute pro-independence leaders. We would leave later, on 5 September, to join 50 000 refugees who had fled to the mountains.

We won, but we were the ones who had to become refugees in the forests and mountains from where we could watch as our houses were looted and burned. Everything the people owned was looted –

cars, motorcycles, appliances, clothes, wedding photographs – and loaded onto military trucks heading toward the western border, to Atambua and then to Kupang. From above in the mountains, we could watch Dili being burnt to the ground, with the smoke thickening as each day passed. Infants cried because there was no milk and they were hungry, their bodies itched from dirt and poor sanitary conditions. Because we had cast our vote on 30 August, life in Timor Loro Sa'e was no longer the same. Grandmothers and grandfathers had to climb tortuous steep mountains, supporting themselves with canes, because they had no other choice if they wanted to continue living, after the military and militias attacked.

Independence day

On 4 September, Saturday, the result of the referendum was announced, and momentarily people were able to celebrate with immense joy, crying and hugging each other. Immediately afterwards they silently grieved for the many heroes and heroines who lost their lives in the struggle to achieve independence. I can only hope that in our efforts to build this new nation, we do not betray them.

Acknowledgments

I wish to thank Professor James J. Fox and Dionisio Babo Soares for encouraging me to write this article. My wife, Jacqueline Siapno, not only translated this text from Indonesian to English but supported me unconditionally throughout the campaign. While it is impossible to mention the names of all the people who were involved in the campaign, I wish to express special thanks to the camaraderie of the following people without whose contributions the campaign would not have succeeded: David Ximenes, Maria Paixão, Felicidade Gutteres, Mar Kairos, Olandina Caeiro, Agio Pereira, Ceu Brites, Ines Almeida, Armandina Gusmão, the Vox Populi team under the editorship of Virgilio da Silva Gutteres, the militantes of Renetil and Impettu, some of whom died during the campaign, Antonio Conçeicão, Joaquim Fonseca, Zeca, José Neves, Anito Matos, Micha Barreto Soares, Graciete, Lita, Lucia Lobato, and my mother, sisters and aunts who never slept until I came home safely during the campaign.

7

Experiences of a district electoral officer in Suai

Catharina Williams

Introduction

During July and August 1999, I was a district electoral officer with
UNAMET in East Timor. In this chapter, I hope to convey some of
the flavour of this experience.

The task of running the popular consultation within East Timor
fell to UNAMET. For this purpose they selected 200 centres, most
of which ended up being run by a multinational team of three – two
district electoral officers and a member of the civilian police. The
latter's tasks included keeping an eye on security, and liaising with the
Indonesian police.

The entire process of preparing for the ballot was of necessity
very fast. By early July, the 200 centres had been selected, regional
headquarters set up, most international staff had arrived at their
respective regional headquarters, and local drivers and interpreters
had been appointed. In Suai it was 8 July (less than eight weeks before
the ballot) before we started voter education, seeking additional local
staff to help with registration, and final negotiations on which building
to use in each centre. Registering the voters started just over a week
later, on 16 July, and continued until 6 August. There were then less
than four weeks until the ballot on 30 August. This period included
two weeks of campaigning (in which district electoral officers in Suai
had very little involvement, even as spectators), several days of
displaying computerised lists of registrations so that people could

check the lists and object to any entries they considered fraudulent, selection and training of local staff for the ballot day, and education of voters about the mechanics of voting. The short time frame inevitably meant that some things had to be made up 'on the run', and led to frustration as information from Dili was sometimes received after we really needed it. Nevertheless, in retrospect, it seems to have had limited impact on the vote, with a very high percentage of the population registering, and 98.5 per cent of those turning up to vote.

As district electoral officer, I was assigned to the region of Suai, in south-west East Timor. (This was relatively close to the West Timor border, where I had earlier learned the Tetun language while working towards a PhD in linguistics.) Initially I was teamed with a Bulgarian colleague and an Irish policeman, responsible for the district of Beco I, on the plains about 30 minutes drive to the east of Suai. We travelled out every morning in a convoy of five UNAMET Landrover Discovery vehicles, accompanied by a truckload of Indonesian police. Our team would drop off the convoy first, along with one Indonesian policeman, while the others went on to the Zumalai district.

Part way through registration I was transferred to Fatululik, in the mountains over an hour's drive north-west of Suai. This district had only just become accessible again by car after a team of 130 local men cut a bypass around a severe landslide. On account of the distance and the difficult roads, the Fatululik team lived locally in the doctor's house for the period of registration, rather than commuting every day. For registration I was teamed with a lady from Zambia and a policeman from Uruguay, while for the ballot I was joined by a Canadian and a Swede.

Site selection

One of the first jobs of each electoral team was to approach the government heads in the area to which they were assigned, and negotiate for a suitable building to use. In some cases this had been done by an advance team. However, I did this for four centres, and was impressed with the co-operation we received. In one case, we approached the sub-district (*desa*) head on a Thursday afternoon, the day before registration was due to start, to ask for a building. Despite this short notice, he came up with the goods, and had the house next to the sub-district office cleaned and furnished in time for registration to start. Sites included schools, government-owned houses, other empty local government buildings, and trading co-operatives.

Voter education

An important part of a district electoral officer's task was to educate the voters about registration and about voting. This was a part I particularly enjoyed, and in which my ability to speak Tetun (albeit not quite the right dialect) proved very useful. Most teams spoke through interpreters; I also sometimes used interpreters to communicate more effectively with Bunak-speaking audiences in Fatululik, as not everyone there understood Tetun well.

We varied our approach from running pre-planned meetings to just walking through the villages, speaking to whomever was available. Response to both varied enormously, both in terms of the numbers attending, and in terms of how freely they expressed interest and asked questions. At one extreme was a village in Suai Loro where it seemed our team was invisible – nobody acknowledged our presence as we walked through, even though we could clearly see women sitting in the doorways of the traditional houses. At the other extreme was the village of Fatuloro, in the district of Fatululik, where 80 people came to listen to us even though we hadn't called a meeting. We never worked out why the response varied so much; certainly in some villages people were strongly warned by the militias against talking with or listening to UNAMET ('or else ...'), but Fatuloro, where the response was so good, was one such village. Perhaps it is no accident that their village head, a prominent member of the militias, was absent the day we went. The fact that many people were afraid to go and work in their more distant gardens no doubt contributed to the high attendances in some villages.

Prior to registration, our primary messages concerned the categories of people who could vote (namely those born in East Timor, with a parent born in East Timor, or married to someone in one of those two categories), the necessity of registering before one could vote, and what documents they needed to show in order to register.

Between registration and the ballot, the focus shifted to the secrecy of the vote, and the assurance that the UN would stay on in East Timor for a period, regardless of the outcome. Both were important in encouraging people to vote; in our absence they were instructed by government and military leaders to vote for autonomy, and the militias constantly threatened that if the people voted for independence, all would die. The message was backed up by displays of guns, shooting into the air, and many other forms of intimidation, all done when foreigners were safely out of the way.

Of particular importance to people was the fact that nobody would ever know how their district had voted; it would thus be impossible for revenge to be taken on any one pro-independence village. In retrospect, with the whole territory voting strongly for independence, this fact did not protect them, but it was very important at the time.

Prior to voting we also gave practical information about the technicalities of voting. In a society with high levels of illiteracy, people were most interested in which symbols would be used for autonomy and which for independence – information that only became available just over two weeks before the ballot. Thankfully the pro-autonomy symbol included the red-and-white Indonesian flag, such that people could readily learn which was which. Three days before the ballot I did a walk-through of several villages in Fatululik to assure myself that the messages had got through. One elderly lady, on being shown the two symbols, insisted that she didn't know which was for autonomy, and which for independence. My heart sank, but then she livened up and said, 'But this one is for Timor, and this one for Indonesia'. In my efforts at presenting all information neutrally and in a politically correct manner (keeping in mind that there were often unsympathetic observers) I had never dared present the issue so baldly, even though I recognised that for many people the Indonesian word *otonomi* ('autonomy') must have been a foreign way of saying 'pro-Indonesia'.

Another issue was how to mark the ballot. At one stage we told people that they would have to mark the ballot with a pen or pencil. This led to considerable unease, and to some humorous sessions in which practise proved that even the elderly *could* in fact draw an 'X' inside a box. Nevertheless it was a great relief when, a few days before the ballot, we were able to tell people that they could punch a hole in the symbol of their choice, just as they had done in the recent Indonesian general elections.

Registration

Registration of voters took place over 22 consecutive days. Each day we were required to be at our offices from 7.00 am to 4.00 pm.

Although some centres remained busy for most of this time, in many it was very quiet for the last week or more. In Fatululik we managed to register 240 people on our busiest day; in Beco the maximum was only about half that, as most registrations were less straightforward.

People born in East Timor needed two documents in order to register. A common combination was an identity card (with photo) and a document from the Catholic church which stated the names of their parents, birth place, and baptism details. The need for these papers led to a document-producing binge, both in local government offices and in the church. It was not unusual for people to drop by the sub-district (*desa*) office to collect their new temporary identity card, and then to go directly to the UNAMET office to register.

Each person was asked their name, place of birth, and place of residence. They then had to show their documents to prove this, before being issued with a registration card. In most cases this was a straightforward matter. There were, however, many mismatches between documents. A common one in Beco (but not in Fatululik, for some reason) was that the two documents shown by the voter had different 'family names'. The fact is that the name which we called a 'family name' could be inherited from a variety of sources, including one's mother, father or one of the godparents. It was not at all uncommon for one of the documents to use the mother's name, and another the name of the godmother. One elderly lady in Fatululik had got someone to write her so-called 'family name' down so that she could pass it to me; clearly it was not a name she ever used.

Another common discrepancy was in birth date, with ages according to the two documents differing by up to 20 years! In practise, age was only an issue if the person was possibly under the minimum age of 17. I saw four cases in which the person was under 17 according to one document, and over 17 according to another. Deciding which one to believe was a problem in such cases. Denying people registration because they were marginally too young was always sad, especially as in most cases the young people didn't seem to realise that they were not yet 17, and at least one was already a wife and mother.

Illiteracy was very high, with the result that most people were unaware of the discrepancies between their documents. However, some younger literate people in Beco recognised the problems, and took it into their own hands to white-out the differences and type the 'correct' name (or age, or whatever) over the top. I don't know how well I convinced them that this was not a good policy, and that they should tell their friends not to do this!

One phenomenon that surprised me was that brand new documents issued by one of the *desa* heads in Fatululik invariably had dates on them that were 12-18 months old. On being questioned about this, he replied that the district (*camat*) head had told him to put old dates on them. From then on he dated his new documents with dates that were six months or so in the future ...

The astonishing thing to me was that virtually everyone turned up with two acceptable documents. This was true even for people who had walked for five hours from villages which were off the road and which the Indonesian police consequently did not want us to visit for security reasons. Clearly, people other than UNAMET were passing the news around in time for people to act on it. One such person was Father Hilario, the senior Catholic priest in Suai. Each week he would speak about the popular consultation after mass, at various times telling people what they needed to do, encouraging them to resist intimidation and vote according to their conscience, and urging the winning side to treat the losing side well.

At Fatululik, which is right on the border with West Timor, we had expected to get a significant number of West Timorese people attempting to register as if they were East Timorese. In the end it seems this did happen, but even the most pessimistic of local informants judged the false registrations to be no more than five per cent of the total. The 'false' papers were genuine documents produced by the sub-district (*desa*) heads, but giving false information. I later heard that both these men were sorry for having issued such documents; one said he had refused twice to give documents to West Timorese, but had succumbed when the militias stood over him until he did it.

As time wore on, we had more and more time in which we had to be present at the registration site, but had nothing to do. At Beco, we always had an Indonesian policeman on guard outside the school, sometimes aided by the local military man. The policeman was a pleasant West Timorese man who was supposed to protect us from attack. He also effectively 'protected' us from anyone who might want to come and talk about the intimidation that was going on in Beco ... In Fatululik, we managed to avoid having an Indonesian policeman on guard, and more often had people come to visit, even though we were within easy sight of the militia headquarters up the road. Here we got to hear complaints of pro-autonomy pressure applied in many ways, requests for help with practical matters like the improvement of the road and the provision of teachers, and the number and distribution of guns. Nevertheless, there were many light-hearted times too, telling 'horror stories', listening to music cassettes, or playing chess with the doctor when he came to visit.

As time went on it became clear that, as in the rest of East Timor, virtually every eligible person who could possibly make it to the registration site had registered to vote. The first few days of registration in both Beco and Fatululik had been chaos, as everyone pushed to get in. Young couples walked five hours each way with infants; old people also walked that far. Some must have walked on empty stomachs – at least one woman who fainted while waiting to register at Fatululik turned out to have walked two to three hours without any breakfast. At Fatululik I was struck by how well dressed most people were, turning up in their Sunday best. This was especially evident one day when some students turned up to collect elderly and infirm people in a truck and bring them in to register. Even people such as militia and government heads, who had previously threatened people that they must not register, themselves turned up and joined the queues (or rather, the crush!). Nevertheless, there were people who were disenfranchised by the requirement (a non-negotiable part of the 5 May Agreement) that people turn up in person to register and to vote, particularly as there was no public transport in Fatululik, some very rough roads, and extremely few vehicles.

The ballot

To run the ballot at Fatululik, it was determined that we needed eleven local staff. Some of these were selected from a list of available people prepared by the office of the *Bupati* ('governor') of Covalima; however about half the people on this list were ineligible to work for UNAMET because they were members of the pro-autonomy party FPDK (which was furthermore strongly connected to the militia). Most of the other staff were mature literate people who had held paying jobs (as opposed to being subsistence farmers). As it turns out, all were men. This was perhaps just as well, since as soon as their appointment became known, all started to receive death threats from militiamen, reinforced by shots (usually in the air) and rocks being thrown at their homes. Most spent a few days sleeping in the jungles at night, while spending the days in their villages. However, all ended up running away to Suai, six hours' walk away, either joining the 2500 refugees in the church, or joining the ranks of some 3500 refugees who were staying with family or friends in the town. When we reported one instance of this to the Fatululik police, we were duly assured that it was merely a problem between brothers, with no political connotations.

As the ballot day approached all our local staff insisted that they were committed to returning to Fatululik to help run the ballot. In this we were fortunate, as local staff at some other centres succumbed to very strong pressure to resign. Nevertheless, we appointed two more people (including a woman this time) in case some wouldn't make it back. Fortunately all reported for work by the evening before the vote. Most had in fact been driven back from Suai by the head of the Fatululik militia (who was, incidentally, also a member of the Covalima parliament). This man had been absent from Fatululik when his members had threatened the UNAMET local staff. Over the few days preceding the ballot, he had participated in reconciliation meetings organised by the Catholic church, and he told us he had promised Bishop Belo to behave well towards our staff.

Since voting was to start at 6.30 am, and our preparatory work had to start at 5.30 am, we spent the afternoon before setting up at the polling site, and slept there overnight. Dinner that evening was a simple but pleasant one hosted by our police guards. In return they thoroughly enjoyed inspecting and devouring one of our ration packs, which we had brought as there were at the time no shops, eating houses or even markets at Fatululik.

We weren't the only people to arrive the evening before. Over the course of the afternoon and evening, people from more distant villages started arriving to spend the night with friends. Two old women who were rubbing their aching legs that afternoon after a two-hour walk up the hill explained to me: 'We knew we couldn't make it up here tomorrow, so decided to come today.'

By 6.30 am on the day of the ballot, the local staff had voted and we were ready for the crowd who had gathered on the hillside in the early morning sun. We had agreed that the first ones to vote would be the East Timorese police and military (out of uniform) and any other men who had been appointed by their village heads to stand guard duty at their villages (as many people had expressed concern that their cattle and goods might disappear over the border into West Timor if their villages were left empty and unguarded). The local staff had built a nice bamboo fence to separate the people into two queues. This was, however, rendered useless within five minutes as old women pushed under it, and others climbed through it. The crush was enormous! Our nicely planned queue control system soon degenerated to some strong men standing either side of the door with a pole between them, letting people through one at a time. (Seeing orderly queues in Dili on TV later filled me with amazement!) By 11.30 am virtually everyone had voted; in the afternoon only one person turned up – a sick but very determined man brought in on the back of a motorbike. Voter turn-out in Fatululik was as impressive as it was elsewhere in East Timor; only ten people out of a total of about 880 failed to turn up, and most of these were known to be ill.

At 4.00 pm we were finally free to do the necessary paperwork and return to Suai with the ballot boxes. We were accompanied by a police escort of half a dozen fully-armed men sitting on back-to-back benches on the back of an open police utility. It was certainly good to hand the ballot boxes on to our supervisors at the end of the day. I was amazed at how exhausted I was!

All the horrors that have occurred since the ballot only serve to emphasise the courage of the East Timorese people as they turned up to vote for what they wanted in the face of constant threats. May they yet receive their heart's desire, along with the peace required to enjoy it.

8

The popular consultation and the United Nations mission in East Timor – first reflections

Ian Martin[1]

On 22 October 1999, Xanana Gusmão, the independence fighter who had assumed the leadership of a seemingly broken Falintil two decades before, who had been captured by the Indonesian army in 1992 and sentenced to life imprisonment, returned to East Timor. Eight days later, he was present at Dili's Comoro airport as the last political and military representatives of Indonesia departed the territory it had invaded in 1975. With him were representatives of the United Nations and of Interfet, the Security Council-mandated multinational force led by Australia – the only Western country which had recognised *de jure* Indonesia's annexation of East Timor. The departing Indonesians left behind them a country devastated by their army and by the pro-integration militia it had created, and East Timorese grieving for murdered relatives and fearing for hundreds of thousands yet to return from their forcible deportation to West Timor – yet a people whose predominant mood was one of liberation.

On 5 May 1999, three agreements were signed in New York, bringing to a culmination 17 years of negotiations facilitated by the

---

[1] Ian Martin was Special Representative of the Secretary-General for the East Timor Popular Consultation and Head of the United Nations Mission in East Timor (UNAMET). The views expressed in this chapter are solely those of the author and do not represent the official views of the United Nations.

good offices of the UN Secretary-General. The overall Agreement between the Republic of Indonesia and the Republic of Portugal had annexed to it a constitutional framework for autonomy as submitted by Indonesia, and was supplemented by two further agreements signed by the Secretary-General as well as by the two parties: an agreement regarding the modalities for the popular consultation of the East Timorese through a direct, secret ballot; and a broad agreement on the security environment. The Agreements had been made possible by an unexpected departure from Indonesia's policy of steadfast opposition to any possibility of an independent East Timor on the part of the interim president, B.J. Habibie: on 27 January 1999, he had announced that if the people of East Timor did not agree to remain part of Indonesia on the basis of the autonomy plan then under negotiation, his government would recommend to the new Indonesian People's Consultative Assembly (MPR) following June elections that the law integrating East Timor into Indonesia should be repealed. The Agreements thus provided that if the East Timorese rejected the proposed autonomy, there would be a peaceful and orderly transfer of authority to the UN, enabling East Timor to begin a process of transition to independence.

Indonesia was insistent that the ballot must be held in time for President Habibie to present the result to the MPR immediately it was first convened, scheduled to be at the end of August. The modalities agreement therefore included a timetable culminating in a ballot on 8 August. This in itself faced the UN with an almost impossible organisational challenge. But the deepest scepticism regarding the Agreements related to their security provisions. In reaction to President Habibie's opening up of the independence option, pro-integration militia had been organised throughout East Timor, and had been killing and committing other human rights violations against pro-independence activists and presumed supporters. The pro-independence umbrella organisation, the National Council of East Timorese Resistance (CNRT), and East Timorese solidarity groups argued that security for the ballot could only be guaranteed by an international security presence and/or the withdrawal of the TNI (Indonesian Armed Forces) from the territory. The Agreements, however, left security in the hands of the government of Indonesia, whose police were to be solely responsible for law and order: the TNI as well as the Indonesian police were to maintain absolute neutrality. The international role was limited to a number of UN civilian police officers to act as 'advisers' to the Indonesian police. This was not because the UN was unaware of or unconcerned by militia violence. Indeed the level of concern was such that as the Agreements were signed, the Secretary-General presented a memorandum to the parties, setting out the main elements that would have to be in place for him to be able to determine that the necessary security conditions existed for the start of the operational phases of the popular consultation. These included the bringing of armed civilian groups under strict control and the prompt arrest and prosecution of those who incited or threatened to use violence, a ban on rallies by armed groups while ensuring the freedom of expression of all political forces and tendencies, the 'redeployment' of Indonesian military forces and the immediate institution of a process of laying down of arms by all armed groups to be completed well in advance of the holding of the ballot. But the judgment of the UN negotiators, Portugal and other key member states, was that any attempt to impose on Indonesia an international security presence would mean no agreement and no popular consultation.

Although the Agreements were signed on 5 May, it was not until 11 June (due to the US requirement to consult Congress) that the Security Council formally mandated the United Nations Assistance Mission in East Timor (UNAMET). The speed with which UNAMET was established on the ground was an administrative and logistical feat of which many thought the UN incapable. Four hundred UN volunteers were recruited to serve under the Chief Electoral Officer and his staff as District Electoral Officers for 200 registration and polling centres, along with some 270 civilian police and 50 military liaison officers – the latter a late addition not envisaged in the Agreements, whose role although confined to unarmed liaison with the TNI would prove invaluable. Together with an information component to conduct a public information campaign and a small political component to monitor the political and human rights conditions for the consultation, as well as administrative, logistical and security personnel, UNAMET's international staff at its peak numbered a little under one thousand.

The unusual speed with which UNAMET was deployed still could not enable it to be ready to open registration on 22 June, as required for an 8 August vote. But the Agreements required the Secretary-

General to ascertain, prior to the start of registration and based on the objective evaluation of UNAMET, that the necessary security situation existed for the peaceful implementation of the consultation process. By mid-June it was clear that this was far from being the case. Although the mission's presence and that of journalists and other international visitors led to a growing normalcy of life in Dili, UNAMET soon witnessed for itself the continuing activity of pro-integration militia, consistent with a flood of reports from around the territory. It became increasingly aware that the TNI was not merely complicit but giving direct leadership to the militia, and that because of this link the police were explicitly excluded from taking action against militia crimes. It confirmed for itself that the estimates of non-governmental organisations that over 40 000 persons were internally displaced were not exaggerated, and discovered that their number was continuing to grow as TNI/militia activity persisted in targeting pro-independence localities. The opening of registration was therefore postponed for three weeks, the UN stating truthfully that this was due both to logistical constraints and the security situation.

The Indonesians were told that the UN required the additional three-week period to be used to bring about a reigning-in of the militia. In fact this period saw direct challenges to UNAMET, as its personnel were subjected to militia attacks on its newly-opened office in the town of Maliana and on a humanitarian relief convoy passing through Liquiça. These well-publicised incidents evoked a strong response from the UN and key member states, but the decision on whether to go ahead and open registration on the postponed date of 13 July had to be taken in the context of clear evidence of continuing militia activity and impunity. The UN was concerned not to play into the hands of those who might want to prevent the popular consultation by intimidating its personnel, but the main concern was the continuing widespread intimidation and harassment of pro-independence Timorese. In particular, the fact that internal displacement was still growing, rather than internally displaced persons (IDPs) returning to their homes, raised serious doubts about the feasibility of the comprehensive registration essential for the consultation.

There were, however, indications of growing Indonesian responsiveness to international pressure, as undertakings were given to the UN and supportive governments at high-level meetings in Jakarta and President Habibie ordered key ministers, including General

Wiranto, the Minister of Defence and TNI chief, to visit Dili. A substantial further postponement would have rendered an August ballot impossible and perhaps imperilled the process, so it was decided to postpone the opening of registration only until 16 July, the latest date still consistent with a vote before the end of August. The Secretary-General publicly made clear that the opening of registration did not imply a favourable security assessment, but that on the contrary security conditions conducive to the consultation still did not exist, and there would be a further security assessment halfway through the 20-day registration period.

At the opening of registration, it seemed impossible that the IDPs, whose number we estimated by then at around 60 000, would be able to register (and then to vote at the same location, as the procedure required), even though the process had been designed to allow persons to register at any registration centre, irrespective of their place of normal residence. In this we underestimated the extraordinary determination and courage of the East Timorese: from the first day they came to register in numbers consistent with estimates for a comprehensive registration, and at mid-point we therefore felt able to continue registration despite the lack of action to address the militia threat. Our concern regarding IDPs continued, but as the end of registration approached it was clear that even they were registering, in part after risking a return to the regions from which they had fled and in part at their current locations. A total of 446 666 people registered, 433 576 in East Timor and the remainder at external registration centres in Indonesia, Portugal, Australia and elsewhere. This exceeded all expectations, and indeed surpassed the total registered in East Timor for the Indonesian election, even though a substantial number of those registered for the latter were ineligible for the popular consultation (being Indonesians without the connection to East Timor by birth, descent or marriage stipulated in the Agreements).

Meanwhile efforts were being made to promote reconciliation among pro-autonomy and pro-independence leaders, in a manner which would contribute to peaceful acceptance of the outcome of the popular consultation. The Bishops of East Timor convened a meeting between leading representatives of the two sides at the end of June, with limited success, although all committed themselves to respect the result of the ballot. Thereafter the leading role passed to UNAMET, and focused on reaching agreement on the establishment immediately after the ballot of an East Timorese Consultative Commission, with equal numbers nominated by the two sides and a small independent element chosen by the UN. These efforts appeared to be successful, securing the commitment of hard-line pro-Indonesia political and militia leaders as well as more moderate pro-autonomy elements, although the former were to repudiate their commitment after the ballot.

Little success, however, attended efforts to promote 'the laying down of arms'. Under the Agreements, the key role was to be played by the Commission on Peace and Stability (KPS), established when General Wiranto visited Dili after militia killings in April. This was dominated by the military, and the UN was deliberately marginalised, despite the role envisaged for it in the Agreements. The KPS never commanded the confidence or full participation of the CNRT and Falintil. The TNI, while seemingly eager to achieve Falintil disarmament, persisted in asserting that there should be reciprocal disarmament of Falintil and the militia, and ignoring Falintil's requirement of reciprocity on the part of the TNI itself, which Falintil insisted should withdraw at least to its district-level barracks. The TNI's demand for the disarmament of Falintil and patently ludicrous claims that militia were disarming diverted efforts from what might have been achievable: a mutual laying down of arms. Falintil carried out a unilateral and largely genuine cantonment of its forces, undertaking that they would not move out with weapons from four cantonment sites. UNAMET sought to encourage some real reciprocity from the militia and TNI, and brokered meetings between TNI and Falintil commanders, and Falintil and militia representatives. Almost on the eve of the ballot, militia and Falintil commanders came together at UNAMET's headquarters to declare publicly that their men would be instructed not to move around with arms, and the Indonesian police and TNI chiefs pledged to enforce this – at last. But we proved right to have little confidence in the effect of these commitments. Falintil however throughout displayed remarkable discipline and restraint, determined not to be drawn into an open conflict that could be presented as 'civil war'.

The Agreements excluded Indonesian government officials from campaigning and required the absolute neutrality of the Indonesian armed forces and police; they allowed East Timorese government officials to campaign only in their personal capacity, without use of public funds and government resources, or recourse to pressure of office. Local administrators had in fact been closely involved with the militia from the outset. When UNAMET arrived, a coercive and persuasive campaign to induce a pro-autonomy vote, involving the full resources of the state, was already under way, employing a range of methods: terror and intimidation, blood-drinking oath-taking ceremonies, forced attendance at public meetings, dismissals of or coerced pledges by public officials, financial inducements. UNAMET put to the authorities substantial dossiers of evidence of the systematic involvement of public officials and use of public funds in these efforts. Apart from some defence of the legitimacy of efforts to 'socialise' (i.e. explain) the autonomy proposal, this evidence and the fact that it contravened the Agreements were not denied. The involvement of public officials and public funds in the pro-autonomy campaigning became somewhat less blatant, but continued right up to the ballot.

Starting from a situation in which most pro-independence leaders were in hiding, UNAMET attempted to promote the conditions for the public functioning of the CNRT. Officials in Dili and most regencies accepted in principle the right of the CNRT to open offices and offered police protection, but it was only near to or after the commencement of the campaign that local CNRT leaders dared to risk this. Negotiations with pro-autonomy and pro-independence leaders gained acceptance of a Code of Conduct for an equitable, non-violent campaign, and the two sides co-operated in ceremonies signing the Code of Conduct and then launching the campaign. Regional campaign committees had some effect in avoiding clashes between rival campaign events. The CNRT limited the number of its public events and the profile of its campaigning, declaring its confidence in its overwhelming majority support.

Nevertheless, a level playing field was never close to existing, and the campaign period was marked by militia attacks on pro-independence campaigners. Pro-independence students who returned from Indonesia or Dili to establish themselves in the districts provoked the fiercest, sometimes lethal assaults, but several of the newly-opened CNRT offices were also attacked and closed. As the end of the campaign period and the day of the ballot approached, an upsurge in militia activity was evident.

The success of the poll on 30 August nevertheless surpassed all expectations. UNAMET's fears that polling stations might be unable to open in districts of the worst militia violence were not fulfilled, and a small number of temporary closures were quickly resolved by co-operation between the Indonesian and UN police. An astonishing 98.6 per cent of those registered voted: indeed, UNAMET estimated that over half of them were already waiting to vote when polling stations opened. This was all the more remarkable in that thousands had again fled to the hills in response to recent militia violence: they came down to vote, in many cases returning immediately to the hills in anticipation of more violence after the ballot. When the count was completed early on 4 September, 78.5 per cent were found to have voted to reject, and 21.5 per cent to accept the proposed autonomy option.

Few doubted before the announcement that the extraordinary turn-out indicated a strong pro-independence majority. The pro-Indonesian hardliners began on polling day itself to prepare to reject the outcome by charging UNAMET malpractice, and went on to boycott the East Timorese Consultative Commission to which they had committed themselves. Violence too was immediate: two UNAMET local staff were killed at the close of polls in Ermera district, and two more were among other killings when militia went on the rampage in Maliana. Elsewhere, including in Dili itself, the announcement of the result was awaited as the signal for the beginning of systematic operations, in which towns and villages were sacked, public and private buildings destroyed, and those East Timorese who did not flee to the interior forced to accept their removal by land or sea to West Timor. A full accounting of the scale of the human rights violations committed must await the reports of the inquiries by the UN-appointed International Commission of Inquiry and by Indonesia's National Human Rights Commission, and the process thereafter of continuing investigation and prosecution. By the end of 1999, hundreds of killings had been documented, as well as accumulating reports of rape. The perpetrators were both Indonesian security forces and East and West Timorese members of militia, but the degree of planning and co-ordination of the operation implied its direction by the TNI, and the removals to West Timor were implemented by the police.

The post-ballot violence was initially portrayed in Jakarta as a spon-taneous reaction to pro-independence bias on the part of UNAMET, whose local staff were among its first targets and victims. The perception of UNAMET bias, in so far as it was held in good faith by some (rather than a deliberate tactic by others who fabricated charges designed to put UNAMET on the defensive), stemmed fundamentally from two factors: our responsibility to push for a level playing field challenged the grip the pro-integration forces had established prior to our arrival; and it was essential for UNAMET to reflect publicly the reality of the security situation (including the scale of internal displacement it had caused), deeply embarrassing as this was to the Indonesians and especially to the TNI and police. The majority of UNAMET's local staff no doubt favoured independence, but this merely reflected the population as a whole and was not the result of any intended bias in recruitment. Their role in the conduct of the ballot was heavily scrutinised by observers, and neither the independent Electoral Commission (which examined pro-integration complaints) nor international observers found any malpractice at all, let alone anything that could affect the outcome.

The key responses of UNAMET's public information campaign to the attempted intimidation of voters had been to emphasise that no-one would know how individuals or geographical areas had voted, and that the UN would remain in East Timor, as the Agreements provided, whether the outcome was autonomy or transition to independence. While the staff of the largest component, the electoral officers, would be withdrawn as soon as the ballot and the count had been completed, the civilian police and military liaison contingents (both of which were unarmed) would be strengthened in numbers, although their mandate would remain one of advice and liaison only, unless and until the UN assumed authority under the independence option. But the post-ballot violence compelled UNAMET to withdraw from the regions one-by-one, bringing to Dili those local staff it could. Prevented by militia violence from moving out of its Dili compound, UNAMET was helpless even to check the destruction of Dili. Its compound became the last refuge of well over a thousand IDPs, desperately fleeing attacks elsewhere, together with the official Portuguese Observer Mission and a few journalists. Most of the large press corps present for the announcement had been successfully frightened out by the militia immediately thereafter, doubtless as part of the well-planned preparations for the violence.

Meanwhile the pressure was mounting for the despatch of an international armed force. First the Indonesian government declared martial law in East Timor and sent additional troops from its strategic reserve command, untainted at least by previous involvement with the militia. But martial law failed to check the violence, and its scale was further exposed when a delegation of Security Council ambassadors visited Dili: their visit and intensive diplomatic efforts by Secretary-General Kofi Annan culminated in the Habibie Cabinet's acceptance on 12 September of international 'assistance' to restore order. The multinational force was mandated by the Security Council on 15 September, to restore peace and security in East Timor using all necessary measures, and its Australian commander and first contingents landed five days later.

By 8 September the degree of risk for UNAMET staff in the Dili compound was judged to have exceeded any level of acceptability. The majority of international staff and all local staff in the compound were evacuated to Darwin on 10 September, but some 80 international staff volunteered to remain with the IDPs. Subsequently Australia agreed to grant temporary admission to the IDPs, and the Indonesian government and TNI were persuaded to allow their departure. On 14 September all but a dozen of the remaining UN personnel were flown out, together with over 1300 IDPs, to return progressively with the deployment of Interfet. When on 25 October the Security Council established a larger and longer-term UN presence, the United Nations Transitional Administration in East Timor, UNTAET subsumed UNAMET's remaining personnel.

The death and destruction which was unleashed upon East Timor after the ballot provoked three major questions, on the part of those of us who had sought to implement the Agreements as well as on the part of external critics. Why was the extent of the violence, of which there were many threats and warnings, not fully foreseen and pre-empted? Was it right for the UN to go ahead with the ballot in security conditions which in no way corresponded to the Agreements? Were the Agreements so fundamentally flawed that they should never have been sanctioned by the UN and become the basis of the popular consultation?

It has been suggested that such violence was not only predictable, but was foreshadowed by specific information received by UNAMET that it was being planned. From the arrival of UNAMET, we were deluged with written and oral reports of TNI/militia meetings allegedly planning specific attacks on pro-independence leaders or neighbourhoods, or on UNAMET itself. With a few exceptions, the events failed to occur as predicted. UNAMET's reporting to the Secretariat, and the Secretariat's reporting to the Security Council, constantly emphasised continuing militia activity and TNI involvement. Many of the predictions were of violence to prevent the popular consultation, which were not borne out. There were also from early on highly public threats, well known to the international community and the media, that a pro-independence vote would unleash bloodshed. The difficulty was to assess the extent to which these threats were designed to affect the outcome without necessarily being likely to be carried out; or were serious on the part of those who made them but would not be carried out against a government desire to avoid international embarrassment; or were indeed deadly serious. Some violence was certainly expected, and this was reflected in the decision to reinforce the military and police components as soon as possible after the ballot.

We believed, however, that the TNI leadership would and could implement government policy sufficiently to check or prevent violence, at least on the scale which in fact occurred. There were positive indications supporting this belief, including the apparent co-operation of senior military and police officers during the registration and campaign periods and on ballot day, and the belated removal of a number of TNI officers whose involvement with militia was most blatant. The indications of a strong pro-independence majority were so clear to all international observers that we assumed that the Indonesians too had come to terms with this outcome, since otherwise violence to prevent the vote would be more rational than violence after it had become an established fact. It transpired that we had underestimated the extent to which Indonesians and pro-integration Timorese had believed that their efforts to induce a pro-autonomy vote could still succeed, or that the outcome could at least be close enough to be repudiated by charges of UNAMET bias. The underestimation of likely post-ballot violence was not the UN's alone: it was shared by most diplomatic observers, and even Xanana Gusmão, who gave strong public warnings of violence, has said that he did not foresee its extent.

Even if the scale of the violence was not foreseen, there could be no pretence that the conditions required by the Agreements for the consultation had existed at any stage. Was it wrong, as it would certainly be in most circumstances, for the UN to decide in August to allow a ballot to proceed when one side had had limited opportunity to

Right: *Refugees (Internally Displaced Persons) camped in the church in Suai prior to the popular consultation*
Below: *Refugees gather outside a wrecked house in Suai*

*District Parliament Building
(Dewan Perwakilan Rakyat
Daerah) in Gleno, Ermera,
destroyed in September 1999*

Above: *Destruction of the
market in Gleno; Pancasila
monument in foreground*
Right: *Burnt-out school
building in Manatuto; the
sign in foreground urges
support for Indonesia's
program of basic education*

campaign and violent threats from the other were prevalent? The apparent paradox is that it was the victims of violence who most wanted the ballot to go ahead. If it were postponed, it was unlikely that the opportunity could be recreated in better circumstances, or at all: the tenure of President Habibie, who almost alone in the Jakarta political elite was committed to allowing the East Timorese a genuine choice, was highly uncertain; and the world attention represented by a huge media presence and hundreds of international observers might be as unrepeatable as it was unprecedented for East Timor. The member states who had most closely supported the operation were unanimous in wanting the UN to proceed; and the CNRT leadership, while calling for an international security presence, preferred a ballot even without one to a postponement. The people of East Timor had shown during registration their determination to defy intimidation: the confidence that they would do so again proved to be well-founded.

There can be no disagreement that the people of East Timor would have been spared one more of the cycles of violence that have marked their history if the popular consultation had taken place with an armed international presence mandated to guarantee security, and the Agreements have been criticised for leaving the security responsibility to the Indonesian police. But it is equally clear that any attempt to insist on an international security presence would have meant no agreement. A stronger stance by key governments on the question of East Timor over time might have been able to change that reality, but the negotiators worked within the reality that existed in early 1999. What is remarkable is not that the Agreements could not include better security guarantees, but that they were ever reached at all: the other reality was that President Habibie's willingness to allow the independence option had little support inside or outside his own government, least of all within the TNI. Once the post-ballot violence erupted, the arrival of the multinational force seemed painfully slow amid the death and destruction in East Timor, but it came only sixteen days after the announcement of the result: this represented almost unprecedented speed, to which the efforts of the Secretary-General and the contingency planning of Australia made the key contributions. It was a bitter blow for the staff of UNAMET that they could not remain in the regions throughout, but UNAMET did remain up to and beyond the limits of acceptable risk for an unarmed mission, and the international attention to its situation helped to ensure that the

UN would fulfil its pledge to stand by the people of East Timor with the armed presence that had become essential.

Those with the most right to answer such questions and to judge the role of the UN in the popular consultation are, however, the people of East Timor themselves. At the end of 1999, even among the ashes of their homes and with relatives yet to return or be accounted for, there seems little uncertainty in their positive judgment.

9

The TNI and East Timor policy

Harold Crouch

As long as President Soeharto remained in power, there was no possibility that the Indonesian government would consider the prospect of an independent East Timor. Soeharto, after all, had been responsible for the initial invasion and could hardly have been expected to disown what he regarded as one of his regime's important achievements. For almost a quarter of a century, Indonesia had borne the world's condemnation while the Indonesian military (TNI)[1] had reduced the guerilla resistance to a few hundred and the captured resistance leader himself had admitted that his forces had been defeated militarily. Although anti-Jakarta demonstrations broke out from time to time in East Timor and occasional military clashes took place, there was no possibility that Indonesia's military forces could be driven out by the resistance forces.

Soeharto's attitude was supported by the TNI. The standard military view was that the armed forces had saved the people of East Timor from communism and protected the rest of Indonesia from possible communist infiltration through East Timor. However bizarre that interpretation may have seemed to the rest of the world, most officers were proud of the sacrifices they had made for the nation in East Timor. They also believed that Indonesia's military intervention in 1975 had saved the East Timorese from civil war and were convinced

---

[1] At that time the military was still known as the Armed Forces of the Republic of Indonesia (ABRI). It was renamed as the Indonesian National Military (TNI) after the separation of the police in April 1999. I wish to thank Kumiko Mizuno and Marcus Mietzner for their helpful comments.

that civil conflict would start again if they withdrew. An overwhelming majority of army officers had served in East Timor at one time or another and some had served three or four tours of duty there. Many officers also felt a deep emotional attachment to East Timor as the place where several thousand Indonesian soldiers had died.[2]

Although the Soeharto government saw no need to offer concessions to world opinion on the East Timor issue, there were, however, signs of growing public scepticism in Indonesia itself. It needs, however, to be emphasised that the average educated middle-class Indonesian citizen had never given much attention to East Timor, whose people made up less than half of one per cent of the total population. For most Indonesians, East Timor was – if it was a problem at all – only one problem among many and by no means the most important. It was only after the Dili massacre in November 1991 – which happened to coincide with the period of political *keterbukaan* (openness) – that readers of the Indonesian press became more aware of military repression in East Timor. But, even then, they tended to see military repression in East Timor as part of an Indonesia-wide phenomenon and not a consequence of the forced integration of that province. Even pro-democracy activists often seemed to believe that the key problem was to democratise Indonesia itself and then the East Timorese would be happy to remain with Indonesia.

Although most educated Indonesians showed little sympathy for East Timorese opposition to Indonesian rule, there was an increasing sense that the East Timor issue was causing more trouble than it was worth. Indonesians did not share the foreign perception of the East Timor issue as a case of invasion and military occupation. Instead they considered it as no more than a nuisance – in the words of the Foreign Minister, Ali Alatas, 'a pebble in the shoe' – caused by a noisy urban minority unrepresentative of the predominantly rural people of East Timor. Many Indonesians were dismayed because the East Timorese showed no gratitude for the many hospitals, schools and kilometres of roads provided by the Indonesian government. Why, they increasingly asked, should we continue to be the target of world criticism just for the sake of the East Timorese who do not appreciate

---

[2]   In September 1999, General Wiranto said that 1500 service personnel had been killed in East Timor and 2400 wounded or disabled (*Kompas*, 13 September 1999).

Indonesian generosity? The *Jakarta Post* expressed this mood in 1995 when it said in an editorial:

> We are detecting the spread of a kind of 'East Timor fatigue' among many Indonesians. Questions such as, how much longer will the East Timor problem continue to haunt us, or, why does East Timor continue to be a running sore even after almost 20 years of integration, are examples of this feeling.[3]

Nevertheless, East Timor was commonly perceived as essentially a failure of foreign policy for which Indonesia's hapless diplomats were blamed rather than a result of the forced integration of East Timor and accompanying military repression.

Lack of sympathy for East Timorese aspirations was particularly apparent in the comments of Muslims who had little sense of identity with the predominantly Catholic East Timorese. The modernist Muslim intellectual, Dawam Rahardjo, complained about 'the impression that the central government treats East Timor as "a favoured son" in the allocation of its budget'.[4] As more Indonesian Muslim civil servants and security personnel moved into East Timor, they became the focus of East Timorese resentment which was expressed in attacks on mosques, violence against 'Muslim' traders in markets and large-scale rioting in September 1995 which forced hundreds to flee East Timor. The Muhammadiyah leader, Amien Rais, complained that Indonesians went to East Timor to provide milk but were given poison in return.[5] Jakarta Muslims initially demanded that the government impose stricter security measures on 'sectarian Catholics' in East Timor but later some seemed to be concluding that the East Timorese were just too different to be accepted in Indonesia. For example, at the end of 1996, Amien Rais proposed that:

> if the East Timorese still want a referendum then I would say it is better to give them a chance to have a referendum. Even if they want to separate from Indonesia. Let it be. It's better for them and better for Indonesia too. I think my government has done its best.[6]

[3]   'The East Timor Issue', *Jakarta Post*, 28 September 1995.
[4]   Dawam Rahardjo, 'Hadiah Nobel dan Diplomasi Indonesia' (*Tempo*, 28 October 1996).
[5]   *Gatra*, 21 September 1995.
[6]   Patrick Walters, 'Let E Timor decide: Muslim chief', *Australian*, 11 December 1996.

And, writing in the Muslim newspaper, *Republika*, another Muslim intellectual, Dr Indria Samego, argued that:

> In recent times we have seen how developmental initiatives initially intended to Indonesianise the people of East Timor have only strengthened the determination of a number of critical leaders to fight for self-determination in the territory.

If all else fails, he concluded,

> Rather than become the target of international criticism, why don't we simply give the opportunity to the East Timorese society to determine their own future?[7]

These sentiments were common among members of the Indonesian Association of Muslim Intellectuals (ICMI) and its think-tank (CIDES) with which the newspaper, *Republika*, was associated. Amien Rais, Dawam Rahardjo, Indria Samego and Dewi Fortuna Anwar (who later became President Habibie's foreign policy advisor) were all associated with ICMI whose general chairman was B.J. Habibie. This is not to claim that Habibie himself shared their views at that time but only to note that these ideas were already being discussed before 1998 in the circles from which he drew his advisors after becoming president.

Even within the military there were some indications of support for a new approach to East Timor, although no military officers appeared to have envisaged the possibility of eventual independence. In 1994, the East Timor resort commander, Colonel Johny Lumintang, admitted to a foreign journalist that 'It is true we have not got the sympathy of the people' and described the Dili massacre as an 'expensive lesson'.[8] Later in the year, Maj. Gen. Adang Ruchiatna, the Commander of the *Udayana* Military Region IX, based in Bali and covering East Timor, speaking at a seminar organised by the Indonesian Institute of Sciences (LIPI), indicated his support for the granting of special status to East Timor.[9] The 'special status' proposal

---

[7]   Indria Samego, 'Politisasi Timtim', *Republika*, 28 and 29 November 1996.
[8]   Lindsay Murdoch, 'Timor not tamed, Indonesians admit', *Age*, 18 April 1994.
[9]   João Mariano de Sousa Saldanha, *The Political Economy of East Timor Development* (1994), pp.371-372; *Australian*, 16 September 1994.

was supported by the East Timor governor, Abilio Soares, who had close military links, especially with President Soeharto's son-in-law, then Colonel Prabowo Subianto. In late 1994 Prabowo discussed the proposal with Xanana Gusmão in gaol but at the end of the year the idea was killed when Soeharto declared his opposition. Nevertheless, indications of military awareness of a need for a changed approach continued to be revealed in occasional public comments by retired officers. For example, Maj. Gen. Z.A. Maulani, an advisor to Habibie, acknowledged that 'the problem at present is that part of the society there feels that it has been treated unjustly' and that 'they believe that our government violates East Timorese cultural values' – although he made it clear at that time that he did not favour a referendum.[10]

It was, however, only after the fall of the Soeharto regime in May 1998 that Indonesian policy began to change. Indonesia's economic condition was desperate when President Habibie came to power and its international reputation had been severely besmirched by anti-Chinese rioting which had culminated in the huge riot of May 1998 that triggered Soeharto's resignation. President Habibie had never shown any particular concern about East Timor during his two decades as a cabinet minister under Soeharto but he was acutely aware of the way in which it continued to harm Indonesia's international reputation and its potential for creating new problems. As part of his effort to improve Indonesia's international image, he decided that something had to be done about East Timor. Thus, he initially proposed that East Timor be granted full autonomy and then proposed the 'popular consultation' that ended with an overwhelming vote in effect for independence.

The autonomy proposal

The possibility of a change in policy was hinted within four days of Habibie's installation as president, when his new Minister of Justice, Muladi, suggested it was now time for Indonesia to make East Timor a 'special region'.[11] Habibie himself quickly asserted in a CNN interview that 'East Timor is an integrated part of the republic ... There is no

---

[10] Z.A. Maulani, 'Kerikil Ini Menyakitkan', *Gatra*, 14 December 1996. After Habibie succeeded to the presidency, Maulani was appointed as head of the State Intelligence Agency (BAKIN).

[11] *Kompas*, 25 May 1998.

need for a referendum, it is Indonesia'.[12] However, a week later in an interview with the BBC, he casually announced that 'I am ready to consider giving East Timor special status like Jakarta, Aceh and Yogyakarta'.[13] It seems that Habibie's offer during the BBC interview was spontaneous and had taken the Foreign Minister, Ali Alatas, by surprise.[14] Later in the month, in an interview with Australian correspondents in Jakarta, Habibie said that in exchange for the granting of special status, the UN would have to recognise integration and 'the whole world should stop making problems'.[15] Alatas soon produced a proposal for 'wide autonomy' which would go far beyond the largely nominal autonomy enjoyed by Jakarta, Aceh and Yogyakarta. East Timor's autonomy would not include foreign affairs, defence and security, and finance but might cover such areas as the economy, education and culture.[16] Habibie seems to have believed that the granting of special autonomy to East Timor would undermine East Timorese resistance to Jakarta's rule and win the endorsement of the international community.

The president's offer of autonomy was greeted by a large demonstration in Dili on 23 June demanding full independence but senior anti-Jakarta leaders were opposed to an early referendum. Bishop Belo declared that 'I do not agree with a referendum now'. 'According to me', he said, 'okay, (in) 10 years, 15 years you can decide it'.[17] Former Governor, Mario Carrascalão, was also opposed to an early referendum. 'If we want to hold it now, it would be suicide', he said.[18] From his prison, Xanana Gusmão also said that there was no need to hold a referendum immediately as 'during the next 5 to 10 years there are several things that need to be done by the Indonesian government in order to prepare East Timor for a referendum'.[19] At the UN, the East

---

[12] *Australian*, 4 June 1998.
[13] *Reuters* in *Canberra Times*, 10 June 1998.
[14] President Habibie's foreign policy advisor, Dewi Fortuna Anwar, had to remind the President after the BBC interview that he should inform the Foreign Minister about his spontaneous offer (interview, 29 July 1999).
[15] *Sunday Age*, 21 June 1998.
[16] *Antara*, 25 June 1998.
[17] *Australian*, 15 June 1998.
[18] *Kompas*, 15 June 1998.
[19] *Tempo*, 27 June 1998.

Timor resistance's overseas spokesman, José Ramos Horta, urged that a referendum be held after a transition of 'two, three, four, five years'.[20]

Habibie's offer and the positive response of Bishop Belo and other leaders gave new impetus to the slow-moving UN-sponsored tripartite talks on East Timor between the Indonesian and Portuguese Foreign Ministers that had commenced in 1992. During the latter part of the year, the two sides drew closer as both accepted the special autonomy idea in which East Timor would exercise authority in all fields except foreign affairs, defence and security, and finance. The unresolved difference, however, lay in whether such autonomy would represent a 'final solution', as the Indonesians insisted, or whether it was just a step toward a referendum, the position that the Portuguese defended.

The 'popular consultation' proposal

The tripartite talks had reached an impasse when, at the end of the year, the Australian government intervened. In a confidential letter sent to Habibie in December, the Australian Prime Minister, John Howard, suggested that some form of act of self-determination be offered to East Timor after a lengthy period of autonomy.[21] Howard's proposal in effect endorsed the position of Portugal and the East Timorese resistance. Habibie was infuriated by Howard's letter which, by making a comparison with French policy in New Caledonia, was seen by Habibie as implying that Indonesia was a colonial power in East Timor. Although Habibie angrily rejected Howard's proposal, its significance lay less in its content than in the fact that Australia was the only 'Western' country that had explicitly recognised Indonesian sovereignty over East Timor.[22] The changed Australian stance seems to have triggered a rethinking of Indonesia's position and, following a cabinet meeting on 27 January 1999, the Indonesian government announced that it would give the people of East Timor the opportunity to accept or reject its autonomy

[20] AFP, 1 July 1998.

[21] Much of Howard's letter is quoted by Paul Kelly in 'Letter that sparked the meltdown', *Australian*, 6 October 1999.

[22] According to Alatas, Howard's proposal 'made Pak Habibie mad, it made Pak Habibie angry, because it came from Australia. Why should Australia get involved?', *Jakarta Post*, 2 November 1999.

proposal later in the year. If they rejected the proposal, the government would recommend to the forthcoming session of the People's Consultative Assembly (MPR) that East Timor be permitted to withdraw from the Republic of Indonesia.

After receiving Howard's letter Habibie called together senior cabinet ministers, including General Wiranto, the Minister for Defence and Security and Commander of the TNI, Ali Alatas and Muladi, on 1 January to discuss the possibility of holding a referendum.[23] Eventually the new policy was finalised by the cabinet's Political and Security Affairs Committee, of which both Wiranto and General Feisal Tanjung, the previous Commander of the TNI and current Co-ordinating Minister for Political and Security Affairs, were members. It was then discussed in a full cabinet meeting at which no fundamental objections appear to have been raised. Much later, however, after appearing before the Indonesian government's Commission of Inquiry into Human Rights Violations (KPP-HAM) in East Timor, Alatas told reporters that 'Although I defended the view that there should be no alternative to Option 1 (wide autonomy), I was outvoted in the meeting'.[24] In a newspaper interview, he said that he had 'advised, among other things, OK we can solve it, but isn't it premature'.[25] In explaining the policy publicly at the time, Alatas said that holding a referendum after 5-10 years would only exacerbate conflict and could even lead to civil war. Further, he implied that Indonesia did not want to subsidise East Timor for a long period and then see it leave the Republic.[26] It appears that most ministers hoped that such a vote would be in favour of integration although a few weeks later Habibie himself hinted that the best solution was 'to grant independence so that we can concentrate on the other 26 provinces that already provide enough problems'.[27]

The details of the planned 'popular consultation' – as the Indonesians preferred to call it – were finally worked out in the 5 May Agreement – one dealing with the consultation itself and the other with security arrangements – signed by the Indonesian and

---

[23] Don Greenlees, 'Howard letter delivered revolution', *Australian*, 27 January 2000. The heading of this article is misleading, to say the least.
[24] *Media Indonesia*, 6 January 2000.
[25] *Jakarta Post*, 2 November 1999.
[26] *Kompas, Media Indonesia*, 28 January 1999.
[27] *Kompas*, 12 February 1999.

Portuguese foreign ministers. The referendum was to be conducted by the United Nations Mission in East Timor (UNAMET) with the support of police and military observers. Despite pressure to place international peacekeeping forces in East Timor during the ballot, the agreement entrusted the Indonesian police with the responsibility of ensuring a 'secure environment devoid of violence or of other forms of intimidation'.[28]

Why did the military accept President Habibie's policy? The military had been strongly committed to retaining East Timor as part of Indonesia. Certainly some military officers had recognised that a change in approach was needed but there had been no sign of willingness to consider a free vote to determine the future of East Timor. However, both Generals Wiranto and Faisal Tanjung had participated in the discussions that led to the announcement of the new policy and had apparently not protested. Wiranto's only public condition was that the correctness of the original intervention in East Timor in 1975 should not be questioned – in view of the sacrifices made by military personnel during the previous two decades.[29] Of the military officers in the cabinet, it seems that only Lt. Gen. Hendropriyono, the Minister for Transmigration, had expressed concern and a few weeks later he said publicly that the holding of a referendum would increase the level of intimidation and 'bring disaster to the people of East Timor'.[30]

Did this mean that the military leadership supported the holding of the referendum? In retrospect, it seems that they did indeed accept the referendum but saw it as an opportunity to settle the East Timor issue once and for all by making sure that the vote would be in favour of continued integration with Indonesia. The stipulation in the 5 May Agreement that 'The absolute neutrality of the TNI and the Indonesian Police is essential', was to be totally disregarded. Although the military leadership accepted the new policy, military officers in general were very unhappy about the prospect of a referendum in East Timor but there was no open military protest against the new policy. In any case, at that time, the military already had its hands full with an intensifying war against separatists in Aceh, increasingly vicious religious and ethnic conflict in Maluku and West Kalimantan, and growing restiveness throughout Indonesia.

28 Paragraph 4 of the agreement regarding security.
29 *Kompas*, 29 January 1999.
30 *Kompas*, 12 February 1999.

The military role in the referendum

Under the overall command of General Wiranto as Commander of the TNI, the officer with primary responsibility for military operations in East Timor was Maj. Gen. Adam Damiri, the commander of the army's *Udayana* Military Regional Command IX (*Kodam*) based in Bali. The officer directly in command in East Timor was Col. Tono Suratman, the commander of the Wiradharma Military Resort Command 164 (*Korem*) based in Dili. Beneath him at the *kabupaten* level were thirteen Military District Commands (*Kodim*), each headed by a lieutenant-colonel, and a network of Military Rayon Commands (*Koramil*) at the *kecamatan* level. Another senior officer involved in East Timor was the former head of military intelligence (BAIS), Maj. Gen. Zacky Anwar Makarim, who was formally appointed as Liaison Officer to UNAMET. Damiri, Suratman and Makarim had all been regarded as close to Lt. Gen. Prabowo Subianto, the Kostrad commander whom Wiranto dismissed immediately after the resignation of Prabowo's father-in-law, President Soeharto, in May 1998.

The military had always been the controlling political force in East Timor. Until the signing of the 5 May Agreement, internal security was the responsibility of the army while the police played only a subordinate role. The military had always worked closely with the pro-integration local elite. The governor and the thirteen *bupati* were all closely allied with the military and appointed with military endorsement. Under the 5 May Agreement, however, responsibility for security was transferred to the police, although TNI forces remained in East Timor.

There had always been considerable confusion about the exact number of troops in East Timor, as official statements were not always consistent with each other. According to credible leaked documents, the total number of military forces (including police) in East Timor in late 1998 was 17 914, consisting of 9976 'organic' (i.e. local) troops and 7938 troops brought in from elsewhere in Indonesia. In addition, if 3711 civilian personnel serving in civilian units are counted, the total number of forces under military command in late 1998 was 21 625.[31]

The civilian units under direct and formal military command – known as *wanra* (*Perlawanan Rakyat* – People's Resistance) – were armed for operations against rebel forces. Naturally the members of

---

[31] I have corrected small arithmetical errors in one of these documents.

wanra were recruited from that part of society which was loyal to Jakarta. In the mid-1990s, however, new paramilitary groups were sponsored by the military but, in contrast to *wanra*, they were not formally incorporated into the military structure. These new units were used to terrorise and intimidate supporters of independence, most notoriously through so-called 'ninja' operations. The most prominent unit was the *Gadapaksi* (*Gada Pemuda Penegak Integrasi* – Youth Guard to Uphold Integration) sponsored by Col. Prabowo, then assigned to the Special Forces (*Kopassus*). By 1998 so-called militias were operating in all 13 of East Timor's *kabupaten*. In many cases, the participants in the new militia were also members, or at least related to members, of the *wanra*. Eventually the various militias were loosely brought together as the *Pasukan Pejuang Integrasi* (PPI – Fighters for Integration Force) under the leadership of the former *bupati* of Bobonaro, João Taveres, as their *Panglima Perang* (War Commander). The PPI itself claimed that the total militia strength was over 50 000 but an Australian diplomat estimated that there were only about 3000 in various militia and another 3000 remnants of *Gadapaksi*. In addition there were about 2-3000 in *wanra*.[32]

It was obvious that the militia forces were closely linked to military officers and government officials. Senior officers and officials made no secret of their good relations with the militia leaders. Thus, Maj. Gen. Adam Damiri, the *Udayana* commander, was quoted as saying that João Taveres' appointment as War Commander of the PPI 'is an appropriate thing and the military will not question it'.[33] In later testimony before the KPP-HAM, Adam Damiri said meetings between military officers and what he called *Pam Swakarsa* (civilian security forces) were routine in order to discuss local security conditions.[34] Leading military officers often appeared at militia rallies. For example, the *Korem* commander, Col. Tono Suratman, attended a militia rally at Maliana in April, only a few days after another militia unit had killed and wounded independence supporters in a church at Liquiça.[35] On another occasion Tono Suratman, the Governor Abilio Soares, and the Police Chief, Timbul Silaen, attended a ceremony in

[32] *Australian*, 10 June 1999.
[33] *Indonesian Observer*, 5 April 1999.
[34] *Kompas*, 28 December 1999.
[35] *Australian*, 10-11 April 1999.

Ambeno where the local branch of the pro-independence organisation, CNRT, was forced to dissolve itself.[36] Local government officials also co-operated closely with militia leaders. According to the testimony before the KPP-HAM of both Col. Tono Suratman and the former *bupati* of Dili, Domingos Soares, the *Pam Swakarsa* or militias were under the supervision of the police and financed by the local governments.[37] In June, the *bupati* of Dili, Domingos Soares, appointed Eurico Guterres, the head of Aitarak militia which had recently rampaged through Dili, as co-ordinator for public security in Dili.[38] Guterres was also appointed as Tavares' deputy in the PPI. And João Tavares, Eurico Guterres and another militia leader, Manuel da Souza, were nominated as Golkar candidates in the June election.[39]

The TNI was often accused of supplying the militia with arms. For example, the general secretary of the Indonesian National Human Rights Commission (*Komnas-HAM*), Clementino Dos Reis Amaral – himself an East Timorese – claimed in January 1999 that the TNI had been supplying militias with weapons since late in 1998.[40] While it is true that some militia members were observed carrying modern weapons, most militia, however, were armed with home-made rifles, machetes, spears and knives. Faced with accusations of supplying arms to the militia, the military admitted that the *wanra* routinely used arms under its supervision but denied supplying arms to the 'private' militias. However, given the overlap in membership between *wanra* and the militias, it was inevitable that some modern weapons were transferred to militia members. And it was impossible to believe that military officers were not aware of this.[41]

---

36   *Kompas*, 3 May 1999.
37   *Kompas*, 22 and 28 December 1999. This claim, however, was denied by the militia chief, João Taveres. The former Chief of Police in East Timor, Col. Timbul Silaen, also denied the involvement of the police in training or supervising the militias. *Kompas*, 29 December 1999.
38   *Australian*, 3 June 1999.
39   Ibid.
40   *Sydney Morning Herald*, 28 January 1999.
41   In an interview in Jakarta in March 1999, a senior lieutenant-general said: In Indonesia we cannot assume that whatever the commander decides is automatically done on the ground. It is quite likely that local military officers are allowing pro-integrationists to have weapons. After all, they have been their friends for many years.

Since the latter part of 1998 conflict between the pro- and anti-integration sides had been increasing and physical clashes had become commonplace. One consequence of rising violence was an increase in the number of refugees either fleeing into the hills or seeking protection in the larger towns. It was widely suspected that pro-integration militias were driving pro-independence villagers away from their homes in order to disrupt the registration of voters for the referendum. The Catholic agency, Caritas, also claimed that refugees in Dili were forced into militia-controlled camps where they had to swear allegiance to Indonesia in order to get food.[42]

That the Indonesian side was attempting to control the supply of daily necessities was indicated in a leaked letter apparently written by Maj. Gen. (ret.) Garnadi to his superior, the Co-ordinating Minister for Political and Security Affairs, General Feisal Tanjung.[43] According to the letter,

> The job of winning over the people of East Timor to support Special Autonomy is in fact not all that difficult because we are competing for floating voters whose demands are very simple, that is the supply of food and medicine. They will follow whoever gives them food and medicine.

But the letter indicated concern because the government's expected monopoly over the distribution of food aid had been broken by the large number of foreign-backed NGOs that were also distributing food and medicine to refugees. The letter argued that 'there is no distinction between a refugee and a hungry person; in fact a hungry man can be made a refugee in a moment under pressure from the anti-integration group'. On the other hand, it complained that 'we are always late whereas the anti-integration side can make use of the opportunity provided by the presence of UNAMET with its extra role as if they are guardian angels *(dewa menolong)*'.[44] What the letter meant was that the presence of UNAMET made it easier for foreign-supported pro-independence NGOs to supply food to refugees and thus enable them to avoid dependence on government aid.

[42] *Australian*, 27 May 1999.
[43] At the KPP-HAM enquiry, Garnadi, who had been the Deputy Chairman of the Task Force to Implement the Consultation in East Timor (*Satgas* P3TT), acknowledged that the signature resembled his and that the stamp seemed genuine but he denied that he wrote it. The enquiry seemed to treat the letter itself as genuine (*Republika*, 29 December 1999).
[44] The leaked Garnadi letter is dated 3 July 1999.

The pro-integration side accused UNAMET of being biased in favour of independence. In particular they claimed that many of its local staff of 500 were known to be supporters of independence.[45] They also said that UNAMET staff themselves were involved in distributing food to supporters of independence. For example, Domingo Soares accused UNAMET of supplying food to pro-CNRT refugees in Sare early in July.[46] Soares' criticism followed an incident on 4 July at Liquiça. A team of NGOs took 13 truck-loads of food and medicine to about 3000 refugees in Fare and Faulara in Ermera *kabupaten*. For protection they were accompanied by personnel from UNAMET and UNHCR. But on their return journey through Liquiça they were attacked by members of the Besi Merah Putih militia armed with firearms, *parang* and stones. One member of the NGO party was shot, four were wounded and the UNAMET car was damaged but neither the military nor the police intervened.[47] The involvement of UNAMET in this incident was criticised by the police chief, Col. Timbul Silaen, who said that UNAMET's authority was limited to holding the 'popular consultation' and did not include the distribution of humanitarian aid.[48]

There is no doubt that both sides were involved in violence against each other but the violence of one side was tolerated by the Indonesian security forces. On many occasions foreign observers – journalists, diplomats, aid workers and UNAMET officials – witnessed incidents in which police did nothing to prevent violence perpetrated by members of pro-integration militias. In May the UN Secretary-General told the Security Council that 'credible reports continue to be received of political violence, including intimidation and killings, by armed militias against unarmed pro-independence civilians' and he noted that the militias seemed 'to be operating with the acquiescence of elements of the army'.[49]

The strategy of the military leadership in Jakarta was to allow local commanders to use the military-sponsored militias to terrorise the population in order to ensure a vote in favour of autonomy. But, despite their endorsement of intimidatory tactics, they did not want

[45]　*Australian*, 10-11 July 1999.
[46]　*Kompas*, 6 July 1999.
[47]　*Kompas*, 5 July 1999; Yayasan Hak statement, 4 July 1999.
[48]　*Kompas*, 6 July 1999.
[49]　*Australian*, 26 May 1999.

the violence to rise to a point where the referendum would lose all
international credibility. General Wiranto assured his cabinet colleagues
that the violence could be controlled and on 21 April, three days after
a murderous rampage through Dili by the Aitarak militia, he organised
the signing of a peace pact in Bishop Belo's house between the two
sides with Tavares and Domingos Soares signing for the integrationists
and Xanana Gusmão, still in prison in Jakarta, signing for the CNRT.
But the violence continued and another TNI-sponsored meeting
between the two sides was held in Jakarta on 15 June. Wiranto also
supported the second church-sponsored 'Dare meeting' in Jakarta on
28-30 June which was attended by thirty participants from each side.

In the end, the military-supported intimidation of voters did not
produce a pro-integration vote. On the contrary, it may have even contributed to the overwhelming rejection of the autonomy option by 78.5
per cent of the voters. As one pro-independence leader explained,

> We practically did no campaigning at all to win the recent consultation ... because
> for more than twenty years anti-Indonesian attitudes have been created by the
> behaviour of the TNI toward our society, to our coffee plantations, to our cattle,
> and to the social fabric which is the foundation of our social life.[50]

Post-referendum destruction

There can be no doubt that the pre-referendum intimidation of voters
was part of General Wiranto's plan to secure a vote in favour of
autonomy. But did that plan also envisage the destruction and killing
that followed the vote against autonomy?

Following the completion of polling on 30 August, General
Wiranto complimented the UNAMET on carrying out its
responsibilities 'successfully'.[51] But, on the ground in East Timor, the
pro-Jakarta militias embarked on a campaign of killing and destruction
even before the announcement of the result on 4 September.
Marauding bands of militia members attacked supporters of
independence and destroyed much of the infrastructure of East Timor.
Although the number killed was probably in the hundreds rather
than early estimates of thousands, the early estimates of hundreds of
thousands of people being forced to flee their homes turned out to

50 *Republika*, 22 September 1999.
51 *Kompas*, 31 August 1999.

be accurate. According to Indonesian figures, about 240 000 refugees entered West Timor while others estimated that several hundred thousand sought refuge in the hills. It was reported that about 70-80 per cent of Dili's business district had been destroyed and 50 per cent of homes had been burnt. The Indonesian newspaper, *Kompas*, described how 'only ruins remain of the lovely and glittering town of Dili'.[52] Other towns and villages suffered a similar fate.

Foreign observers, such as those of the Carter Center, reported that their members 'have on numerous occasions witnessed militia members perpetrating acts of violence in full view of heavily-armed police and military personnel who either stand by and watch or actively assist the militias'.[53] But it was not only foreigners who were shocked by what they saw. *Kompas* reported that 'The Indonesian security forces often seemed to do nothing when violence broke out'[54] and several Indonesian journalists' associations claimed that 'violent attacks on journalists were launched quite openly by pro-autonomy militia without the slightest attempt by the police or TNI to prevent them or to take action against the perpetrators'.[55] *Komnas-HAM* also noted that terrorist activities took place 'directly witnessed and permitted by members of the security forces'.[56] *Suara Pembaruan* reported that 'The police, military and militia are seen to have taken control of the streets. The police can be seen greeting and chatting with militia members'.[57]

General Wiranto, however, adamantly denied that his troops were supporting the militias. 'It is not possible that the TNI is backing the militias', he declared. 'From the beginning we have said we are neutral', he asserted somewhat unconvincingly.[58] The security problem in East Timor, he explained later, was due to the dissatisfaction of the pro-integration side with what they saw as electoral violations perpetrated by UNAMET.[59] He even suggested that 'This dissatisfaction is proper, and has been expressed in the form of spontaneous actions'.[60] On

---

52   *Kompas*, 12 September 1999.
53   Carter Center Weekly Report on East Timor, No. 18, 6 September 1999.
54   *Kompas*, 2 September 1999.
55   *Kompas*, 3 September 1999.
56   *Kompas*, 9 September 1999.
57   *Suara Pembaruan*, 5 September 1999.
58   *Kompas*, 3 September 1999.
59   *Kompas*, 7 September 1999.
60   *Kompas*, 2 September 1999.

another occasion he told a journalist that 'You can see and feel yourself how a disappointed person, who has been treated unjustly before their own eyes, whose complaints have been ignored, in the end will be disappointed and angry. Then they express their disappointment.'[61]

Wiranto was referring to the pro-integration side's claim that the referendum had been conducted fraudulently. The *bupati* of Dili, Domingos Soares, detected an 'international conspiracy' behind the defeat while the pro-integration *Forum Persatuan dan Keadilan* (Unity and Justice Forum) accused UNAMET of bias. It was alleged that UNAMET's local staff were mainly supporters of independence while it had refused to accept observers from Indonesia.[62] One respected Indonesian observer, Benyamin Mangkoedilaga, of the *Komnas-HAM*, supported these accusations. He said 'violations and injustices really happened and were done in front of our eyes by certain UNAMET individuals' who were locally recruited and 'obviously pro-independence'.[63]

The pro-independence militia leaders threatened to go to war if the referendum decision were implemented. João Tavares, the War Commander of the PPI, announced that 'we will declare war and take up arms'. His colleague, the governor of East Timor, Abilio Soares, was equally bellicose. 'We are ready for war', he said but also suggested the partitioning of East Timor as an alternative.[64]

Was the post-referendum killing and destruction a spontaneous reaction of disappointed supporters of integration as claimed by General Wiranto? Or was it part of a contingency plan prepared in advance by the TNI? And if part of a TNI contingency plan, at what level in the TNI was it prepared?

The much-quoted 'Garnadi document', dated 3 July, has been interpreted as evidence that the destruction was planned at the highest level in the Indonesian government. But the document is open to a less culpable interpretation. Its author foresaw the possibility that the vote might be against autonomy and, therefore, proposed a

---

61 *Republika*, 5 October 1999.
62 *Waspada*, 6 September 1999. UNAMET had rejected 24 Indonesian NGOs which offered to send referendum monitors on the grounds that some were not genuinely independent of the Indonesian government. *Kompas*, 26 August 1999.
63 *Kompas*, 10 September 1999.
64 *Suara Pembaruan*, 5 September 1999.

contingency plan to meet such an eventuality. The plan envisaged the evacuation of vulnerable civil servants and immigrants before the announcement of the result and the preparation of facilities for refugees in West Timor. It also proposed that preparations be made to secure a route for withdrawal including 'if possible, the destruction of vital facilities'. Later Human Rights Watch (HRW) publicised a telegram sent on 5 May (the day on which the UN-sponsored agreement between Indonesia and Portugal was signed) by the Deputy Chief of Staff of the army, Lt. Gen. Johny Lumintang, to the Bali Regional Commander in which he instructed that preparations be made to evacuate refugees in the event of the people voting against autonomy.[65]

Neither the Garnadi document's proposals nor Lumintang's telegram are obvious blueprints for the destruction that followed the announcement of the referendum result. Indonesian elite opinion at the time was quite genuinely expecting the referendum to trigger a civil war. Although most were confident that the pro-integration side would win, the Garnadi memo explicitly envisaged a situation in which autonomy was rejected and the pro-integration minority was being massacred by the victorious pro-independence majority. The letter can be read as proposing that 'vital facilities' such as bridges, communications equipment etc. should be destroyed to allow pro-integration supporters to flee to safety in West Timor. There is nothing in the letter to suggest the 'scorched earth' destruction – including public buildings, houses, shops, hotels and so on, let alone mass killings – which actually happened. Similarly the evacuation envisaged in Lumintang's telegram is explicitly placed in the context of measures to prevent the widely expected civil war.

This does not mean, of course, that TNI officers on the ground in East Timor had not given thought to exacting revenge if the vote went against integration. In May, *The Australian* published a story about a document which said 'Massacres should be carried out from village to village soon after the announcement of the ballot if the pro-independence supporters win'. This document also promised aid in the form of M-16 rifles as well as support from the air force.[66] But it is not clear that this was a real plan of action or just part of the general intimidation to persuade voters to support the autonomy

[65] Human Rights Watch (HRW), Indonesia/East Timor: Forced Expulsions to West Timor and the Refugee Crisis, Vol. 11. No. 7(c). Appendix.
[66] *Australian*, 24 May 1999.

option. And even if some officers were considering such action, it does not necessarily show that the TNI leadership was committed to this policy. In any case, in May the TNI leaders were still confident that the vote would be in favour of autonomy.

In August, however, as officers and militia members faced the increasing likelihood that the vote would go against them, there are more indications of plans to exact revenge on the pro-independence side. The disaffected former *bupati* of Covalima, Rui Lopes, claimed that shortly before the referendum military and police officers had ordered militias to attack the UNAMET office in Suai, burn the town and drive the population into West Timor.[67] Rui Lopes' claim was made after reports that about 100 people, including three priests, were killed by militias in Suai on 6 September. Leaked reports from foreign police personnel attached to UNAMET also described plans prepared by local military and police offers to attack pro-independence supporters if the vote was in favour of independence.[68] This suggests that military officers and their militia friends planned some sort of retaliation but it leaves open the question of whether the violence had been planned long in advance at the highest level in the TNI.

As the referendum approached, the Indonesian government made preparations for a possible influx of refugees into West Timor. The Justice Minister, Muladi, said that he expected 200 000 or more refugees to flee from East Timor if the pro-independence side won and the Minister for Social Affairs, Yustika Baharsyah, announced that her department had prepared facilities for 200 000 refugees in West Timor.[69] It has sometimes been suggested that such large-scale preparations indicate that the post-referendum destruction was planned well in advance. But it seems no less plausible to believe that the Indonesian government was worried that the outbreak of civil war would force refugees to flee. That facilities for 200 000 refugees were prepared in advance does not indicate that the mass destruction by pro-Jakarta militias was planned by the government.

As it happened, the post-referendum chaos was indeed accompanied by a huge exodus of refugees to West Timor. Although many were forced to leave by militia and military threats, it also needs to be recognised that a substantial number were supporters of

[67] Carter Center East Timor Weekly Report, No. 9, 13 September 1999.
[68] Paul Daley, 'What the UN knew', *Age*, 9 October 1999.
[69] *Kompas*, 3 September 1999.

autonomy who may well have felt a genuine fear for their safety after the referendum. In all about 240 000 refugees – about one-third of the indigenous population – were transported to West Timor. It has been pointed out that this number is much larger than the 94 000 who voted for autonomy and the conclusion has sometimes been drawn that most of the refugees, therefore, were coerced supporters of independence. But this overlooks the fact that many refugees were children who had not been eligible to vote in the referendum. If we assume for simple illustrative purposes that all 94 000 supporters of autonomy fled to West Timor and took their children with them, the total number of 'willing' refugees could easily have exceeded 200 000. It is possible that many of these refugees had been convinced that a civil war was about to break out in which they would be subjected to violence by the victorious majority. They therefore gratefully accepted TNI assistance to escape to West Timor. After several months in refugee camps and having seen the restoration of order in East Timor, many decided to return although by January 2000 about 50 000 refugees had opted to remain in Indonesia.

Although an uncertain proportion of refugees was 'willing', there is also plenty of evidence indicating that the military was involved in forcing many others to leave for West Timor. Interviews conducted by HRW in November with returning refugees in Dili indicated that many had been forced by militia members to move to West Timor during the three weeks after the referendum before the arrival of Interfet troops on 20 September. Refugees told HRW that militias, 'often accompanied by local army officers, forced families at gunpoint into the district or subdistrict army headquarters', after which their houses were burned and they were taken by car or truck to West Timor.[70] The HRW account is consistent with the observations of UNAMET officials and Western journalists. It is also supported by reports in the Indonesian press. For example a *Kompas* reporter asked refugees in Dili why they were leaving. One answered, 'Because I was told to leave. They said it would be better if we leave'.[71]

But, was the forced evacuation of refugees part of a long-term plan to destroy East Timor after the referendum? HRW argues that 'The logistics involved, the similarity of the process from one end of East Timor to the other, and direct witness testimony all point to a planned and systematically implemented operation'.[72] As discussed

[70] HRW, op.cit.
[71] *Kompas*, 19 September 1999.
[72] HRW, op.cit.

above, there is in fact no question that the military had given consideration to the possibility of mass evacuation and was prepared to evacuate over 200 000 people to West Timor. What needs to be explained is why the military felt it necessary to force so many people to become 'unwilling' refugees.

The available evidence is not sufficient to provide convincing support for the view that the destruction that followed the referendum was part of a long prepared military plan. It seems that many officers, at least until about July or early August, were still quite confident that the intimidation carried out by the militias under their guidance would secure a pro-autonomy vote. It was only as the referendum drew close that most must have realised that the referendum might indeed be lost. But even then it seems that they expected the result to be quite close. It is of course possible that military officers planned to encourage militia violence well in advance but it seems quite likely that their support for the destruction, killing and forced deportation was a reaction to their realisation that the referendum would be lost.

Even on the evening of the ballot, pro-integration supporters had begun their campaign of killing and destruction. That the TNI and police made no serious attempt to prevent the violence is obvious. That some elements in the military – particularly local East Timorese soldiers – participated in the violence is also clear. And there are indications in some areas at least – such as Suai – that military officers actively encouraged the violence. That the violence took place throughout East Timor indicates a degree of territory-wide co-ordination that would have required military approval and probably assistance. And it is clear that TNI personnel played a major role in forcing unwilling refugees to cross into West Timor.

At this stage we can only speculate about military motives.

First, the TNI had worked closely for two decades with the pro-integration sector of society from which the militia members were drawn. Why were the security forces unable to stop the rampaging militias? According to President Habibie, 'It must be acknowledged that they (TNI) faced obstacles which were more psychological than military'.[73] The loyal support of *wanra* and the militias over many years had imposed on the TNI what Wiranto called a 'psychological burden ... because they had to confront a section of the Indonesian people themselves who felt that they had been treated unjustly'.[74]

[73] *Republika*, 13 September 1999.
[74] *Suara Pembaruan*, 20 September 1999.

Wiranto said 'it is not possible that our close relationship with the fighters for integration could be cut off just like that. We could not avoid this and we honestly admit it'.[75] In a later newspaper interview he even asked 'Must we confront them with force?'[76] Wiranto's loyalty to the TNI's militia allies was such that he could not bring himself to turn on them in the new circumstances. But, as an editorial in the *Jakarta Post* asked, if Wiranto knew that his troops could not control the militias, why did he accept responsibility for maintaining order under the 5 May Agreement in the first place?[77] And, the 'psychological burden' does not explain the active involvement of TNI troops in forcing refugees into West Timor.

A second possible explanation is also psychological. The TNI leadership had accepted Habibie's policy of holding a referendum because they were confident that they could secure a victory for the pro-autonomy side. Military officers had also conveyed that sense of confidence to the pro-integration East Timorese and to their civilian colleagues in Jakarta. Thus it came as a huge shock to most Indonesians when the pro-autonomy side was not only defeated but defeated by a margin of nearly four to one. As Ali Alatas explained much later, 'They always reported that we were going to win. So they too were shocked, maybe ashamed.' The TNI leaders then claimed that they lost because of electoral violations permitted by UNAMET but, as Alatas again pointed out, the violations were 'not to the point that you can change 78 to 22 per cent'.[78] Angry and humiliated by their overwhelming defeat, it has been suggested that military officers then gave a free hand to their men and the militias to exact some sort of revenge on the East Timorese people who had so decisively rejected integration with Indonesia.

Another explanation suggests more rational calculation. Indonesia had always justified its initial intervention in East Timor as motivated by the need to stop a civil war in East Timor. And they continued to justify the heavy military presence in East Timor as being necessary to prevent the resumption of that war. After Habibie introduced his new policy in January 1999, many military officers continued to argue that a civil war would break out if East Timor won its independence. The overwhelming vote

75 *Republika*, 13 September 1999.
76 *Republika*, 5 October 1999.
77 *Jakarta Post*, 13 September 1999.
78 *Jakarta Post*, 2 November 1999.

in favour of independence, however, undermined much of the credibility of the 'civil-war' justification. Instead of a neutral arbiter between more or less evenly matched warring factions, the TNI now appeared to be the oppressor of the vast majority of the people in order to protect the interests of a small minority. In a desperate attempt to legitimise its long involvement the TNI may have aimed to convince not only the rest of the world but also the Indonesian people that there really was a civil war by themselves creating a huge exodus of refugees. Having announced preparations to receive 200 000 refugees, the TNI had to make sure that the refugee camps were filled.

A fourth explanation, often put forward by foreign observers, was that the destruction of East Timor was intended as a deliberate warning to other restive provinces which might seek independence, particularly Aceh and Irian Jaya. If, however, as suggested above, the decision to allow the destruction to take place was taken rather late in the process – because Indonesian leaders had been confident of winning until the last month or so – it seems more likely that the policy was driven by the situation in East Timor itself rather than possible consequences in faraway Aceh and Irian Jaya. The impact on other provinces was probably no more than a secondary consideration.

At what level was the decision taken to permit the destruction of East Timor? General Wiranto himself has stated that the TNI's 'psychological burden' prevented it from taking measures to repress the rampaging militias. It is obvious, however, that military officers in East Timor gave explicit support and encouragement to the militias and that soldiers, especially those of East Timorese background, participated in the destruction. Did orders come from Jakarta, Bali, Dili or local commanders? Both the United Nations and the Indonesian government established commissions of inquiry which reported on these questions. The answers will only be clear if charges are laid and officers brought to court.

Curbing the violence and the intervention of the UN

There were signs that the massive destruction taking place in East Timor was going far beyond anything that members of the government had expected. On 5 September, President Habibie sent the Political and Security Affairs group of ministers (including Faisal Tanjung, Wiranto and Alatas) to East Timor where they met representatives of both the pro- and anti-independence sides but reportedly did not venture outside the airport. In a later interview Alatas said of the post-referendum violence that 'It shocked the world, it shocked us too frankly' and he asked 'why it was not stopped immediately'.[79] According to one report, militia leaders angrily confronted Wiranto and accused him and the government of betrayal. Wiranto, they apparently believed, had previously assured them that the referendum would result in a victory for autonomy.

At this point it seems that Wiranto began to take steps to regain control of the situation. He ordered six Kostrad battalions to go to East Timor and persuaded the President to introduce martial law in East Timor at midnight on 6-7 September. Earlier on 6 September, Habibie had raised the possibility of martial law at a meeting with the parliament (DPR) but the response was generally negative. He then discussed the issue in cabinet but failed to obtain endorsement[80] – although one inside source asserts that the proposal was not specifically rejected by the cabinet. However, in briefing the press, the Minister for Information, Lt Gen Yunus Yosfiah, gave the impression that the cabinet had rejected the martial law option. Thus, when the introduction of martial law was announced at midnight, it seemed that General Wiranto had imposed his own wishes on the president. Rumours even circulated about the possibility of a military coup.

In fact there had been no serious conflict between Habibie and Wiranto on this issue. Habibie initially felt constrained by the 5 May Agreement that required Indonesia to use the police, not the army, to maintain security. He had then contacted the UN Secretary-General and explained that the police no longer had the capacity to control the situation. Under Indonesia's emergency law, it was possible to declare a civil emergency which would place full power in the hands of the regional governor but the governor, as noted above, was one of those threatening to launch a civil war. And, in any case, as Wiranto pointed out, 'the governor has already fled'.[81] The only alternative, therefore, was to introduce martial law. Kofi Annan then accepted the declaration of martial law but warned that 'the international community will have to consider what other measures it can take if Indonesia fails to bring the situation under control within 48 hours'.[82]

[79] *Jakarta Post*, 2 November 1999.
[80] *Kompas*, 7 and 8 September 1999.
[81] *Republika*, 13 September 1999.
[82] Keith Richburg, 'Mayhem Continues in East Timor', *Washington Post*, 8 September 1999.

Wiranto appointed the army's Assistant for Operations and former East Timor *Korem* commander, Maj. Gen. Kiki Syahnakri, as martial law commander. It seems that by now Wiranto was persuaded that Indonesia's international reputation was at stake and that firm action should be taken to restore order. Pro-integration militia leaders were called to a meeting with Maj. Gen. Adam Damiri in Bali where, according to Wiranto, they were told that 'there is no longer a need to engage in actions or activities that violate the law'.[83] João Tavares then announced that all operations ceased on 9 September.[84] Wiranto himself met Guterres and Abilio in Dili on 11 September and reiterated that all activities which 'ruin the good name of East Timor' should stop.[85]

By now the international condemnation – fed by newspaper reports and television broadcasts throughout the world – was putting enormous pressure on the Indonesian government. In the face of demands to accept international troops to restore order, Indonesian leaders continued to insist that they could do the job. Wiranto declared that 'We have the capacity to handle the situation'[86] and Alatas pleaded that 'For Indonesia, we have pride that we can carry out our obligations and we request that we be given the opportunity to complete that task'. He added that 'it will only create a very bad image if, before we are given the opportunity, we give up and agree to the sending of foreign troops although according to the international agreement, it is in fact our task to carry out that duty'.[87]

In response to growing international concern, the UN Security Council sent a five-member mission headed by the British ambassador to the UN, Sir Jeremy Greenstock, to Indonesia where they visited Dili on 11 September in the company of General Wiranto. Initially Wiranto told the mission that there was no need for international troops. 'Conditions in East Timor are already good', he said, 'there is no more killing, burning and destruction'. But, after accompanying the mission on their tour of Dili, he seemed to back down and agreed that 'The offer to speed up the entry of peacekeeping forces must be considered as one of the choices for the government of Indonesia'.[88] The mission members were amazed by the destruction that they saw

83   *AFX-Asia*, 8 September 1999.
84   *Kompas*, 12 September 1999.
85   *Kompas*, 12 September 1999.
86   *Washington Post*, 8 September 1999.
87   *Kompas*, 10 September 1999.
88   *Kompas*, 12 September 1999.

and noted that 'The mission had the distinct impression that when the General travelled to Dili along with the mission and toured the city, he had not been prepared for the extent of destruction'. They concluded that the Indonesian security forces were incapable of restoring order. The mission leader said that 'I don't think anybody here has any doubt that there has been complicity between elements of the defence forces and the militias. In some areas, there is no difference between them in terms of action and motivation'. The mission therefore recommended that an international force be sent to East Timor 'without delay'. It also recommended that 'apparent abuses of international humanitarian law' be investigated.[89]

As the violence in East Timor continued, the UN Secretary-General said that Indonesia would be responsible for 'crimes against humanity' if it did not immediately accept the dispatch of foreign troops. This was backed by the US President, Bill Clinton, who declared bluntly that the Indonesian military was backing the militias while the US ambassador to the UN, Richard Holbrooke, explicitly blamed the TNI 'under the leadership and command of General Wiranto' for what happened in East Timor. Meanwhile, the Chairman of the US Joint Chiefs of Staff, General Henry Shelton, had been speaking daily by telephone with Wiranto. Ominously the IMF suspended the visit of an aid team to Indonesia and both the IMF and World Bank expressed their concern about the situation in East Timor.[90] Finally, on the evening of 12 September, the Indonesian cabinet agreed to accept the international force in East Timor.

On 15 September the UN Security Council authorised the formation of the International Force in East Timor (Interfet) to be commanded by Australian Major-General Peter Cosgrove with a Thai Deputy Commander. Around 4500 of its 7000 strength was Australian. Cosgrove arrived in East Timor on 19 September and troops began to land on 20 September. Cosgrove and the Indonesian commander, Kiki Syahnakri, seem to have co-operated well together. Although the 5 May Agreement provided for Indonesian forces to retain responsibility for security in East Timor until the MPR had made a final decision on East Timor's future, the Indonesian presence declined rapidly and all had left by early October.

---

[89]   *AFP*, 13 September 1999.
[90]   *Kompas*, 11, 12 September 1999.

With the MPR preoccupied with its vote on President Habibie's 'accountability speech' on 19 October and the presidential election on 20 October, the reversal of the 1976 MPR decision incorporating East Timor into Indonesia was passed unanimously without debate by the weary MPR members shortly before midnight on 19 October 1999.

Reference

Saldanha, João Mariano de Sousa, 1994. *The Political Economy of East Timor Development*. Jakarta: Pustaka Sinar Harapan.

10

East Timor: the misuse of military power and misplaced military pride

John B. Haseman

On 20 October 1999, the Indonesian parliament ratified the results of the United Nations ballot in East Timor, thereby creating Asia's newest independent entity. Not yet a country – several years of UN administration is likely to follow – East Timor has finally gained its freedom after almost 400 years of colonial rule by Portugal and 23 years of failed integration as a province of Indonesia.

The path has not been easy and the price paid by the East Timorese has been very high. The euphoria that began with Indonesian President B.J. Habibie's January 1999 announcement of 'autonomy or independence' quickly vanished. A process that could have been relatively painless, had good will been expended on both sides, instead became painful for all sides. Instead of implementing a peaceful program to educate and persuade the East Timorese population of the advantages of autonomy within Indonesia, Indonesia implemented a forceful 'security approach' of intimidation, violence and terror.

The final result: a discredited Indonesian government, disgraced Indonesian armed forces, a deployed Australian-led international peacemaking and peacekeeping force, and a lengthy and expensive program of reconstruction in East Timor, is about the worst possible outcome that could have been imagined.

There are many complex and interrelated issues involved – political, economic and military. The issue that has gathered the most attention has been the military-supported campaign of violence and intimidation in East Timor. An examination of the military issue must look at both the international and the Indonesian audiences, however, in an attempt to determine the 'why' and the 'who' of the viciousness that overwhelmed East Timor.

When the International Force in East Timor (Interfet) began its work to restore security to the devastated people and infrastructure of East Timor, the primary and complex question to be answered was 'what went wrong?' Eight months later, after Interfet's successful operation and a transfer of security responsibility to the United Nations, the question remains unanswered and subject to both Indonesian and international investigation.

How did Indonesia, having jettisoned the autocratic Soeharto government in May 1998, and having held one of the world's most remarkable democratic elections in June 1999, so indelibly and inexplicably allow violence to bring international disgrace to itself, its leaders, and to its armed forces at a time when it is moving toward becoming the world's third-largest democracy?

As it turned out, a lot of things went wrong. But 'wrong' in the case of East Timor depends very much on the audience, and there are many audiences for which the events in East Timor in recent months by no means hold the same meaning. There is first the international audience, second the Indonesian audience, third the Indonesian armed forces audience, and sadly but lastly, there is the East Timor audience. This analysis looks primarily at the Indonesian armed forces and attempts to analyse why the tragedy of East Timor happened, what elements of the armed forces were involved and more importantly which were not, and what the objectives of the campaign of violence may have been.

It must be recalled that despite the resignation of President Soeharto in May 1998, Indonesia at the start of 1999 had changed but little. President Habibie was the longest serving Soeharto cabinet member and his hand-picked vice-president, so close to Soeharto he was often referred to as a surrogate son to the former strongman.

The military, though it had raised to senior levels a number of reform-minded generals, still had the mind-set of a force accustomed to having its own way and beset by a strong sense of automatic obedience to superior officers, no matter how wrong the decisions may be. Indonesia's political power elite had suffered from the lack of alternative leadership for three decades, its 'reform cabinet' consisted almost entirely of hold-overs from the last Soeharto government. There was no effective counterbalance to nearly unlimited executive power.

There was a major policy decision made at some level of government to apply a 'security approach' rather than a 'political approach' in East Timor in an attempt to gain a favourable pro-autonomy vote. Instead of using its vast information and propaganda network to persuade the East Timorese populace of the considerable advantages of autonomy within Indonesia, the military was directed to apply the tough use of force that characterised most of its prior actions in East Timor. Policy decisions of this magnitude are not taken in isolation in Indonesia. This decision was probably reached by consensus at the cabinet level, pushed by hard-liners but eventually approved by at least part of the cabinet. It is not clear whether President Habibie approved of the policy decision, or even knew of it. There has been no explanation of why the decision was made to implement a campaign of intimidation and fear in East Timor, rather than to make an effort to persuade the populace of the benefits of the autonomy proposal.

It is quite possible that this decision was based on a major intelligence failure. The hard-line security approach must have been based on an estimate that the pro-Indonesia segment of the population, reinforced by a campaign to terrorise enough of the neutral and pro-independence segments of the populace into approval of the autonomy proposal, would gain a favourable majority in the 30 August ballot. Instead the vicious militia campaign caused a huge number of East Timorese to go to the polls and reject the proposal by a four-to-one margin. All indications are that the Indonesian military and the government were stunned by the magnitude of the anti-Indonesia vote.

Both the civilian and military government has consistently misread public opinion in East Timor. I recall on many occasions when, after my frequent visits to East Timor as U.S. Defense Attaché, I reported to Indonesian military officers my impressions that the sentiments in East Timor were not so much anti-Indonesia as anti-army. Virtually every East Timorese had experienced a negative relationship with the army because of mistreatment or slights to themselves or their family and friends. My observations were always summarily rejected by intelligence officers who insisted that my impressions were in error and that I had not spoken to the right people. Indonesia's military intelligence network has always failed to appreciate the degree to which the East Timorese have hated the Indonesian army. On 30 August, the population voted to get the army out of East Timor, pure and simple. And Indonesia's intelligence agencies either failed to make a correct estimate of the probable outcome, or used its certain knowledge of coming rejection to reinforce those who supported a 'security approach'.

The same type of intelligence failure occurred in Burma in the run-up to the 1990 parliamentary elections in that country during my assignment as the U.S. Defense and Military Attaché. The all-powerful Burmese military intelligence agency, the Directorate of Defense Services Intelligence (DDSI), consented to a national parliamentary election in 1990 in part because the military was confident that the government's National Unity Party (NUP) would win the election. The foreign diplomatic community was briefed that the NUP would get at least a plurality and probably as much as 60 per cent of the vote, based on their own intelligence estimates and country-wide polling.

Instead, the Burmese people went to the polls in June 1990 and gave a huge mandate of more than 85 per cent to the National League for Democracy and its associated regional parties. The Burmese military government responded first by ignoring the election and then by declaring it a 'referendum' and not an election. The parliament elected in 1990 has never been allowed to meet.

The DDSI was sure it would win in Burma, and so apparently did the Indonesian hard-liners think they could win in East Timor. In both cases they totally failed to read the true will of their target populations.

In my view, based on information available and analysis of information and events, the months of violence that destabilised and brutalised East Timor was a deliberately planned covert operation carried out in accordance with orders issued by someone in authority over at least some elements of the armed forces. The likely strategic objective was to attain a pro-integration vote in East Timor or, failing that to either negate that vote or so destabilise the territory that it would take years of time and a huge financial investment by the international community to make a viable country of East Timor.

That operation was forced by a powerful group of hard-liners made up of active and retired military officers as well as well-placed civilians. The operation was well-financed. Elements of the intelligence apparatus and covert operations assets from the Army Special Forces

Command (Kopassus) and the police were utilised to implement most of the operation. They used as their primary tool a basic militia organisation in East Timor that was originally raised and supported by the army in the 1980s to assist in security and intelligence for the military. Organised by Kopassus and intelligence teams, that militia base was expanded greatly by recruitment of both East Timorese and non-East Timorese and then directed and supported as a surrogate force to intimidate the populace into supporting integration.

An as yet unknown number of covert military and police personnel supported the operation. TNI soldiers, ethnic East Timorese from the two territorial battalions and the territorial structure permanently assigned to East Timor, who either deserted from their units or were under orders from the covert operation agents, were also involved. This force perpetrated most of the violence and physical damage in East Timor prior to the announcement of the voting results in early September as well as afterwards.

The vicious months-long campaign of the militia forces was a strategic failure. The operation – dubbed *Operasi Sapu Jagad*, or 'Operation Clean Sweep' – may have succeeded in killing many pro-independence East Timorese and destroying much of East Timor's infrastructure and towns, but it failed to achieve its objective of gaining approval for autonomy within Indonesia.

It was also a tactical failure. A cardinal component of any covert operation is the need for 'plausible denial'. Those in the Indonesian military directing the operation failed to achieve 'plausible deniability' to its claims of non-involvement. Western intelligence agencies, non-government organisations, and the United Nations itself were all aware of the involvement of military and intelligence covert operatives in organising, recruiting, training, and directing militia force activities. World-wide television showed police and soldiers standing by while militia forces wreaked violence on a defenceless populace. Too many people – non-Timorese and closely resembling military personnel – were seen using sophisticated radios and telephones to direct events. A vivid television news clip broadcast around the world showed a crew-cut non-Timorese man leaning against a utility pole taking a cigarette break, then pulling on a huge wig of long unruly Timorese-style hair and romping down the street, weapon in hand. Foreign soldiers assigned to the UN monitoring mission watched as a group of 'militia members' drew up in military formation and marched with precision onto a C-130 aircraft at the Baucau airfield, to fly away, most likely back to their army special forces unit on Java.

In short, the perpetrators of the covert operation attempted to conduct their efforts using the rules and standards of 20 years ago and completely failed to take into account the impact of instantaneous communication and an open society.

The East Timor fiasco was a military leadership failure. There is a cardinal principle of military command which holds that any military commander, including the armed forces commander-in-chief, is responsible for what his men do or fail to do. By this standard, General Wiranto must bear responsibility for what men in the pay of his army did in East Timor. Elements and personnel of the TNI, acting under the orders of *somebody* in authority, conducted reprehensible acts in East Timor, failed to perform their mission to provide security and order in the province, and failed to fulfil the commitment of their nation given to the United Nations to guarantee security in East Timor prior to, during, and after the balloting.

The involvement of some elements of the armed forces, even though a tiny percentage of total military strength, brought international disgrace to a beleaguered military, already reeling from domestic revelations of past human rights atrocities in its security campaigns in Aceh, Irian Jaya, Jakarta and East Timor.

The Sapu Jagad Operation was not implemented by itself without higher command approval. Either General Wiranto obeyed cabinet orders to run the operation, or he ordered it himself without approval of his civilian superiors, or the operation was ordered without his approval by others, outside the military chain of command, with the power to do so – a very small group indeed. No matter which of these circumstances obtained, it reflects leadership failure at the very highest levels of the Indonesian armed forces.

However, and this is an important caveat, it is wrong to blame all of the Indonesian armed forces for what happened in East Timor. The majority of TNI personnel, while distressed at the 'loss' of East Timor, are dismayed and angered by the atrocities committed by TNI elements and their militia surrogates in East Timor. That atrocious behaviour has brought humiliation for Indonesia, to the TNI as a whole, and international criticism and disgrace for the TNI as a professional military organisation. Years of efforts to build professionalism within the TNI have been badly damaged in the eyes of the outside world. And it has brought the added embarrassment of international inquiry and a domestic investigation that implicated 33 members of the armed forces, civil government, and non-official civilians. Indonesia's internal judicial inquiry began in March 2000 and will no doubt result in controversy no matter what the final results might be.

That is the view of the international audience. But recall that there are many audiences to the events in East Timor. Perhaps not everything that happened there is considered a failure by at least some of those audiences.

Many analysts hypothesise that at least one strategic objective of the security approach was to set an example of the fate that will befall other separatist-minded regions of Indonesia if efforts to secede persist.

The international community is not without blame. With considerable intelligence input from those already on the ground in East Timor, the involvement of military and police in the militia depredations, and the degree of violence that might be suspected, was known and should have been disseminated with greater speed. Several countries admitted that they had received such reports, but had relied on repeated assurances of the Indonesian military leadership that they could control the situation. This was a failure in foreign intelligence estimates.

And what of the implications for Indonesia? What might be seen from the Indonesian audience that may well differ from conclusions drawn by the international audience?

To understand the implications of the army's role in East Timor, it is important to look beyond the international view of this tragedy and its 'failures', and instead look at it from the inside, as most Indonesians will do. A large segment of Indonesian society simply does not understand either the short term events of the past several months, or the conditions that have existed in East Timor for the past 20 years.

The reason is because the situation in East Timor has been, over the years, a more important issue overseas than it has been in Jakarta. Most Indonesians look at East Timor as a security issue, not a human rights issue. There has never been the same degree of concern in Indonesia about human rights violations in East Timor as in Aceh or Jakarta. To analyse the East Timor problem as a security threat to Indonesia as a whole, the possible strategic objectives of the military become more clear, particularly to the Indonesian public and the military audiences.

First and foremost, if there was ever any doubt that the armed forces is the most powerful and influential element in a post-Soeharto, more 'open' Indonesian society, those doubts have been erased. Within the army and some important political forces in Indonesia, there is a primordial fear that allowing East Timor to secede from Indonesia will lead inexorably to a breakdown in national unity and possible disintegration of the country. This is the primary reason why the military so strongly opposed the sudden decision by President Habibie to equate rejection by the East Timorese of his autonomy package with separation and independence for the province. The fear of national disintegration is so strong in the armed forces that some elements in the military have been willing to risk strong international criticism, withholding of loans from international financial institutions, and the loss of its international military-to-military programs.

There are other reasons for the military's opposition to President Habibie's 'autonomy or independence' policy as well, more parochial to military interests both institutional and individual. The army in particular has strong emotional and psychological ties to East Timor. A huge percentage of the officer corps has served in East Timor, senior officers went there time after time. The army fought and sacrificed thousands of its men's lives to integrate East Timor into Indonesia. The military also feels strong loyalty to the tens of thousands of East Timorese who supported the military and the civil government over the past two decades.

Finally, there were substantial financial interests at stake, reportedly primarily those of the Soeharto family and its cronies, to which the military may well have access.

Another blunt fact of the matter is that East Timor's 800 000 people make up less than one-half of one per cent of the Indonesian population. Neither the military nor the Indonesian government was willing to allow that tiny percentage of the country to, in their view, destroy the viability of the other 99.5 per cent of Indonesia.

Therefore, ever since President Habibie's surprise announcement that he would grant independence to East Timor if its people rejected his autonomy proposal, the military began planning its own strategy to negate the adverse effects – as the armed forces saw them – of the decision. That the military leadership was not consulted on the decision, and its after-the-fact advice disregarded by the president, added the important psychological element of 'face' to the impetus for planning and implementing the hard-line security approach to ensuring the retention of Indonesia's 27th province.

The strategic objectives of the military's covert campaign in East Timor appear to have been, first, to negate the decision to free East Timor and second, failing in that, to give an unmistakable lesson to other potentially secessionist regions elsewhere in Indonesia that the consequences of attempting to secede from the country are far too high. In achieving either or both of these objectives, the military also drives home the clear fact that it is still a powerful force to be reckoned with in the post-Soeharto political equation.

There were several important components to the covert operation to retain East Timor as an autonomous province of Indonesia. First, it was necessary to destabilise the security situation in East Timor so that society there could be portrayed as a violent one in which clans, regions and political factions are constantly fighting with each other. Official Indonesian briefings have contended that only the presence of a strong security force could keep violence under control. This led to an expansion of the use of thugs, dignified with the term militia, as surrogates for the army. The army has used these tactics frequently in its covert security operations, not only in East Timor but throughout the country.

By portraying East Timor as in a state of civil war between pro- and anti-independence forces, the next step in the strategic campaign may have been to attempt to discredit the results of the UN-sponsored ballot as biased and to demand a second round of voting. Though a claim without merit to the international community, it would have played well in Indonesia, where a substantial element of the population is prepared to believe that international political and economic conspiracies are at work against their country.

This portion of the strategic plan failed because the pro-independence Fretilin guerrilla force and its huge clandestine support army kept its promise to foreswear combat operations and remained in its agreed-upon encampments. The pro-independence Fretilin forces showed remarkable restraint in the face of great provocation. By not responding to militia violence, it proved impossible to show 'civil war' in the province. That left the militia forces with only an unarmed civilian population to fight. The pro-integration militia forces quickly lost the moral high ground when violence spiralled out of control. Instead the world saw violent thuggery at its worst and Indonesia's credibility and that of its military forces sank to an all-time low.

International pressures for a peacekeeping force became too great for the Indonesian political and military leadership to withstand. And tragically for the East Timorese people, they became the unfortunate pawns in the political battle for the national unity of Indonesia and the retention of power and influence on the part of the Indonesian military. Virtually every element of power and decision-making within Indonesia was willing to sacrifice any part of that tiny one-half of one per cent of the country's population if doing so is portrayed as saving the other 99.5 per cent of the nation.

But what of the implications for the future? Indonesia is simultaneously attempting to implement major political, economic and military reforms. Just one of these tasks is a major undertaking but Indonesia has been forced by circumstances to deal with all three at the same time. Indonesia is in the throes of a transition toward greater democracy and openness after more than three decades of darkness during the autocratic Soeharto era. Its economy was the hardest hit by the region's recession.

A stable, united Indonesia is of great importance. Indonesia is the world's fourth most populous nation, the largest and most moderate Islamic country in the world, and a country of great economic potential. It occupies a strategic location between Asia and Australia, between the Pacific and Indian Oceans. This is no tiny impoverished and unimportant mini-state. It is potentially a political and economic giant with an important role to play in the world. Nobody expected that Indonesia's transition from dictatorship to democracy would be easy or that the simultaneous economic, political and social challenges it must face could be quickly solved.

Indonesia, like all countries, needs a respected and respectable security force for its national defence, internal unity, and international contingencies. As the United Nations Transitional Administration in East Timor (UNTAET) expands its operations to maintain and improve security and meet the huge humanitarian requirements there, it is ironic but important to recall that Indonesia has been one of the most reliable supporters of United Nations international peace-keeping operations elsewhere. As indelible images of the damage wrought by some elements of the TNI continue to emerge daily from East Timor, it is difficult now to apply the adjectives 'respected and respectable' to the Indonesian security forces. But the key words here are 'some elements'.

The atrocities committed in East Timor were carried out by only a tiny number of people taken from only some elements of the military. A vengeful cabal of hard-liners directed the violence for a variety of potential objectives well analysed in the international media. That policy was carried out with unspeakable ruthlessness by some elements of Indonesia's military and police intelligence apparatus and some of its special forces personnel, who organised and supported militia forces as surrogates. But the great majority of the Indonesian armed forces was *not* involved in the East Timor tragedy of recent months.

It is more important than ever before to keep in mind the imperative need for constructive military-to-military relationships between the Indonesian armed forces and the military establishments of the Western democracies. Dozens of senior Indonesian military officers with reformist credentials have the intellect and international sophistication to make a real difference in Indonesia's halting efforts to implement meaningful reforms. The world community must encourage and support these reformists. Dialogue and co-operation with a moderate government and military leadership would help to isolate and eliminate the hard-line faction from positions of power once and for all.

Indonesia's armed forces remain the most powerful and influential element of Indonesian society. It is crucial that the TNI be encouraged to continue a reformist agenda and to prevent control by hard-liners and their extensive monetary resources.

Now is the time to encourage a moderate military leadership. Now is the time to enhance dialogue between reform-minded senior Indonesian military officers and the military leaders of the Western world's leading nations. To isolate the entire TNI because of atrocities committed by a minority cabal would only encourage those hard-liners to persist in efforts to regain control of the country. The international community should help them to reform the Indonesian defence establishment so that what happened in East Timor will never, ever happen again, anywhere.

11

The strategic implications of an independent East Timor

Alan Dupont

East Timor's independence and the turmoil that has enveloped Indonesia since President Soeharto's political demise in May 1998, will have far-reaching strategic implications for South-east Asia and Australia's relations with Indonesia. It is sobering to recall that only a few years ago, the region was still basking in the glow of its economic and diplomatic successes. There was much talk of Asian economic miracles and a growing belief that South-east Asia was in the midst of an historic transition to peace and prosperity based on the establishment of a genuine security community and enhanced intra-regional trade. National economies were expanding at impressive rates and ASEAN was on the verge of bringing all ten South-east Asian states within its protective embrace. The sense of optimism was palpable, reinforced by significant progress in developing multilateral security structures like the ASEAN Regional Forum and the successful management of long-standing regional conflicts.

Today it is the fear of implosion rather than the inevitability of transition that dominates political discussion about the region. 'Arcs of crisis' have supplanted 'economic miracles' as the dominant theme of countless newspaper editorials and opinion pieces. Some consider that 'the Pacific century is now officially on hold' (Friedman 1999:8). However, just as the metaphor of an economic miracle failed to encapsulate the complexity and realities of South-east Asia's development over the past two decades, so too the evocative image of an arc of crisis exaggerates the region's predicament. Democracy, admittedly flawed and hesitant in its progress, has spread its fledgling wings over much of the region including in Indonesia, where the election of Abdurrahman Wahid represents a decisive break with the authoritarian past. Most South-east Asian states are gradually returning to positive economic growth and the region is still relatively conflict-free if judged by the standards of its modern history. Nevertheless, Indonesia's uncertain future and the violent aftermath of the United Nation's-sponsored ballot on East Timor underlines the challenge to regional order posed by continuing instability in the archipelago.

Australian security concerns

Of all Indonesia's neighbours, Australia was the country most affected by the turmoil in Indonesia and East Timor's bloody transition to independence. Whatever his domestic sins, Soeharto's great strategic virtue was that he presided over an unprecedented era of stability and predictability in Indonesian foreign policy. East Timor's descent into anarchy was an unpleasant reminder to Australians of how benign their immediate strategic neighbourhood has been for most of the Soeharto period. The ferocity of the militia assault on East Timor, aided and abetted by elements of the Indonesian armed forces (TNI), not only killed many innocent people and almost completely destroyed the province's infrastructure; it was also a major setback for Australia's relations with Indonesia. The violent aftermath of the ballot led to the unravelling of the strategic partnership between the two countries, painstakingly constructed since 1992. The failure of this bold but flawed initiative in regional confidence-building was dramatically symbolised by Indonesia's unilateral decision in September 1999 to abrogate the 1995 security agreement with Australia.[1] The security agreement foundered because Australia was ultimately unable to reconcile two conflicting national interests – the desire to deepen defence and security ties with Indonesia and the conviction that the East Timorese were entitled to a genuine act of self-determination.

Australia faces three major challenges in East Timor. First is the danger of a military confrontation between Australian members of the UN security force in East Timor and the pro-integration militia.

---

[1]   For an analysis of the 1995 Agreement on Maintaining Security, see Alan Dupont, 'The Australia-Indonesia security agreement', *Australian Quarterly*, 68(2), Winter 1996, pp.49-62.

Concerns that the Indonesian army might support a guerrilla campaign from West Timor aimed at destabilising East Timor have eased since Wahid's election as Indonesia's fourth president. Nevertheless, as long as armed militias operate with impunity across the poorly demarcated border, the risk of military confrontation and miscalculation remains. An armed clash resulting in Australian or Indonesian casualties, as occurred in October 1999, could easily set off another round of recriminations and jeopardise the tentative rapprochement that has taken place since Wahid's election. Second, there has been a marked, negative shift in Indonesian sentiment towards Australia that will take a long time to dissipate and will impede the reconciliation process. Many Indonesians wrongly believe that Australia precipitated East Timor's march towards independence and the adverse international reaction to Indonesia's management of the East Timor problem which followed. Third, public and elite opinion in Australia towards Indonesia has been soured by the violence in East Timor which will circumscribe and complicate the Howard government's attempts to rebuild the relationship.

ASEAN's dilemma

A once robust and assertive ASEAN has suffered a major loss of credibility and influence since the economic crisis which has been exacerbated by Indonesia's travails. Enlargement, the absence of Indonesian leadership, and divisions over the organisation's future direction and guiding principles have diminished its coherence and reduced its ability to play a stabilising role in the region. Gone is the euphoria and sense of optimism that prevailed before the economic crisis and the widespread belief that ASEAN could provide a significant counterweight to the great powers. This is now a more distant prospect. Australia's advocacy on behalf of the East Timorese has accentuated differences between Australia and South-east Asia about how best to handle East Timor and has further weakened ASEAN, which has had little to say publicly about events in Indonesia or East Timor.

The notable exception has been Malaysia's outspoken Prime Minister, Mahathir Mohammad, who castigated Australia and Western nations for their alleged hypocrisy in rejecting Indonesia's occupation of East Timor while turning a blind eye to similar transgressions by other countries. Mahathir accused the West of seeking to break up

Indonesia and asserted that Australia would be 'the main beneficiary'.[2] The Malaysian Prime Minister's comments failed to elicit much support regionally but they underline South-east Asian uneasiness about the wider strategic ramifications of East Timor's violent separation from Indonesia. Although many South-east Asian states have made significant contributions to Interfet and its peacekeeping successor, they are primarily in East Timor because of Jakarta's wish that Asian states be represented in both forces, not through any abiding concern for East Timor. On the other hand, there is a growing recognition that East Timor is a regional problem that requires a regional response.

ASEAN's reluctance to criticise militia violence in East Timor reflects a desire not to offend its most powerful member. It should not be forgotten that the main reason for ASEAN's establishment in 1967 was to place regional reconciliation with Indonesia 'within an institution- alised structure of relations' (Leifer 1995:50). There is concern in South- east Asia that Australia has put East Timor ahead of its relations with Jakarta and that in doing so, it has contributed to instability and encouraged separatism in the archipelago. An additional worry, in the weeks after the ballot, was that the International Monetary Fund, the World Bank and the Asian Development Bank would cut off funds to Indonesia, and Western nations might withhold aid and investment in order to punish Jakarta for its behaviour in East Timor (MacIntyre 1999:13). Pessimists feared that if this happened, Indonesia's nascent recovery could quickly stall, worsening domestic political instability and heightening the possibility that other parts of South-east Asia could be drawn into ethnonationalist conflict. Worse still, Indonesia might eventually break up in much the same way as Yugoslavia and be replaced by a number of chronically weak and unstable successor states.

Although misplaced, these anxieties are understandable. Since Soeharto's fall, the severity and incidence of ethnic, religious and political strife has risen alarmingly throughout the archipelago, especially in Aceh, Kalimantan and Ambon. None of this means that Indonesia will necessarily fracture and disintegrate in the manner of Tito's Yugoslavia. On balance, Indonesia should muddle through, but the risk is greater than at any time since the 1950s, when Jakarta faced powerful secessionist movements in West Java, Sumatra and Sulawesi. The Balkans' analogy fails to capture the

2   Mahathir also predicted that East Timor would become 'Australia's Vietnam'. 'Timor will be Australia's Vietnam, says Mahathir', *The Straits Times,* 14 October 1999, p.23.

gravity of Indonesia's potential break-up. Even before its dissolution, Yugoslavia was a relatively small country located on the periphery of Europe. Indonesia, on the other hand, dominates South-east Asia geo-politically because of its size, population and its strategic location at the region's maritime crossroads. It sits astride the crucial sea lanes through which passes much of East Asia's trade with Europe, the Middle East and Australia. The situation in Indonesia today is more analogous to that of the Soviet Union in the late 1980s. Like the Soviet Union, Indonesia is more an empire than a country. Its political weight and strategic importance in Asia far exceeds that of Yugoslavia in Europe.

While East Timor's independence is unlikely to lead to the 'Balkan-isation' of Indonesia, the handling of the issue by the Habibie govern-ment and the armed forces leadership under General Wiranto, was an unmitigated disaster for Indonesia. The violence and intimidation carried out by the TNI-sponsored militia prior to the ballot, and the scorched earth policy conducted after the overwhelming vote against autonomy undermined international confidence in Indonesia's political process, threatened the country's fragile economic recovery and renewed doubts about the military's commitment to reform. East Timor's independence has already provided encouragement to 'freedom' movements else-where in the archipelago, especially in Aceh and Papua (Irian Jaya). However, the key to the successful resolution of these long running conflicts rests with the Indonesian government. Greater political autonomy and a more equitable distribution of Aceh and Papua's rich natural resources would go a long way towards defusing anti-Javanese feelings and reducing the impetus for independence. No regional state will want to become involved in either dispute. Australia has made it quite clear that East Timor is a special case and that there are no parallels with Aceh or Papua. International support is therefore unlikely to be forthcoming. Without it, neither the Free Aceh Movement nor its Papuan counterpart, the Free Papua Movement, have the political or military strength to win independence in the face of Jakarta's obduracy. Nevertheless, both insurgencies will continue to fester until such time as the government seriously addresses their underlying causes.

The Wahid factor

President Wahid clearly recognises the importance of tackling head on the grievances of regional Indonesia. His election, and that of

Megawati Sukarnoputri, represent Indonesia's best hope of reuniting the country and bringing to an end the sectarian strife and political turmoil which has plagued the nation since Soeharto's departure. In taking on personal responsibility for Aceh, Indonesia's new president has signalled the importance his administration attaches to bringing the outer provinces back into the fold of a unitary state. If he can satisfactorily resolve Aceh, the other rebellious provinces are likely to fall into line. Failure to meet the political, economic and religious aspirations of the Acehnese would undermine Wahid's presidency and bode ill for a speedy return to stability throughout the archipelago.

There are many other domestic challenges that the new government will have to meet, notably kick-starting a moribund economy, reining in endemic corruption and maintaining what is still a fragile coalition in the national parliament. There are three competing centres of power in post-Soeharto Indonesia – the military, secular nationalists and those who want to see an end to the separation between Islam and the state. Since no one group has sufficient strength to dominate the political agenda as Soeharto was able to do, Indonesian politics will be hostage to the tensions between them for many years to come. Wahid, however, brings to the presidency several important political assets. As head of the 35 million strong Nahdlatul Ulama, the largest Muslim organisation in Indonesia, he is one of the few Indonesians with experience in the art of mass politics and the skills to match. These skills were clearly in evidence during the frantic manoeuvring which preceded the presidential vote. Wahid played a consummate game of political poker with opponents and allies alike, seeing off the challenge of the incumbent, Habibie, and then cobbling together enough votes to win the ultimate prize. In doing so, he demonstrated an impressive ability to draw support from a broad coalition of parties and interests across the political divide, from the Muslim right to the secular left.

Wahid has the legitimacy and moral authority that Soeharto and Habibie lacked and is widely respected within the country. Even though he heads a conservative religious organisation, he is at heart a moderate and a nationalist who opposes the establishment of an Islamic state for fear that it would promote disunity and inter-communal violence. The new president has three of the attributes considered vital for a successful Indonesian leader. He is male,

Javanese and has impeccable Muslim credentials. But his health is poor following a serious stroke and an unsuccessful operation to arrest his failing eyesight. The major question mark over Wahid's presidency is whether he has the physical resilience to withstand the pressures of national leadership. That is why the choice of Megawati as his vice president was so crucial. If Wahid is unable to serve out his full term because of illness or death, under the constitution, she will assume power.

Wahid has moved quickly to assert his authority over the military whose reputation at home and abroad has been severely tarnished by its excesses in East Timor, Aceh and Java. The issue here is how to reform the armed forces and make it more accountable without emasculating its legitimate security functions. The appointment of a civilian, Juwono Sudarsono, as Defence Minister and the elevation of a naval officer to the position of armed forces commander, indicate that Wahid is determined to accelerate military reform. His end game is to professionalise TNI and eventually transform it into a modern, apolitical defence force. This will not be easy. Hard-liners will resist modernisation and will be supported by conservatives in the political parties and bureaucracy as well as the still influential armed forces' retired officers' association (PEPABRI). There is no guarantee that the new armed forces commander, Admiral Widodo, will be able to impose himself on a truculent and resentful army long accustomed to being the pre-eminent service. What is required is no less than a fundamental change in Indonesia's military culture. The armed forces will eventually have to accept that their national security function must be subject to the rule of law and their leaders accountable to an elected president and national assembly.

Internationally, Wahid's election has been genuinely welcomed. He is relatively well-known in South-east Asia and regarded as an able and moderate leader. His long-standing association with Australia has been generally warm and productive notwithstanding his criticism that Canberra has been too assertive, diplomatically and militarily, in responding to the East Timor crisis. The silver lining in the political storm clouds that have hung over Indonesia for the best part of two years is that Wahid has begun his term of office unencumbered by the East Timor issue. The removal of arguably the major irritant in Indonesia's relations with Australia, Europe and the US for the past quarter of a century provides the basis for a much sounder relationship with the West. This will be critical for Indonesia's future because Wahid's government inherits a fragile and poorly performing economy that will require substantial foreign investment for years to come.

Will an independent East Timor be viable?

Much the same could be said about Indonesia's new neighbour. The crucial difference is that Indonesia retains the capacity to shape East Timor's future as an independent nation while Dili will have little clout in Jakarta. A hostile, resentful Indonesia would make it extremely difficult for East Timor to prosper and the embryonic nation has many other challenges to overcome if it is to progress, economically and politically. There are many who doubt East Timor's economic viability, especially since the massive destruction of infrastructure and essential services wreaked by the militia. East Timor's gross domestic product is only US$113 m. Spread over its population of 830 000, this gives the East Timorese a per capita GDP of around US$138, less than half that of Indonesia, making it one of the poorest states in the world (Murphy 1999:46).[3] The local economy is heavily dependent on coffee. Arabica coffee beans from East Timor command a high price on the international market because of their blending qualities, but coffee alone cannot sustain the economy. Unfortunately, apart from coffee and a little sandalwood, there is not much else of economic value. East Timor will also have to make do without the substantial sums of money pumped into the economy by Indonesia since 1975. It will therefore begin life as a very poor country and will struggle to survive for the first few years of independence without substantial foreign aid.

On closer examination, however, the country's economic prospects are not quite as grim as these statistics suggest. There are grounds for optimism that East Timor may not necessarily suffer the fate of other struggling micro-states. Half of East Timor's budget during Indonesia's occupation went towards paying for a bloated bureaucracy which at its height numbered around 24 000 civil servants (Murphy, McBeth and Lintner 1999:20). Australia and Portugal have committed themselves to making up East Timor's financial shortfall during the transition to independence. The World Bank and the Asian

---

[3]   These figures are for 1997.

Development Bank are also likely to grant generous development assistance. This will provide a much needed economic breathing space for the new government and allow it time to begin rebuilding infrastructure and attracting foreign investment which is the key to East Timor's longer-term economic future. There is also potential for diversification into tourism and agribusiness. In conjunction with rehabilitation of non-productive coffee plantations and proceeds from oil and gas from the Timor Gap, within a decade East Timor could have the makings of a small but vibrant economy, sufficient to provide a modest standard of living for most of its population.

Ultimately, however, East Timor's future will be determined by politics rather than economics. Political stability will be critically dependent on the capacity of East Timor's elites to reach an accommodation with one another. Xanana Gusmão's National Council of the East Timor Resistance (CNRT) will need to provide assurances to erstwhile opponents that there will be no vendettas or discrimination against them. As part of the peace process, the CNRT will probably have to accept the incorporation of some militia units into an integrated East Timorese constabulary in exchange for the militia's agreement to disarm and refrain from hostile acts. For their part, former pro-integrationists will have to demonstrate their commitment to the new East Timor and to renounce their loyalty to Indonesia. The establishment of new political institutions and the development of a political culture that encourages broad-based participation and ends the feudal practices of the past 400 years will be an important early test of leadership for an East Timorese government.

East Timor's future external orientation is an issue of more than passing concern to its neighbours. One of the reasons for Indonesia's occupation of East Timor in 1975, and Australia's tacit approval, was fear that a Fretilin victory could promote pro-communist and anti-Western influence in South-east Asia. Even today, many TNI officers passionately believe that the CNRT is really just a front for a left leaning Fretilin leadership which will pursue policies inimical to Indonesia and Australia once entrenched in power. In reality, however, these fears have little substance. For a start, East Timor will be run by the UN transitional administration (UNTAET) for at least three years and possibly five before an East Timorese government assumes power. As a small nation, sandwiched between much larger neighbours that are endowed with abundant resources and possess overwhelming military strength, East Timor is hardly in a position to directly threaten the vital national interests of the two preponderant powers of the south western Pacific, especially as the East Timorese leadership will be preoccupied with the demands of nation-building for at least a generation, and dependent on Australia and Indonesia's continuing good will for vital economic and political support. East Timor's new leaders have already indicated their intention to seek membership of the Pacific Island Forum and ASEAN. Given the often stated commitment of the CNRT to the rule of law, respect for democratic institutions and the maintenance of good relations with its neighbours, it is unlikely that an independent East Timor would become a hot-bed of political radicalism or pursue a foreign policy significantly at odds with Australia or Indonesia.

The real danger is that East Timor could become a weak state rather than a rogue state. Much will depend on the attitude of Indonesia and the level of support provided by Australia and the international community. A weak and chronically unstable East Timor could present opportunities for unwelcome external power involvement by states with anti-Western leanings, although it is difficult to see the circumstances under which such a scenario might be played out. In any event a policy of destabilisation would be directly counter to Indonesia's own strategic and political interests. There is a much greater risk that poverty, intercommunal tensions and entrenched political violence could lead to social unrest which would inevitably spill over East Timor's borders creating friction with Indonesia and other regional states. Another possibility is that an impoverished and anarchic East Timor would provide opportunities for transnational criminal organisations dealing in drugs, people-smuggling and money laundering as has occurred elsewhere in the Pacific.

One problem for the new government in Jakarta is that the East Timor issue has become so politicised domestically that it will be difficult for Wahid to develop a constructive relationship with Dili. A premature attempt to do so could invite condemnation by extreme nationalist elements, inevitably drawing accusations of betrayal and selling out to foreign interests. The dilemma for Indonesia, however, is that continued intransigence towards East Timor will risk alienating those nations most able to provide the economic assistance that Indonesia desperately needs, namely the US, Japan and the Europeans. Thus, even as an independent nation, East Timor's future will be inextricably tied to that of Indonesia and to a lesser extent Australia. If Australia and Indonesia remain at loggerheads, the prospects for East Timor will be bleak indeed. Improved Australia-Indonesia ties must therefore be a primary foreign policy objective for East Timor's new government. Without progress in this area, no amount of foreign aid or investment will bring about the transformation in their lives that the long-suffering people of East Timor desire and deserve.

References

Dupont, Alan, 1996. 'The Australia-Indonesia security agreement', *Australian Quarterly* 68(2), Winter, pp.49-62.

Friedman, Thomas L., 1999. 'Southeast Asia has turned into an arc of instability', *The International Herald Tribune*, 10 September, p.8.

Leifer, Michael, 1995. *Dictionary of the Modern Politics of Southeast Asia*. London and New York: Routledge, p.50.

MacIntyre, Andrew, 1999. 'Asian wariness compromises our regional role', *The Australian*, 30 September, p.13.

Murphy, Dan, 1999. 'Perky future', *Far Eastern Economic Review*, 18 February, p.46.

Murphy, Dan, John McBeth and Bertil Lintner, 1999. 'Economy of scale', *Far Eastern Economic Review*, 11 February, p.20.

12

East Timorese refugees in West Timor

Januar Achmad

Exodus from East Timor[1]

The gunshots started on 3 September 1999, one day before the result of the referendum was known. Residents of Dili had already started to leave their homes, although all the shops were still open. Most of the Indonesian bureaucrats' families had left for West Timor before the 30 August referendum. At 9.15 am, in Dili, on 4 September 1999, the result of the referendum was announced by Kofi Annan, the Secretary-General of the UN in New York. Despite the Habibie government's naive belief in a positive outcome, the pro-independence group had won with a huge 78.5 per cent of the vote.

The gunfire intensified on the night of 4 September. More people were leaving their homes on foot, on motorbikes and in cars, seeking refuge in the nearby churches and schools within their neighbourhoods. Sister Yulia ADM from Los Palos was in Dili with her congregation at SCMM (one of the many orders of sisters in East Timor) on that

[1] The information in this chapter on East Timorese refugees' settlement in West Timor and repatriation to East Timor is based on the author's observations in the field as a medical officer working together with eleven doctors from Yogyakarta in the refugee camps along the border between West and East Timor from October 1999. The information was gathered through in-depth interviews with refugees, priests, nuns, militia leaders as well as with Indonesian military and civilian leaders.

night. As she reports, the church compound was full of refugees. The houses of pro-integrationists were burnt by their owners themselves, as well as by the militia as revenge for their loss in the referendum.

Sister Yulia packed her belongings and tried to leave Dili for Los Palos on 5 September. On her way to Baucau, she witnessed thousands of militia gathering near the museum as she continued her journey. After a while, her car was stopped by a group of young people who warned her that she must be careful because at Hera, 50 km in the direction of Los Palos, there was a road block set up by Aitarak militia. This information turned out to be true. At Hera, her car was stopped by two men armed with samurai swords.

> My heart was trembling so hard. I prayed God would protect me and the driver and I bowed our heads as the Balinese Hindu do when they ask for mercy. That was how I asked for permission to pass the checkpoint in front of these young men. I thought I would be killed instantly. If that happened, I was mentally prepared since my mission was only to serve God. Finally, it seems my prayers were answered. The militia just let the car pass without comment.

Meanwhile in Dili, another Indonesian, Yeni Rosa Damayanti was in her office, Solidamor (Solidarity for East Timor). She was the chairperson for the Indonesian Independent Electoral Watch for the Referendum in East Timor (or *KIPER* in Bahasa Indonesia). She also felt unsafe in her office on 5 September 1999. She decided to move to the predominantly Indonesian official residential area in Delta Komoro. She assumed it would be well protected by the Indonesian security forces since most of the residents were Indonesian officials and their families working in East Timor.

As Yeni explained, 'On 6 September 1999, the shops in Dili were looted, ransacked and destroyed by the militia. Most of the merchandise was moved out and transported in military trucks.' Meanwhile, as she reports, her friend came in the early morning to warn her to leave immediately for the church, because there were rumours that the Delta Komoro area would soon be burnt down. So Yeni and her friends made another move to the Protestant church. The church was already full of refugees.

The idea was to leave nothing for these ungrateful East Timorese who voted overwhelmingly for independence. As one pro-integration leader stated: 'Why should we leave all these things built by Indonesia for these Timorese people who choose to leave us? Let the Falintil build from scratch' (pers. comm., 20 January 2000). This was the justification behind the destruction of all of the official houses, offices and public utilities which had been built by the Indonesian government since 1975. Even some of the doctors in Belu district, West Timor, helped to empty the government store house for medicine in Suai district, East Timor. Moreover, the destruction was wider than the official buildings, and included private empty homes too, after they were looted by the militia and elements of the military and police force.

The Indonesian police came the next day on 6 September 1999 to the Protestant and other churches in Dili. They warned the refugees that the churches were not safe any more and they must immediately move out to the police stations, military camps, seaport and airport for transit to West Timor and other places in Indonesia. Those who did not want to be evacuated soon left the churches and went to the mountains to hide. Most of these people were pro-independence supporters. They believed that they would be killed on their way to or in West Timor.

Sister Yulia meanwhile arrived safely in Los Palos on 5 September 1999. Soon after she arrived in Los Palos, she was told to go to the seaport and to wait for evacuation. A farmer, who came from Los Palos, illustrates how the people in East Timor were forced to leave their homes. He was a refugee at the Tuapukan refugee camp outside Kupang. His name was Fernando da Costa from Zaeivaca, Zoro village, Los Palos, East Timor. His story was very similar to those told by many refugees interviewed in West Timor during these last three months.

> The militia and elements of the military invited all the villagers in Los Palos to come for a meeting at the village hall. The message was clear that everybody must immediately register and then leave East Timor. Those who stayed on would be considered pro-independence followers and would be killed. In one case, the militia took all the medicine from the hospital in Los Palos and forced three nurses working there to register at Los Palos district military office. If not, they would kill all their family members. The objective was clear. The militia needed the nurses to help them in exile in West Timor.

> All buildings constructed after the integration in 1975 must be destroyed. Our things such as food, clothes, or any belongings that could not be taken away were left behind. Livestock were killed and burnt. Many people, before they left, tried to hide their belongings by burying them. The militia came to search and later on dug them up and destroyed them.

For Sister Yulia in Los Palos, each day she had to suffer more anguish.

The militia and soldiers from the indigenous East Timorese army battalion 742 came to intimidate her into registering for evacuation at the district military (*KODIM*) headquarters in Los Palos. It was alleged that those who did not register would be killed. Finally, Sister Yulia went to complain directly to the battalion commander. She told the commander that as a sister she could only take orders from her superior in the Catholic order. She would not obey a military order. Without the consent of her superior she could never leave her work place. The deputy commander was very sympathetic and allowed her and her fellow sisters to stay on in their convent in Los Palos. She came to Kupang, West Timor, at the end of December 1999 to visit people from the Los Palos parish, who were then in the Tuapukan refugee camp. She came to persuade them to go home. Many did immediately follow her home. One of those who followed her back was the farmer, Fernando da Costa. He left Tuapukan secretly and silently together with 18 others at night and went to the Catholic church for transit in Kupang organised by the Jesuit Refugee Services. This was the first group to leave Tuapukan in the last days of December 1999.

Fernando had to leave his house, farm and his entire herd of 30 cows, pigs and chickens in order to survive. All his livestock was killed by the militia. He and his family of nine people were then evacuated by the Indonesian navy ship from Com, Los Palos, on 14 September 1999. They arrived in Kupang the next day after one night's journey at sea. He and his family were transported by waiting military trucks to Tuapukan, one of the most crowded refugee camps in West Timor. He left the camp for Los Palos one day after Sister Yulia visited them in December 1999.

In Dili, the evacuation started *en masse* immediately on 4 September 1999 by land, sea and air for the refugees already gathering at the seaport and airport as well as in police stations and the military camps. In Baucau the evacuation by the military started on 9 and 10 September 1999. Yeni and her colleagues left Baucau on 10 September 1999 by Indonesian airforce Hercules to Kupang. In the western part of East Timor and Ambeno, the enclave surrounded by Indonesian territory where a large number of the population were pro-integration, people spontaneously moved to West Timor together with their leaders.

On Christmas eve, I went to visit refugees in Tuapukan carrying presents for the children of Januario from Los Palos and his relatives. Suddenly, a woman approached me and asked my help to find her husband, who had been a truck driver for one of the shops in Los

Palos. He had disappeared on 2 September while at Batugade on his way to Los Palos from Atambua, West Timor.

As the story goes, he entered East Timor with a convoy of four trucks full of merchandise from Atambua on 2 September 1999. But he never reached Los Palos that day nor did his eleven companions, including the shop owner's son. No one knows what happened to them, even though the trucks they had driven have been sighted in Kupang many times. The families assume that the men were killed by elements of the Indonesian military and their trucks confiscated in Batugade, East Timor.

One of the last refugees to leave from Dili on 19 September 1999, the night before Interfet arrived in East Timor, was a retired senior medical doctor. Dr Longuinhos Monteiro was one of two doctors to remain in East Timor in 1975 after the territory was seized by Soeharto's regime. He was originally from Goa, India, and had married a local East Timorese woman. His brother-in-law is Lt General Yunus Yosfiah from Kopassus, the former Minister of Information during President B.J. Habibie's tenure. I met the doctor and his wife, Rosa, the night before they went back to Dili from Kupang at the end of October 1999.

I asked him then why his powerful and infamous brother-in-law did nothing to protect him and his family in Dili. It was surprising to see him, a senior doctor and a relative of an Indonesian minister now living as a refugee in the small room provided by the Catholic church together with other refugees. He did not answer my question directly. He said the family sent many trucks from Atambua to help evacuate them, but they failed to reach Dili.

> Many of the trucks were robbed by the armed militia, and especially the military and police personnel on duty in East Timor before and after 4 September 1999. The robbers used the trucks to transport the goods they looted from the shops and wealthy families in East Timor. It was always the case that shops or houses were burnt only after the perpetrators first emptied the buildings of any valuables.

This story is also confirmed by other documented cases from the Tuapukan refugee camp.

On his last day in Dili, Eurico Guterres, the Aitarak militia leader, came to visit Dr Monteiro and his family to warn them to leave immediately. This was on 19 September 1999. But the couple did not want to leave since the husband was too sick and too old to travel.

They thought their powerful brother-in-law, the Minister of Information in Indonesia, could protect them. They were wrong.

At around 6.00 pm, on 19 September 1999, the Red and White militia (*Merah-Putih*) from Liquiça came to their house and took away their cars. Everything that could not be taken away was destroyed in front of them. The couple was then forced to leave Dili by truck together with others. That was how they reached Atambua at midnight, the day before Interfet arrived in Dili. No one was spared in East Timor, not even the relatives of the powerful in Jakarta. Dr Monteiro has lost everything even though he was awarded the model-doctor prize by the Indonesian government in the 1980s. In just two weeks, much of East Timor was depopulated by the militia by ravaging, ransacking and destroying the land under the blind eye of the Indonesian military and police force.

Dispersal

Most of the refugees were located by the government of Indonesia in the districts of Belu and North Central Timor (*Timor Tengah Utara:* TTU) and on the surrounding islands in the province of Nusa Tenggara Timur (NTT). Some of them were dispersed as far as Irian Jaya and Sulawesi, depending on the availability of the ships that passed by Timor at the time.

According to the local NTT government official report at the end of September 1999, there were more than 259 268 people displaced in NTT. However, there were also many East Timorese refugees who voluntarily moved to West Timor. This includes the 1188 Indonesian farming families who were transmigrants from Java and Bali, as well as businessmen, civil servants, and about 6000 members of the military and police forces with their core and extended families.

Many families were separated during this mayhem. Thousands of husbands lost their wives and children. From early September until the end of December 1999, the International Red Cross (ICRC) in West Timor as well as in East Timor, has helped thousands of children to track their parents and families.

The camps

On 4 September 1999 the first shipment of 1000 refugees arrived in Kupang harbour and was received by the governor of the NTT district. After disembarking from the ship, Fernando and his family, together with his fellow residents from Los Palos, were transported to Tuapukan refugee camp by military and police trucks. Here, 25 km outside of Kupang, these pro-independence supporters were housed together with the evacuated militia members, army personnel and their dependants. This is a typical profile in the refugee camps.

Initially, only a few tents were available, so most of the refugees were settled in the football stadium, government buildings and schools. More just slept in the open air with no shelter at all for a few weeks. The wealthy East Timorese families first stayed in hotels. Later, they rented houses in the city and villages around the camps. The cost of renting immediately skyrocketed 100 per cent. Some of the refugees also moved out from the camps and rented rooms or houses in the villages where they could. The peasant farmers stayed in churches, empty offices, or public camps. They could improve their housing problem by building their own traditional huts with materials readily available from nearby woods. Palm trees and leaves are locally used to build roofs, especially in camps outside the city.

Self-help projects

One project in Tuapukan was pioneered by a military sergeant, Januario, from Los Palos. He rented a room in a house from one of the local villagers for his own family. Later on, he built more huts near the main refugee camps at Tuapukan for his relatives, which totalled 80 people. Most of the local people prevented the refugees from using their toilet facilities in Tuapukan after the first week of their arrival in early September 1999. I supported Januario's various efforts to construct permanent toilets and water tanks for drinking water for these 80 people. In the beginning the women just asked for a bucket to carry water. I offered them a water tank if they were willing to build it themselves. Through donations by the Indonesian corporation *Lippo*, and by *Kompas* and *Suara Pembaruan* newspaper readers, I was able to provide the construction materials.

Once they had finished the toilet and water tank with a storage capacity of 5000 litres, I gave mattresses to the workers and was able to increase their electric power for their huts as a bonus, using the same source of funding. This water and sanitation project became a model for other refugees around Noelbaki and Tuapukan, two of the biggest refugee camps in West Timor. Then, others began to request similar aid in constructing their own sanitation and water facilities. By providing these facilities, the refugees also rebuilt their own self-esteem through helping themselves and their neighbourhood. The Indonesian government worked closely with national and international NGOs to help build these toilet facilities in the refugee camps.

Indonesian government responses

In August 1999, the local government of Nusa Tenggara Timur (NTT) province had anticipated the worst scenario of the referendum. The governor of NTT, Piet A. Tallo, believed that the pro-integration group could only win at most 30 per cent of the vote. It seems he had a better understanding of local East Timorese people's aspirations than his counterparts in the military and central government.

He had prepared the local government to accommodate the refugees. On 12 August 1999, the Minister of Social Welfare, Justika Baharsjah, visited Kupang to discuss the preparations to accommodate an estimated 22 000 families totalling about 100 000 refugees from East Timor. Despite the expectation of large numbers of pro-integration refugees, the provincial government had never prepared for the actual number of refugees at the peak time at the end of September. The actual number reached nearly 270 000 people because of the forced exodus of pro-independence supporters too.

After the news of the referendum was announced on Saturday, 4 September 1999, the governor of NTT, Piet A. Tallo, immediately called an urgent meeting between the civilian and military authorities at 11.00 am in his office to discuss and co-ordinate the plans to evacuate Indonesian and government officials and their families from East Timor. The first refugee camp in Kupang at Noelbaki was prepared to accommodate this first group of refugees.

In addition, the governor of NTT had ordered each government department to contribute five staff members every day to help the refugees disembark from the ships and airplanes. The Department of Social Welfare distributed 400 grams of rice and 1500 rupiah to each refugee. Fernando received 5 kg of rice the day after he arrived at Tuapukan camp.

The International Red Cross distributed kitchen and family kits, consisting of sleeping mats, sarongs, blankets, buckets, and cooking utensils. In total, the ICRC had distributed 150 000 family kits to the refugees in West Timor (NTT). For those who did not receive rice assistance from the Department of Social Welfare, World Vision distributed 50 kg of rice for each family. Other NGOs, such as the Salvation Army, provided milk porridge. Yayasan Belu Sejahtera extended their existing program in West Timor to accommodate the East Timorese refugees with supplementary foods and with soybean powder. The Ministry of Public Works and World Vision, both built water tanks and toilets in the refugee camps.

In Kupang, the local municipal government immediately organised health services with health posts and mobile clinics to serve the influx of 23 621 refugees (see Table 1). In total, six health posts with 24-hour services were set up, three in the sports stadium and three in the sports authority building. Each health team consisted of one doctor, two nurses, one midwife, one nutritionist, and one sanitation expert. MSF (*Medicins sans Frontières*) Belgium had constructed 120 public toilets in these two places. The total refugees housed in the stadium and arts buildings were more than 1000 people each; the sports authority building had 1500 refugees, and the rest were living in hotels, with relatives, or among villagers in Kupang municipality. By the end of January 2000 there were only 100 families left behind in the stadium in Kupang (GOR); the rest had returned to East Timor.

Conditions

The most desperate refugee groups were those evacuated by Indonesian airforce planes. They could bring hardly any of their personal belongings due to limited space. They needed more assistance than those who were evacuated by boats or military trucks over land. Many of these refugees settled in the open without tents and roofs. Although many international agencies and the Indonesian government worked hard to support the refugees' basic needs, it was clear that there was no advanced plan to cope with the refugees on this scale.

NTT is one of the poorest regions in eastern Indonesia. Suddenly the population increased dramatically at the end of September 1999. The central government could only provide rescue funds and foreigners, especially Caucasians, were not welcome by the militia, especially in Belu district where most of the refugees resided, see Table 1.

For example, MSF doctors from overseas came to Atambua but were too scared to work in the refugee camps. ICRC staff too were

TABLE 1: *Distribution of refugees in NTT province by 3 October 1999*

District / Municipality	3 October 1999		Changes Minus *		8 November 1999	
	Families	Persons	Families	Persons	Families	Persons
Belu	29 175	144 933	319	1 374	27 120	135 689
TTU	7 444	32 878	-	-	9 630	44 335
TTS	1 652	5 474	-	1	1 228	6 255
Kupang	4 209	23 621	-	25	7 956	36 338
Municipality of Kupang	7 733	44 983	-	-	516	2 173
Alor	692	2 851	-	-	701	2 886
East Flores	90	960	-	-	200	935
Sikka	394	1 646	-	-	349	1 326
Ende	146	771	-	-	524	2 395
Manggarai	130	612	-	-	270	1 620
Ngada	93	430	-	-	93	430
Total	51 158	259 168	319	1 400	48 587	234 391

Note: * The number of refugees who moved in and out of shelters.

Source: Ministry of Social Welfare, NTT, dated 16 November 1999.

forced to evacuate their Caucasian expatriate staff from Atambua to Kupang in September 1999 due to the increasing security risk. The main threat was the militia, who considered all Caucasians were white Australians. Australians were alleged to have helped the pro-independence group to win the referendum unfairly. Thus Australians were the enemy.

I arrived in Kupang on 22 October 1999, after securing funding in Jakarta for the medical team to work in West Timor. At that time, Kupang was relatively calm and militia were no longer roaming the city armed with guns. However, the residents of Kupang and West Timor were still cautious and shops generally closed earlier than usual. In this tense environment, I arrived to prepare my work for the refugees in Belu and TTU districts near the border with East Timor.

It seems the Indonesian local government in NTT was also concerned with security and the safety of the refugees and general public. So, in mid-September, the religious leaders in NTT as well as S.K. Lerik, the Mayor of Kupang, complained directly to Major-General Adam Damiri, commander of the Udayana Military Command that the government must confiscate all arms from the militia. Despite this, security was still a major issue, as my own experiences show.

After meeting with the archbishop of Kupang to get his advice, I decided to travel to Belu and TTU districts to observe the situation in the field and to meet with the health authorities assigned to the border area. One nun from Memisa, Holland, one staff from a Catholic volunteer organisation *(Perdhaki)* from Jakarta, myself and the driver were assigned the archbishop's car for the drive from Kupang to Atambua on 26 October 1999. To illustrate the security conditions in West Timor, I give my own experience in Kupang.

On the outskirts of Kupang, the provincial capital city of NTT, we stopped at the petrol station to fill up. While waiting in the queue, suddenly we were surrounded by twelve East Timorese militia. Their leader questioned our driver in Tetun, so we did not understand the conversation. However, I could see he was terrified by this uninvited guest at his car window.

Immediately I could sense the potential for danger unfolding in front of us by looking at the militia's faces. They all looked very cool, cruel and intimidating. I asked the leader what the problem was. He told us that my companion was an Australian who was not wearing her habit. The militia were everywhere in West Timor threatening to kill any Australians they could find because they believed that most of the UNAMET staff were Australians and they had organised the referendum unfairly. They believed this bias was what caused the pro-independence result of August 1999 in East Timor. Despite these open threats from the militia, by the end of January 2000, there were no reports that any Australians or Caucasians were killed in West Timor.

Violence against the refugees

Atrocities committed against the pro-independence followers started in East Timor long before the refugees arrived in West Timor. Only after the new government had been sworn in, in Jakarta, did the local situation in West Timor improve significantly. In September 1999, every person suspected of being a pro-independence activist, especially university students, former UNAMET staff, or UN agency staff were pulled out from trucks at the check points along the way to Atambua. In Atambua, one of the International Red Cross (ICRC) local staff from East Timor was kidnapped soon after he crossed the border and has not been heard of since.

The same applies to those who were preparing to board planes at the airport in Dili and Baucau and embark on ships in the seaports in

East and West Timor. They were taken away and remain missing. According to Amnesty International, many were killed at sea during the evacuation. Many more were kidnapped from the refugee camps each night and disappeared in the first month after arriving in West Timor. Some of their bodies were found in the bamboo forest in Belu district. The militia searched for their enemies in the refugee camps as well as the church compounds. However, the Catholic church in NTT played an important role in saving lives. They hid, protected, and later, evacuated the high risk refugees who came together with their families and were targeted by the militia soon after they arrived.

On 18 December 1999, the local people found a female corpse at Salore hamlet, Kabuna village, West Tasifeto subdistrict in the Belu district close to the border with East Timor (*Surya Timor*, 21 December 1999:9). This woman was a pro-independence activist who was killed because she tried to persuade fellow refugees to return to East Timor (pers. comm., 26 December 1999). Most of the women including the militia's wives wanted to return to East Timor, but most of the militia were too afraid to go home by the end of January 2000. They believed the pro-integration militia members would be killed and/or jailed for being a members of a militia. In mid-January 2000, I witnessed a group of young people waiting outside the refugee transit camps in Dili to attack the returning militia. The pro-integration activists demanded that they be provided the western part of East Timor for their resettlement in East Timor, so they could maintain their close social, political and cultural links with Indonesia.

For the local TNI and the police in West Timor, the killing of the East Timorese refugees was not their concern. It seems the Indonesian local security forces left the refugees to solve their own political differences without actively stopping any conflicts. They considered the issue an East Timorese internal family affair and turned a blind eye to any conflicts erupting around them. It is obvious and natural that most of the Indonesian security forces would be sympathetic to the pro-integration group and they were reluctant to confront the armed militia in West Timor.

Many of these crimes against the refugees were also witnessed by the health centre medical officials (Puskesmas staff) in Betun in the Belu district who performed many autopsies on the bodies found in the bamboo forest near Betun. A female medical officer also reported treating one rape case (pers. comm., 28 October 1999). However, in some cases, the Indonesian police tried to help and protect rape victims despite extreme difficulties.

In September 1999, for example, some women from the camp brought a gang rape victim to the police station in Betun for protection. She had been kidnapped and gang raped by three militia the night before. The police protected her from further harassment from the militia who came back to the camp looking for her the next day. Unfortunately, at the time the militia returned, only one police officer was on duty. So he did not have the courage to arrest the rapists and admitted that he was scared of the men. The police officer explained to the health centre doctor that he did not want to intervene. This was not their jurisdiction any longer since the victim was East Timorese. Even though they resided in West Timor and were subject to Indonesian law, the police stated that the refugees chose to solve their own problems when they voted for freedom from Indonesian rule. The same happened in places such as Tuapukan camp in Kupang when the UNHCR staff were attacked by the militia. In general the police attitude was to watch, but to do nothing to stop anyone wanting to prevent the UN staff doing their job in the refugee camps. Moreover, the militia was clearly not afraid of the Indonesian police.

Health

I came from Canberra with the purpose of establishing and leading a medical mission to West Timor. Soon after arriving in Indonesia, I recruited a medical team consisting of 11 young medical graduates from the University of Gadjah Mada, Yogyakarta. They worked in the Belu and TTU districts from mid-November 1999 to the end of January 2000.

Our medical reports reveal a preponderance of upper respiratory tract infections, diarrhoea, malaria and malnutrition in children under five. Health conditions were made worse by the poor distribution of staple foods, such as rice, to the refugees at the end of November 1999. The Ministry of Social Welfare, for example, stopped distributing food in the area. The Catholic Relief Service was suddenly responsible for all the refugees in Betun and has continued to be responsible for them.

Co-ordination was poor. My medical team and I witnessed thousands of refugees starving in Kletek refugee camp in Betun in early December 1999. These refugees had only mango and cassava porridge for several weeks to fill their stomachs before many of them returned home after the border was opened at the end of November 1999.

In general, health services for the refugees were adequate. There were no serious incidents of epidemic outbreaks in the camps in West Timor, except in Tuapukan where the international health authorities worked hard to contain a cholera outbreak that struck in November 1999. Nearly 100 people were reported dead, most of them children under five. By the end of January 2000, the outbreak was under control. The nutritional status of the children under five was similar to that of the local population.

Initially, sanitation facilities were inadequate due to problems of security, but improved significantly. Many NGO field workers were afraid to work in Tuapukan camp. I was asked by Father Andre Soegijopranoto, the Director of Jesuit Refugee Service in Kupang, to help them to penetrate the camp in early November 1999, so they could persuade the refugees to go home. This Jesuit organisation played a crucial role in helping the refugees to go home. I started with a water and sanitation program for the soldiers and their families, which eventually brought us into close and friendly contact with them and the militia. In addition, many local and international NGOs and particularly the government health system, responded well to the health needs of the refugees. Health posts were established near the refugee camps with 24-hour emergency services.

Among the NGOs who worked in Belu district were medical teams from the Philippines, the University of Atma Jaya in Jakarta, the Christian Children's Fund, the Red Cross and University of Gadjah Mada medical volunteers who worked directly with the refugees and supported the existing government health services. There were adequate medical supplies despite a twofold increase in refugee numbers at the health centres in the Belu district. All the medical services were free of charge to the refugees. In the initial stage of the refugee influx, for six weeks, there were only government health centre doctors in the field available to help the refugees. For example, at Betun, the number of outpatients increased from 100 to 500 in September 1999 with only one doctor and a dentist who acted as doctor due to the lack of additional medical officers. I have to salute these young government doctors who dedicated their profession to help the refugees. This is especially true for those doctors who were working in the border areas, where there were no incentives for overtime, overwork, or danger.

Mortality in some camps, such as Tuapukan, was high with crude estimates of 2.1 deaths/10 000 population/day (Bradt *et al.* 1999) and mortality rate of 9.2 deaths/10 000 population/day, for under-fives. In Namfalus near the border town with Suai, East Timor, six per cent of children less than one year old were categorised as severely malnourished and 43 per cent mildly malnourished. 4.5 per cent of children in the under five group were categorised as severely malnourished and 50 per cent mildly malnourished. Poor nutrition, sanitation and personal hygiene, with crowded conditions without proper ventilation, were the underlying causes of acute respiratory infection and death, especially for the children under five.

Repatriation of the refugees

In general, the West Timor community and government received the refugees well from early September onward. Despite this, most of the refugees wanted to return home. The opportunity came when Mrs Sadako Ogata, the High Commissioner UNHCR and her staff from Geneva, paid a visit to the camps on 19 September 1999 accompanied by the Indonesian Co-ordinating Minister of Welfare. Soon after that, UNHCR was allowed to set up offices in Kupang and Atambua, with the Indonesian government providing the security for field staff working among the refugees. On 22 September, President Habibie agreed to allow the refugees to choose to settle in Indonesia or return home to East Timor. From that time, the refugees began leaving West Timor and other parts of Indonesia by air, sea and land. At the end of January 2000, a total of 140 000 refugees had returned home to East Timor.

The government provided a special army unit battalion 432 Kostrad from Makassar to protect the refugee convoys organised by UNHCR and MOI in the first week of November 1999. I was there when the first group of more than 1000 refugees went home by ship from Atapupu. The army appeared very disciplined and prevented the militia from harassing the refugees. This was the same unit that had previously been stationed in Baucau, East Timor, and had successfully prevented serious damage to that town, the only town still intact after the mayhem in September 1999. They were given a farewell send-off by the people of Baucau on 22 September 1999 (pers. comm., 15 January 2000, Dili).

Conclusions

Despite accusations and evidence of compliance in the destruction of East Timor, the Indonesian government, the West Timorese people, the Catholic and Protestant churches all significantly helped the refugees in West Timor to survive the first months of their ordeal. Soon after that, local, national and international aid agencies took part in the rescue and aid operation. There were no serious epidemic outbreaks nor mass starvation, except in Tuapukan camp in Kupang district and the Kletek camp in Betun in the Belu district.

After the new democratically-elected Indonesian government was sworn in, in early November 1999, the security situation improved dramatically and repatriation programs for the refugees were accelerated by opening the border in three places in Belu and TTU districts. This political development in Jakarta had a positive impact on the East Timorese refugees. The military also changed their attitude by assisting the refugees to return to East Timor. Every day thousands of the refugees crossed the border, both spontaneously and with assistance by UNHCR.

More than 100 000 refugees had gone home by the end of January 2000. Many of the rest were militia and their families, former Indonesian government civil servants, and military personnel from East Timor (*Kompas*, 11 February 2000). These civilian, military personnel and militia members and their dependants are more likely to settle in Indonesia permanently. Some of these refugees have already settled in the various districts of West Timor.

For those who have decided to live in Indonesia permanently as Indonesian citizens, the government of Indonesia has planned to relocate them from the refugee camps in West Timor through the local transmigration resettlement projects. Here, they will mix with the local population in each district within NTT province. As for the East Timorese returnees, the process of rebuiding their shattered nation has begun.

Acknowledgments

I feel privileged to have been associated with such outstanding professionals as Professor James Fox and his colleagues from the Australian National University, Canberra, who encouraged me to write this chapter. I owe special gratitude to Dr Oki Fitriani and Dr Oryzati Hilman for collecting information and comments, as well as to Laine Berman and Evelina for polishing my English and making suggestions on this chapter; to Drs Bambang Subroto, Dr Felicianus, ICRC-

Kupang, General Moerwanto, Colonel Sutarno, Drs Suryadi, drg Kuswartini M. Suhel, Piet Alexander Tallo SH, S.K. Lerik, Herminio da Silva da Costa, Father Andre Soegiyopranoto, Dr Moudy Luminta, Sister Brigita, Sister Yulia ADM, Yeni Rosa Damayanti, Father Piet Olin, Father Simon Suni, Father Yoesef Sievers SVD, Sister Yasintha Hour Asa RVM, Father Gregory Neobasu and Dr Sonya Roesma who provided me with information for this chapter. To all of them I am most grateful.

References

Bradt, D. *et al.*, 1999. 'WHO/UNICEF health situation report', 12 August, p.1, mimeogragh.

Government of Indonesia-Departemen Sosial, 1999. '*Laporan status pengungsi Timor Timur di NTT*', Jakarta, 16 November, p.1.

Kompas, 2000. *'Pengungsi TimTim Membebani NTT*', 11 February, p.23.

Surya Timor, 1999. '*Wanita misterius ditemukan tewas*', Kupang, 21 December, p.9.

Tallo, P.A., 1999. '*Penjelasan kronologis penanganan pengungsi Timor Timur oleh pemerintah daerah tingkat I Nusa Tenggara Timur kepada presiden Gus Dur*', Kupang, 9 November.

13

Reconciling worlds: the cultural repositioning of East Timorese youth in the diaspora

Fiona Crockford

It is Saturday 13 November 1999, a world away from Dili, as East Timorese in Sydney gather to commemorate the eighth anniversary of the Dili massacre. As usual, St Mary's Cathedral in the city's centre provides the focal point for the public mourning of the scores of young Timorese who were massacred at Santa Cruz cemetery on 12 November 1991. For Sydney's East Timorese community, St Mary's has become a familiar landmark, part of a diasporic landscape upon which they have faithfully reinscribed their collective trauma and memory over their years in exile. And yet, this year's commemoration of martyred youth has a remarkably different feel. For the first time in twenty-four years, Timorese here join their compatriots at home to celebrate a fragile peace and an unfamiliar freedom. Inside the cathedral, the congregation even looks different. Many familiar faces are missing. As East Timor transforms from a context of war to one of 'reconstruction' and 'reconciliation', some long-term exiles have already returned, as they always said they would, to help rebuild their shattered country. In their place are a large number of Timor's most recent refugees, airlifted out of the post-referendum tumult and chaos by Australian Interfet troops. They look bewildered, still in shock, as if they have not quite grasped the suddenness of their uprooting.

Outside, on the cathedral's forecourt, the atmosphere is convivial. Everywhere, the talk is of return – who's gone, who's going, confessions of nervousness and apprehension. And then, a moment of irony as young Timorese aslyum-seekers are presented with a mock 'Certificate of Citizenship'

on behalf of Australia's Aboriginal community. The gesture of solidarity
aimed at unsettling the authority of the Australian state, also anticipated
the Australian government's withdrawal, on 19 November, of an appeal
against the earlier Federal Court decision in favour of the asylum-seekers.
Far from signifying a victory for the asylum-seekers, the withdrawal may
be seen as a stalling strategy while the government secures legislative
changes to immigration. The new legislation – primarily aimed at
stemming the flow of 'boat people' to Australia – will impact upon
Timorese applications for refugee status, some of which have been
pending for almost ten years. Most of the applicants are young. They are
concerned that their applications will be rejected given that East Timor is
now free and they no longer have grounds for claiming refugee status. In
the meantime, they must continue to wait, living their lives in a permanent
state of temporariness.

This chapter focuses on the personal and political dilemmas of young
Timorese, particularly in diasporic Sydney, now faced with the very
real possibility of an imminent return home; with the difficulties of
having to reconcile the different worlds of 'home' and 'away'; with
the pressures and responsibilities involved in negotiating the
expectations of Timorese families and communities, both at home
and in exile, that they will, indeed that they should, return and help
rebuild an independent East Timor. For young Timorese asylum-
seekers in Australia,[1] who currently await the outcome of convoluted
political and legal judgments that will determine their fate, these issues
are especially potent, but they are provocative issues, too, for Timorese
youth who have lived here longer and who feel more established in
their identities as 'Australian-Timorese'.

The identities young Timorese have constructed in exile,
underscored as they are by mythologies of home and return, are
profoundly unsettled in this current period of uncertainty and instability
within East Timor itself. Bereft of the very thing that has given
Timorese exile its meaning and coherence – the struggle for
independence – notions of home and belonging are in flux, as
complex and conflicting emotional attachments and ambivalences
now emerge to destabilise pre-ordained itineraries that insist on 'return'.

[1]   I am referring specifically here to East Timorese who have sought political
asylum in Australia during the 1990s and not to the most recent refugees who
arrived following the referendum in August 1999.

The struggle for independence gave Timorese lives, however they might have been lived, definition. That struggle was one thing. The struggle for 'survival' as a new nation now suddenly looms as a different reality altogether. Young Timorese in Australia privately express anguish at the difficult question of shared responsibility for it; at the prospect of 'starting over'. *Now we can go home, but do we really want to? Now we can return, but to what? Normality?* In the madness of post-independent East Timor, as aid agencies and carpetbaggers scrabble for opportunity and scarce resources, what place will there be for latecomers, even those that are supposed to belong?

As young Timorese ponder these questions, there is, for some, a sense of resignation, but even this may mask a deeper trepidation since the questions themselves may be too confronting, almost unspeakable in their contravention of parental and communal expectations. Refusing the rhetoric of 'return' may be interpreted within the wider Timorese community as unpatriotic, the ultimate betrayal, and may in fact confirm the corruption of Timorese youth by an impoverished and self-centred Australian culture. Outside East Timor, in diasporic Sydney at least, older generation Timorese lament the 'loss of culture' among the young.[2] Here, young Timorese are criticised for being too 'Australianised', for 'forgetting' the struggle, for being apathetic, apolitical, undisciplined, too materialistic. It is, indeed, their very adaptation to the cosmopolitan contexts in which they find themselves which is perceived as problematic.

Yet the experience of exile can also provide a space of creativity and critique which can lead to a critical self-awareness. Arguing against the revival of Portuguese language in East Timor,[3] Ivete de Oliveira,

[2] Indeed, the 'loss of culture' among the young is a recurrent theme among older Timorese, both within and outside of East Timor. On a visit to Timor in 1998, older people I spoke with frequently expressed their deep dismay at the declining moral order and loss of public 'etiquette' since 1975, contrasting their own childhood experiences with what they saw as a culturally and morally impoverished upbringing under the Indonesian system.
[3] This issue has caused deep resentment among Timorese youth both inside and outside of East Timor. For young Timorese educated within Indonesian schools and universities, the Timorese leadership's cultural preference and nostalgia for things Portuguese appears deeply suspect. In Baucau and Los Palos, Timorese youth have refused to attend Portuguese language classes, apparently rejecting the imposition of alien cultural values they perceive as meaningless to their current needs (Ceu Brites, pers. comm.).

210   *Fiona Crockford*

a young Timorese anthropology graduate educated in diasporic Java, is quoted in *The Sydney Morning Herald* (5/11/99) as saying:

> We think it is more useful for us to use Indonesian ... I think the older leaders have a strategy of keeping the young people down ... Maybe they are scared we want to join the leadership. We're very angry about this.

Her comments echo the concerns of a young, Canada-based, Timorese activist, Bella Galhos. Speaking at a conference in Sydney in April 1998,[4] she had argued that the range of political identifications then available to Timorese youth were too limiting given the changed, and changing, contexts in which they lived. In particular, she argued for the need to educate young women politically, in order to equip them for effective participation in formal political processes. She suggested that young women's reluctance to engage publicly in the political domain was partly due to cultural constraints that placed strict limits on their roles and behaviours. Thus, she had called for Timorese leadership to adopt a more flexible and democratic approach that would encourage the active inclusion of all young Timorese in decision-making processes.

Her criticisms caused considerable tension among Timorese participants at the conference. In keeping with the general tone of the conference, which took 'struggle' and 'solidarity' as its twin themes, others had kept the discussion within the frame of the nationalist struggle – in terms of a conflict between a Timorese 'us' and an Indonesian 'them'. Galhos, on the other hand, had interpreted the conference brief more broadly, raising questions concerning basic human rights and the democratic management of difference 'within' the Timorese community. For a community still engaged in unrelenting political struggle, Galhos's probing critique may almost have broken a taboo. Yet, as Timorese now begin to unravel and dismantle their colonised (Indonesian/Portuguese) selves and resituate themselves as citizens of a new nation, the democratic management of difference will become ever more pressing. Such important internal cultural debates, however, are too starkly framed in terms of inter-generational schisms. Cultural tensions do not solely exist along generational

---

[4] Bella Galhos was speaking as the co-ordinator of the Canada-based East Timor Alert Network (ETAN) at the Asia Pacific Solidarity Conference hosted by the Democratic Socialist Party, in a workshop entitled *Solidarity and Strategies for Victory in East Timor: Youth Perspectives*. She is now the Executive Director of the East Timor NGO Forum in Dili.

lines. Indeed, the focus on inter-generational conflict within the wider East Timorese community tends to obscure the complexity of social dynamics and overlooks the diversity of experience among Timorese youth itself.

Of the more than 1500 Timorese asylum-seekers currently in Australia, the majority are young people who have arrived since the 1991 Dili massacre. Indeed, many are survivors of the massacre. Their own socialisation as Indonesian-speaking Asians marks them off, not only from older generation Timorese socialised in a Portuguese colonial context, but from other Timorese youth born and/or educated in diaspora. As such, newer arrivals tend to draw a distinction between themselves as 'nineties' Timorese and young 'seventies' Timorese who have lived in Australia since 1975. Indeed, this difference is remarked upon by 'nineties' Timorese living elsewhere in diaspora. For example, young Timorese interviewed in the United Kingdom (who mostly sought asylum at foreign embassies in Jakarta in the mid-1990s) referred to their difference from Lisbon-based 'seventies' arrivals.

Conversely, 'seventies' Timorese youth have their own perspectives on and acknowledge their difference from 'nineties' Timorese who have been socialised in a completely different cultural, historical and, therefore political, context. While some defer to the 'authenticity' of 'nineties' Timorese experience and acquiesce to a perception of themselves as privileged, even spoilt, others are more defensive, sensitive to criticisms or judgments that may place their own Timoreseness, and experience, in question. And yet, these two groups are not, in reality, distinctly bound off from each other. In the Australian context, 'seventies' Timorese may include 'eighties' arrivals who may have translocated via Portugal, for example. More critically, other social relations may cut across these demarcation lines to reveal common experiences, according to gender, class, ethnicity and so on.

It is true that young 'nineties' arrivals articulate a sense of being closer to the struggle than 'seventies' Timorese youth and that, as such, they not only provide a vital link between home and diaspora but that they actively embody it. Recalling traumatic events, for example, scars on the body may be used to endorse testimonies. The physical body itself then becomes a site of remembrance whose authority cannot be denied: I am the evidence of the brutality of the Indonesian military regime. Among 'nineties' Timorese youth who have been active in the resistance and who continue to be involved in campaign work, there is also a sense of frustration with other Timorese youth in diaspora who are not active in, or who may have chosen to distance themselves from, the struggle, that they do not know real suffering and hardship. Many of these young people refer to their own lives in the diaspora in terms of 'struggle' and 'sacrifice';

> I do not feel psychologically free ... I realise life is a struggle that we must face and fight for our lives wherever we are. We must be courageous and suppress our feelings in order to keep going (*Doli*, Sydney, July 1999).

At the same time, they characteristically subordinate their own personal suffering and sacrifice to the trauma experienced by those 'at home';

> Psychologically it's awful because we're a long way from our families ... but it's not as bad for us as for those in Timor. Sometimes we feel guilty living [in diaspora]; we can go to movies, we are free ... (*Dino*, Dublin, September 1999).

> Young Timorese have to think about [the struggle] in general, not personal terms. If we compare our plight [in diaspora] with Timorese in Timor, especially Falintil, we have a different situation. They face the enemy. For us it's psychological pressure. It's different for exiles since '75. They have become more assimilated (*Kupa*, London, September 1999).

There is a discernible 'hierarchy of suffering' here which would seem to be integral to the construction of 'Timoreseness'. Prior to the Indonesian invasion of East Timor in 1975, there was little sense of a collective East Timorese identity. If it is true that the invasion served as a defining moment in the development of an East Timorese self-consciousness, when the people of East Timor began to recognise themselves as a true collectivity, united by the shared experience of their traumatic confrontation with Indonesia, then being a 'real' Timorese must partly be predicated on 'suffering'. This suffering is not just hierarchised, but spatialised in such a way that it must be continually re-inscribed in diaspora as a necessary condition of exile, with the notion of 'home' as an abiding destiny. Resident in Australia, but 'not-here' to stay,[5] the East Timorese community has routinely engaged in processes of 'remembering' and 'reliving' the past, most notably in their marking of evocative dates in their recent history and by re-enacting traumatic events (such as the Santa Cruz massacre).

[5]   I borrow the expression from James Clifford's discussion of diaspora discourses and the condition of simultaneous 'separation and entanglement' (1994:311) diasporic experience implies.

For young Timorese who have grown up here there is often a deep sense of responsibility for these unexperienced events:

> [my family have] continuously reminded me of the suffering of my people, reminded me of my identity, and to take full advantage of the opportunities offered here in Australia, so that one day I can return and help build East Timor (Santos 1996:25).

For some young Timorese, then, the 'weight' of responsibility has served to create a link to a home they barely remember or have never seen. Notions of 'home' and return may now appear less simple than they once did but, as permanent residents in Australia, they will have some measure of choice about how and when they return. For young Timorese asylum-seekers, however, as 'return' looms more imminently on the horizon, 'home' is no less simple as a concept and as a reality and choices are far more circumscribed. While many speak of their longing to be reunited with family and with the land, there is much to reconcile. There is the disjuncture between the physical homes they remember and those they will return to. There is the estrangement of the experiences of home and diaspora; the disentangling of lives lived in exile and the reassembling of lives as 'returnees'.

It is one of the tragedies of their specific displacement that young asylum-seekers have sacrificed their education, both in East Timor and in universities across Indonesia, only to be excluded from tertiary education within Australia. The Australian government's refusal to grant asylum-seekers permanent residency means that they have been classified as 'international students' and therefore expected to pay substantial fees for tertiary education. It also means that they have been unable to fulfil the specific task ascribed them by the leadership, namely, *to educate ourselves in order to empower ourselves with knowledge* (Exposto 1996:34). Their unresolved status here means that many continue to rely on Red Cross funding, or find employment where they can. Their options are limited. Some have undertaken TAFE vocational and English language courses, assisted by Catholic church organisations. Some currently work in unskilled and unstable jobs in factories, or as cleaners, or gardeners, as carers in nursing homes. As such, there is a general feeling of ambivalence and lack of preparedness for the 'return home'.

When asked how they feel about returning most will say that of course they *want* to go home but talk of deferral in order to finish, or to get, an education. Indeed, among 'nineties' Timorese youth, this is repeated like a mantra throughout the diaspora, from Dublin to London, to Lisbon, to Sydney:

> There is no doubt ... that [we] have the commitment to go back. There's a reason that some of us stay longer because [we] want to study and [we] want to get experience ... We're all concerned to return. The main concern is what we bring to East Timor. The people there need help. What kind of help are we going to give them? I can go there and build houses – this is the easy answer. But, in ten years' time, people [will] need people who have skills to transfer, to develop East Timor ... There's nothing to avoid – you have to go back (*Arsenio*, London, October 1999).

> We want to go back, but we want to go back *with* something (*Ligia*, Sydney, November 1999).

> I have to finish my diploma ... I want to bring something to my mother's grave [at Santa Cruz cemetery] (*Doli*, Sydney, November 1999).

> I haven't got any specific skills at the moment. I'm concerned about what is my profession. Because people will say 'you left the country for six years and what have you done there?' And I'm not going to say that I have been campaigning, because everybody's fighting for their country, not only me ... I would say most people who want to go back to Timor are people who left after 1990, or late 1980s. But from 1975 ... I think the youngers [sic], they will go to Timor to visit, not to stay. They can say 'I'm Timorese' but they don't have to go back ... I think that this will also be the work of the independent government of East Timor, how to convince these people to go back. You have to create possibilities. It is also the problem of reconciliation. The problem of re-encountering people again, Timorese in Portugal, in Australia, with Timorese who are in East Timor ... (*Boaventura*, London, October 1999).

As the last respondent suggests, after years of learning to survive as Timorese inside and outside of East Timor, and of coping with the different kinds of suffering those experiences entail, there is the additional problem of reconciling the different experiences – and perhaps 'cultures' – of home and exile; of war and peace. To fully grasp the realities of young Timorese lives, it seems necessary to develop an understanding that brings into focus, not only the complex relations of power that may operate to marginalise youth, but also the social relations that cut across those relations, to reveal commonalities. Underpinning the tensions and contradictions of their experiential diversity are fundamental

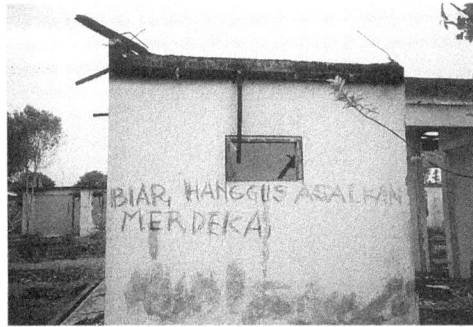

'Biar Hanggus Asalkan Merdeka' – *'Let them burn us out, just as long as we are free'; grafitti on an East Timorese house destroyed during the mayhem of September*

Above: *Refugee camp in Oecussi, marked with CNRT posters*

Left: *Reconstruction - young men carry away burnt timber as they begin to rebuild*

Right: *Xanana Gusmão
speaking to a gathering
in Baucau*

Below: *'People's
Citizenship for East
Timorese' – East
Timorese at a gathering
in Sydney*

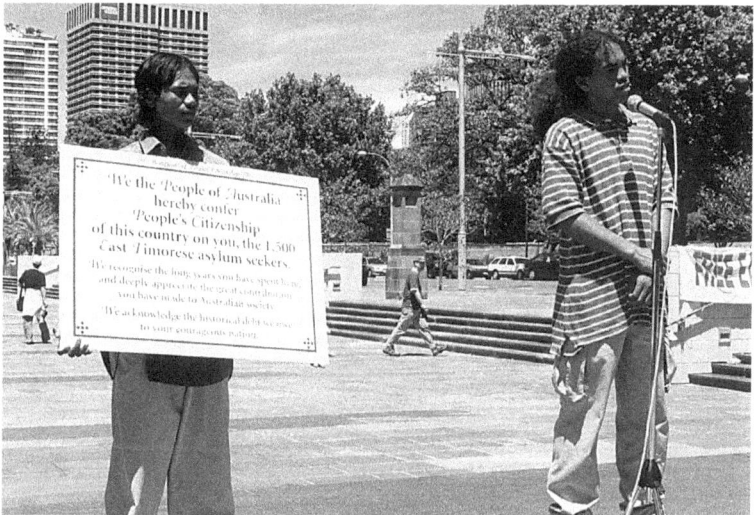

questions of identity. The challenge for a truly democratic leadership will be how to affirm and encourage a collective sense of East Timorese identity, while acknowledging the validity of the multiple dimensions of 'Timorese-ness'.

Acknowledgments

The ideas in this chapter are drawn from my doctoral research on youth identities in the East Timorese diaspora. Although my primary field site is in Sydney, I have also conducted fieldwork in the United Kingdom, in Ireland and in East Timor itself. I am indebted to the many young Timorese who have shared their thoughts and feelings with me over the past two years. My special thanks to Doli, Ligia, Kupa, Dino, Boaventura and Arsenio for giving me permission to include their words here, and to Bella Galhos for her generosity of spirit. I would also like to thank Professor James Fox and Dr Christine Helliwell for their editorial comments. Finally, this research would not have been possible without the support of my good friends at ETRA (East Timor Relief Association) in Sydney, especially Agio Pereira, Ines Almeida, Ceu Brites and Kieran Dwyer.

References

Clifford, James, 1994. 'Diasporas', *Cultural Anthropology* 9(3):302-338.

Exposto, Elizabeth, 1996. 'What it means to be Timorese', in *It's Time to Lead the Way: Writings from a Conference on East Timor and its People*. Melbourne: East Timor Relief Association, pp.32-35.

Santos, Maria Teresa, 1996. 'Personal experiences, thoughts and views about East Timor', in *It's Time to Lead the Way: Writings from a Conference on East Timor and its People*. Melbourne: East Timor Relief Association, pp.23-26.

Newspaper Articles

Lague, David, 1999. 'Colonial Divide Splits Timorese', *Sydney Morning Herald*, 5 November, pp.1, 12.

14

An international strategy for the new East Timor: some preliminary thoughts

Andrew MacIntyre

East Timor is an unlikely candidate for statehood. It is very small, very poor and war-torn. It has very little human capital, very little infrastructural or administrative capacity and a very large and possibly antagonistic neighbour. And yet a new state is indeed in the process of being born. Economic circumstances dictate that aid will be indispensable for the foreseeable future. Political and strategic circumstances dictate that the cultivation of international supporters willing to come to its assistance in the event of threats to its national security will also be indispensable for the foreseeable future. How East Timor positions itself and the terms on which it interacts with a range of countries and international organisations will have important consequences for the ultimate task of pursuing political stability and economic development. In short, an effective international strategy will be critical to the birth, development and survival of East Timor as an independent state.

In this brief essay, I attempt to think through the international outlook from the perspective of a new East Timorese government. The hurdles faced by this prospective state are truly daunting. The preliminary thoughts offered here are intended as a contribution to the discussion that must now go on among East Timorese leaders as they craft a strategy for engaging the region and the world. A strategy that serves the interests of a resistance or independence movement is unlikely to be a strategy that serves the interests of a new state.

There are important details about the 'shape' of the new East Timor which are not yet known and which will inevitably have a significant bearing upon the design and conduct of international strategy. For instance, we do not know what institutional framework of government will be adopted, we do not know what coalition of interests will be dominant in the new government, and we do not even know when the East Timorese will be able to begin governing themselves given the uncertainty about the scope and duration of the expected UN administrative mission. Although we are missing important pieces of information of this sort, we can nevertheless identify a range of issues that are going to be important for East Timor's interaction with the outside world. We can infer these from East Timor's domestic, political and economic circumstances, from the 'structure' of its international circumstances, and also from experiences from other parts of the world.

In broad terms, the leaders of the new East Timor have an acute need to seek friends internationally, on both a bilateral and multilateral basis. Without international support the new state will very probably fail at its two most fundamental and intertwined tasks: providing stability and security, and facilitating economic growth and development. Set out below is a brief discussion of a range of items that should be high on the agenda for discussion by East Timorese as they contemplate international engagement. These stretch from dealing with key countries and UN peacekeepers, through to questions of membership of multilateral organisations, border negotiations and human resources.

Perhaps the single most pressing international issue for East Timor is its relationship with Indonesia. No amount of aid will help East Timor to grow economically if domestic resources and the attention of policy-makers are tied down by protracted conflict with Indonesia. Private capital simply will not enter such an environment. It would be very easy for a hostile Indonesia to destabilise East Timor with cross-border raids or to continue active support for pro-integration militia groups or to obstruct air and sea access to East Timor. A key question, therefore, is: will Indonesia be actively hostile to East Timor?

If we look to other international experiences for insight, the nearest analogy is a post-colonial situation. In most cases, however unhappy the severance, it is very rare for colonial powers to actively harass their former colonies or to attempt to reverse the separation. The primary exception to this is cases in which there is a sizeable dispossessed émigré population that cannot be reconciled to the new situation and is able to exercise political influence within the former colonial power. Cuba and Ireland are among the few examples. It does not appear that this will be the case with East Timor. Although there has clearly been a genuine pro-integration portion of the East Timorese population – landholders, some business people, government officials, etc. – these people appear to have either abandoned their previous views or left East Timor for West Timor and other parts of Indonesia. There is little evidence at this stage to suggest that they are in a position to mount a rearguard action. Importantly, this group does *not* include the pro-integration militias who, for the most part, are hired thugs with changeable loyalties. With the departure of Indonesia, it is not at all clear that the militia have any real political constituency or social base inside East Timor.

If there appears not to be a critical mass of truly committed pro-integrationist émigrés capable of influencing Indonesian policy, there remains the possibility that the Indonesian government, or perhaps a section of the Indonesian military, might for its own reasons harass East Timor or provide remnants of the pro-integration militia with the resources to do so. Although there appears to be some activity of this sort still underway at the time of writing, in my judgment, it is very unlikely once the separation and human resettlement processes are *completed.* There are several reasons for believing this. First, Indonesia faces many deeply pressing problems of its own that will require enormous attention. Second, the great majority of Indonesians have little interest in East Timor and wish it no harm, so there is little domestic demand in Indonesia for an anti-East Timor posture. (This is in marked contrast to the situation in, for instance, China, where there is widespread and strong public sentiment that Taiwan is part of China.) Third, Indonesia stands to lose a great deal of international financial assistance were it to conduct or sponsor a campaign of violence or destabilisation against East Timor. Although quite unlikely, it is not impossible to construct scenarios under which this might happen, depending on how Indonesia's own political circumstances evolve.

What should East Timor do in this situation? East Timor has a clear interest in good rather than bad relations with Indonesia. If possible, in its direct dealings with Indonesia, East Timor needs to pursue a policy of functional diplomatic engagement. Notwithstanding the past violence and tension, as a matter of priority East Timor needs to work to find a means for diplomatic coexistence and, if practicable, co-operation. The bilateral relationship with Indonesia is unlikely ever to be close, but it is not unreasonable to think that it might be functional. There would be many advantages to East Timor if this were so.

Striving to build a working diplomatic relationship with Indonesia is, at best, only one component of an overall international strategy. East Timor also needs to have regard for the defence of its own national security. However, unlike other small states with large and potentially worrying neighbours – Cuba, Singapore, Israel – East Timor is simply not capable of developing a substantial indigenous defence capability in the near term. Self-help is not a realistic option for the time being. This points clearly to the need for East Timor to work assiduously to cultivate international support from key countries and agencies. In the short term, the most important such challenge is East Timor's relationship with the United Nations. This is particularly complex.

Without the involvement of the United Nations, East Timor would not now be separating from Indonesia. Equally, without the involvement of the United Nations, East Timor will face an extremely uncertain short-term future. The current UN-sponsored International Force in East Timor (Interfet), armed with a Chapter 7 mandate for active peace-enforcement, has been essential to pushing back the threat posed by the departing pro-integration militia. This Australian-led force will soon be replaced by a UN administrative mission and peace-keeping operation. Although less potent in military terms (working with a milder Chapter 6 mandate) the expected peace-keeping mission would be a significant element in deterring the possibility of serious Indonesian-sponsored destabilisation efforts, since this would almost assuredly trigger punitive action against Indonesia by the international community.

UN involvement is thus of vital importance to East Timor. But, perversely, the UN is also a potential hazard for the new state. There is a danger that the planned UN bureaucratic presence in East Timor will stifle or retard the political processes that East Timorese leaders and the East Timorese population need to work through for themselves. The nation-building and state-building tasks ahead of East Timor involve much more than neutral monitoring and peace-keeping activities. Hard political bargains need to be reached on fundamental issues like constitutional design, the creation of an indigenous security force and so on. If, as is quite likely, the UN has complete authority in the 'administration' of East Timor and local political leaders are kept to the side in a tame consultative capacity, there is a real danger of artificial and politically unsustainable outcomes being reached. By comparison with its international record for peace-keeping and election monitoring operations and even peace-enforcement operations, the UN's record for state-building is poor. The experience in Somalia is a stark illustration of this. Unlike Somalia or Cambodia, the UN will in effect have a clean political slate in East Timor, since the previous political elite has departed. This may mean that the UN mission will assume broad ranging government powers. No matter how well intentioned, the potential for unsustainable political arrangements to be imposed is considerable.

This creates a delicate dilemma for East Timor: on the one hand it desperately needs UN involvement, but on the other it must be very wary of a stifling and prolonged UN presence once it arrives. Accordingly, at the same time as working closely with the UN to facilitate the rapid establishment of the new peace-keeping mission, East Timorese leaders will need to push hard to maximise their voice in the conduct of the mission. As my colleague Peter Timmer puts it in his companion essay on developmental priorities in this volume, East Timor will need to ensure that there is a clear exit-strategy for the UN.

Looking beyond the UN involvement, because East Timor cannot sustain a self-help strategy, it is imperative that it work to build an extensive and diverse network of international support. This will be important for both security and economic development. The wider the network of international support – especially among wealthy countries – the greater the access East Timor is likely to have to economic assistance. And the wider the network of support, the more focused pressure can be brought to be bear upon Indonesia, should this actually be necessary.

The two countries with the greatest commitment to supporting the birth of East Timor are Portugal and Australia. East Timorese leaders will need to build close and effective ties with these two countries and may, to some extent, be able to play them off against each other in order to maximise financial assistance. In addition to material support, Portugal also matters because of its potential to help mobilise wider support within the European Union. Australia matters greatly too, because in addition to aid, it is the country most likely to come quickly to East Timor's assistance in the event of a serious external threat. However, as with the United Nations, very close involvement with either of these countries also carries risks of excessive dependency for East Timor. The chronic problems of nearby Papua New Guinea are a reminder that too close an embrace from even a well-intentioned aid-giver can compound rather than alleviate developmental problems.

Geographic proximity suggests that this is more likely to be a problem with Australia than Portugal. For instance, a possibility that may well emerge in discussion in the near future is that East Timor should enter a security agreement of some form with Australia. In my view this is a bad idea and should be rejected by East Timor's new leaders. A defence agreement with Australia is both unnecessary and very probably also harmful. It is unnecessary because Australia is already heavily invested in the successful birth of an independent East Timor. For many years there was a bipartisan consensus in Australia to resist the idea of an independent East Timor as unwelcome and unrealistic given political realities in Indonesia. This position was reversed as circumstances in Indonesia and East Timor changed radically in the wake of the financial crisis and the fall of Soeharto. Having invested heavily in helping to uphold the outcome of the referendum for East Timorese independence by sending a large military contingent, and with this new position enjoying wide support within Australia, Canberra is most unlikely to ignore calls for assistance if East Timor's security is seriously threatened. Quite simply, given the military and moral commitment Australia has now made, provided East Timorese leaders manage the bilateral relationship with Australia carefully, a security agreement would be superfluous. But more than this, not only would a formal agreement add no additional increment of security, it may in fact carry significant costs. A security agreement with Australia would increase the danger of a PNG-like dependency, it would increase the likelihood of difficult relations with Indonesia, and it would reduce the ability of East Timor to forge its own path and identity in South-east Asia. East Timor already enjoys a de facto Australian security umbrella; formalising this would bring no benefits and possibly significant costs.

While cultivating relations with Australia and Portugal, East Timor will also need to reach quickly beyond them and build working links with a range of other global and regional players. The key candidates are obvious: the United States and Japan. The United States is pivotal because no significant international peace-keeping operation can take place without its support and because it is able to use its leverage within the International Monetary Fund and the World Bank to bring pressure to bear upon financially dependent countries. The United States will not be a leading provider of aid for East Timor, but it could be the ultimate guarantor of its security. The reverse is true of Japan. Japan demands attention because, unlike the United States, it is a very large provider of aid, particularly in the Asian region. Japan has already promised to provide US$100 m to support the planned UN peace-keeping mission. Although Japanese development assistance typically follows Japanese corporate investment abroad, even modest assistance would have major significance for tiny East Timor. Ideally, a diverse international consortium of donors (modelled perhaps on the Consultative Group on Indonesia) will emerge to help finance the rehabilitation and development of East Timor's economy.

Beyond the United States and Japan, three other countries warrant special attention from East Timor's leaders: the Philippines, Thailand and China. The Philippines may be a natural ally for East Timor, as the other Catholic nation in the region and, moreover, one with a strong commitment to democracy. Similarly, Thailand's strong commitment to democracy may engender natural sympathy for the plight of East Timor. Both Thailand and the Philippines have assumed an openly pro-democracy posture with ASEAN and been outspoken on the need for a more critical intraregional approach to human rights problems. While not being able to provide substantial financial support or security guarantees, the Philippines and Thailand may be able to provide valuable advocacy within South-east Asia on East Timor's behalf. This will be important if East Timor is to evolve into a truly independent state in its own right rather than, for instance, a frail Australian dependency.

The most interesting and least obvious potential diplomatic target of opportunity for East Timor is China. Given China's authoritarian political framework and the questions surrounding the status of Tibet and Taiwan, China may seem an unlikely target for diplomatic efforts by East Timor. Further, there are obvious potential difficulties with this given the periodic tensions in China's relations with both Japan and the United States. Nevertheless, China does have the potential to

be an important interlocutor for East Timor. It is important to keep
in mind that without China's consent, neither the current UN peace-
enforcement mission nor the planned peace-keeping mission could
proceed. As a member of the UN Security Council, China could
easily have exercised its veto privilege. Indeed, many observers were
surprised that China did not do so, given the Tibet issue. Building a
friendly relationship with Beijing may help if the Security Council is
called upon again to make another pivotal decision on action regarding
East Timor. The principal opportunity cost of this strategy would be
that East Timor would have to forgo any offer of financial assistance
in exchange for recognition by Taiwan.

Turning from countries that are likely to be of particular
importance for East Timor, three other more general issues require
attention: membership of multilateral organisations, border
negotiations and human resources. Small- and medium-sized states
are typically enthusiastic joiners of multilateral institutions. This will
be particularly important for a very vulnerable state like East Timor.
Membership of the United Nations is the first priority, as an
affirmation of East Timor's formal credentials as a new member of
the community of states. I would argue that the second priority is
membership of ASEAN. Membership of ASEAN would help to
cement East Timor's credentials with the region as an entity
independent from Indonesia; it may carry some modest developmental benefits if plans for South-east Asia-wide economic co-
operation gain real momentum; and it would also help East Timor
avoid becoming locked into an Australia-centric orbit. There will, of
course, be some resistance from within ASEAN to East Timorese
membership, but good working relations with the Philippines and
Thailand may well help here.

Along with membership of some potentially helpful multilateral
organisations, an issue that the new East Timor will have to face fairly
quickly is uncertainty about some of its borders. There are two
dimensions to this: one concerns Indonesia, and the other Indonesia
and Australia. With regard to Indonesia, the immediate issue is the
historical enclave of Ambeno (Oecussi) on the north coast of West
Timor, which is officially to be part of East Timor. This historical
anomaly has the potential to be a source of major difficulty for East
Timor. Not being geographically contiguous to East Timor it will be
very costly to service and defend. Given that relatively few people

live there and it has no major economic significance, it may well be that East Timor should consider trading this small geographical outpost with Indonesia for some suitable territorial or policy concession. It may be that this can be profitably tied in with the second border issue – the handling of the 'Timor Gap' maritime border zone. Under an earlier agreement between Australia and Indonesia it was decided that the oil resources believed to lie beneath the seabed in the disputed zone would be jointly exploited. It may be that there will be a frictionless deal to transfer Indonesian territorial rights vis-à-vis Australia and the treaty zone to East Timor. However the situation could easily become much more messy and contentious. Although not an immediate priority, this is an issue that is going to require careful attention.

Finally, complicating all of these questions, is the issue of human resources. It is all very well to produce a shopping list of foreign policy priorities, but pursuing the various objectives outlined here requires financial resources and appropriately skilled personnel. Maintaining embassies and servicing even minimal membership obligations in international organisations would place a severe drain on foreign currency resources for East Timor. Even more difficult will be finding the personnel to conduct these international operations. Given that East Timor will not be able to maintain many permanent missions and has only a very small number of internationally experienced personnel on which to draw, great care will be needed in selecting a small team of individuals who can perform these tasks on a moving basis. There are also questions of style and tactics. Until now, international strategy for the East Timorese resistance movement has been largely conducted by the exiled Nobel Laureate José Ramos Horta. The tactics he has successfully employed in the past are very unlikely to be the tactics that will serve now that East Timor is achieving statehood. Searing criticism that captures the attention of the international media will increasingly need to be replaced with quiet bargaining that captures the attention of international bureaucrats and politicians.

The challenges ahead for the world's newest state are truly daunting. There are many acute domestic problems needing urgent attention. But critical to many of these will be the ability of the country's new leaders to craft an effective strategy for dealing with the outside world. In this essay, I have attempted to view the world from the perspective of a policy-maker in the new East Timor and have outlined some key ingredients for consideration in the construction of an international strategy. There will be some hard choices here as East Timor struggles to weigh up competing priorities. Nevertheless, these are choices East Timor's leaders will have to confront as they struggle to make the transition from a disparate resistance movement to a fledgling state.

Acknowledgments

This chapter has benefited from discussions with Saleh Afiff, Miles Kahler, João Mariano de Saldanha, Peter Timmer, Barbara Walter and Nancy Viviani.

15

Questions for the United Nations team managing East Timor

C. Peter Timmer

East Timor is starting from scratch. Even in the context of war-torn societies, the historical record is sparse indeed on lessons for a new country with so little in the way of institutions, physical capital and experienced civil servants with which to form a government. What follows then is a series of questions for the UN managers in charge of the transition process from the burned out shell of the Indonesian (and Portuguese) legacy to a sustainable and independent East Timorese government. Some speculation on plausible answers is provided, but as much to stimulate serious thinking very early in the development process as to defend particular approaches. These questions, and the rough attempts at answers, draw heavily on two sources: the paper by Jonathan Haughton (1998), and my own experience in the early stages of transition economies in East and South-east Asia (and Russia).

It is difficult to categorise the questions into economic or political, domestic or international. For example, a fundamental question facing the new country will be its relationship with Indonesia, with whom it will share a land border to the west, access to sea lanes from its ports, and concerns about control of airspace for commercial and military aircraft. A hostile Indonesia will virtually guarantee that East Timor remains poor and undeveloped, as investors, tourists (and even donors), will not brave hostile fire on ships, aircraft, or personnel. How to maintain the territorial integrity of East Timor is obviously a political question, but one fraught with economic dimensions as well, both because of the cost of an independent defence force and the burden to a trade-oriented economy of severely restricted commercial access. The example of the United States' embargo of Cuba highlights the potential problem that East Timor could face if a peaceful arrangement with Indonesia cannot be negotiated and enforced.

Based on the experiences of other societies trying to build a development-oriented government in the wake of devastating wars, as reported by Haughton, the problems build from broad and philosophical to narrow and specific. The problems are partly a matter for domestic politicians to resolve as peace is established, but the donor community also tends to play very extensive roles in the initial transition from war to peace and from destruction to development. This community ranges from the IMF and World Bank, with expert teams, technical assistance and development loans, to emergency relief agencies engaged in feeding the hungry and tending to their wounds. A very basic question for these donors, and a question that is particularly acute for the UN Mission about to undertake the entire management of East Timor for two to three years, is when should they leave? Equally important, who will decide?

Put another way, what criteria can be established now that will determine when the reconstruction phase has been a success, and an independent East Timor can be treated as a small but viable country on the road to economic well-being? Are these criteria primarily political, so that when honest elections have selected a representative government, it will be time for the UN team to go home? Or should the criteria primarily be economic, so that the UN agenda is not complete until, say, per capita incomes have returned to their previous peak? The time horizons of the two different criteria are likely to vary considerably. Haughton suggests, for example, that economic recovery to previous levels takes at least a decade after peace is restored, and this is in societies with more human and physical capital intact than in East Timor. By contrast, there seems little doubt that an election in an independent East Timor could select a popular and representative government within six to twelve months if that were the UN agenda. The likely president of this independent East Timor, Xanana Gusmão, has articulated a vision of a free and open society with an economy based on agriculture, trade, mineral development, and tourism. This vision sits comfortably with Western donors and argues for heavier weight on political stability as the main criteria for the departure of an interim UN administration, rather than a return to previous economic levels.

Still, even if the UN time horizon is shorter rather than longer in terms of its resident mission, East Timor will need donor funds for reconstruction and development for decades to come. Indonesia still receives massive funding from the World Bank and other donors; there is no reason to believe that East Timor can outgrow similar needs any faster. Where will this money come from, after the world's attention has moved on to the next televised crisis? Indonesia is a large and important country in both geopolitical terms and, at least potentially, in economic terms. It commands attention for its size and importance, although the United States was very slow to recognise this. East Timor is tiny on both counts, but it has touched the world's conscience and a groundswell of public opinion more or less forced the Western powers to intervene. But such opinion is short-lived and will not be the basis for long-term attention from aid donors. Somehow a case needs to be made for continuing substantial amounts of aid (in per capita terms), a case that will get more difficult as East Timor establishes its own voice and progressively begins to reject the kind of conditionality that is now commonplace with nearly all donors. Although Gusmão is now using the very language that donors like to hear – Western-style democracy, open institutions, diversified economy driven by exports, and so on – he is also rejecting a 'culture of dependency' that the society could easily be prone to if its affairs and finances are managed for long by outsiders. Real tensions are going to erupt over the need for foreign resources for faster growth and control of the country's destiny.

Part of these tensions will be over the size of government itself. There is surprising diversity in both the developed and developing world on the scale and scope of government. If the neo-liberal consensus argues for a small government focused on tasks unique to the need for collective action (and commensurate with the human capital available to staff a civil service), a political economy perspective would argue that the institutions supporting a larger role for the private sector and civil society are conspicuous by their absence in East Timor, and they take a long time to build. A competent government can be built more quickly, especially since it starts from zero and thus faces little hostility from an entrenched bureaucracy. From the beginning, then, a larger and more aggressive role for government may be both popular and successful. In this debate, the donors may need to take a back seat despite fairly clear preferences, especially at the World Bank. The bank's views will be important not just because of the money it brings to the table but also because of the intellectual forces the bank can bring to the debate. East Timor may also want some technical assistance in dealing with donors and their advisors.

Part of the debate over the role of the government versus the private sector in war-torn economies is simply empirical – how quickly can commodity and factor markets get back to work, and who will have earliest access to them? Just as there is considerable opposition in Asia to selling off 'national treasures' at distressed prices to satisfy IMF conditions for emergency loans during the financial crisis, so too do vulnerable societies feel cheated when outside capital and expertise is able to take advantage of newly emerging market opportunities faster than impoverished inhabitants. 'What did we fight for?' then becomes a political rallying cry for curbs on foreign trade and investment, curbs which are unlikely to form the basis for rapid and equitable economic growth. Putting sensible guidelines in place early on is thus crucial, but obviously depends on a competent government with both the mandate and human resources to design and implement such a regulatory structure. Although 'positive' political economists may cringe at the opportunity thus generated to collect economic rents, the dilemma is real enough and cannot be hidden under a market-oriented mantra. Despite the fact that 'sustainable development' has come to have an environmental connotation, political sustainability of growth-oriented policies and institutions arguably comes first.

What policies and institutions need to be developed first? Even though initially in the hands of the temporary UN mission, the early development efforts are likely to have considerable inertia, so it is important to point the entire institution-building and policy-making process in the right direction. Haughton argues that the institutions underpinning macroeconomic stability and credibility with investors, foreign and domestic, should come first, but that might be a particularly economic perspective on the question. Especially in East Timor, which starts from almost zero in all institutions except the Roman Catholic church, social and political institutions may be equally important. If the UN mission is successful in stabilising the economy, even at a low level, through its flow of resources and appropriate management, building trust among neighbours and establishing local political dialogue are likely to pay very high dividends in terms of long-term sustainability of the society. These civic and political institutions are just as important as economic institutions to East Timor's success. Accordingly, they deserve substantial attention right from the beginning by the UN mission.

A number of less general, but still important, issues will need to be faced quite early on in the reconstruction process. Property rights are at the top of this more specialised list, for two reasons. First, there is real confusion over what legal code to use and the validity of historical claims to property, especially land. Second the presence of much deserted land and urban (shells of) buildings in the wake of owners fleeing or being killed is likely to start a spontaneous squatter process that will be difficult to reverse. Without clear guidelines on property rights and ownership, the UN peace-keeping forces will be powerless to stop this process. In the slightly longer run, without clear property rights, investors will be reluctant to start the rebuilding process except for emergency repairs to basic shelter.

A final topic that needs immediate attention and agreement from an interim East Timorese government is what currency the new country will use. There is an obvious temptation to establish a central bank and the country's own currency, but there are two reasons for caution in this direction. First, the cost of maintaining an independent currency and central bank are substantial and the East Timorese economy will be quite small. Second, management of a domestic currency and the main-tenance of a competitive exchange rate are difficult tasks, easily captured by special interests who gain from currency manipulation or over-valuation. Although there is substantial academic debate over the relative merits of fixed versus floating exchange rates, for East Timor a simpler option would be to adopt the US dollar as the domestic currency.

The details of dollarisation would need to be worked out, but the de facto reality is that most trade is denominated in dollars, most aid will be converted to or paid directly in dollars, and most savers and investors will use dollars to avoid the uncertainty and instability of possible alternatives, such as the Indonesian rupiah or a new East Timorese currency. Both economic growth and stability are likely to be served by not driving the dollar economy underground, but by making it the legal as well as de facto currency. Local coins and notes could be issued on the basis of dollars held in reserves to facilitate day-to-day transactions, but dollarisation would help the country avoid one of the major sources of instability and rent seeking in the new economy.

Many questions have been raised, and few answers offered with any sense of confidence. How is a new government to know what to do? When a new regime starts in an established country, such as Indonesia in 1967, China in 1978, the Philippines in 1986, or Vietnam in 1989, there is a combination of old institutions, policies, and people that represent continuity, at the same time that new opportunities are created by the mandate for change. Economic history offers important lessons to these transition economies, but much is being learned from them as well. A similar situation exists for East Timor, but with important differences. East Timor is not a 'transition' economy. It is a new economy, building institutions, policies, human and social capital, and political legitimacy almost from scratch. Haughton's survey of the issues facing war-torn economies finds a remarkable body of research on these issues from a distressingly large sample of countries – 42 countries damaged by war since 1970.

East Timor has the opportunity to learn and benefit from this research, but it can also contribute to the future development of other similar examples – and there will be others – by allowing, even encouraging, research on its own efforts at nation-building. Some plans will work, others will fail. It will be important to know why. Entrepreneurial initiative will emerge serendipitously or be squashed by authorities – how can it be channelled productively rather than seen as a threat to a new government? If there is any benefit at all to starting over in the wake of the devastation visited on East Timor, it will be the opportunity to learn from this extraordinary set of circumstances about how people and institutions respond to challenge and crisis. Godspeed.

Reference

Haughton, Jonathan, 1998. 'The reconstruction of war-torn economies', HIID/CAER II Discussion Paper No. 23, June.

16

The Joint Assessment Mission and reconstruction in East Timor

Sarah Cliffe[1]

On October 29, a group of 24 people drove into Dili from Comoro airport. They watched through the windows of the UN bus as a vista of burnt houses, bombed banks and businesses and waving kids spread out before them. For some of the group, this was their first visit back to the country in 24 years – for all it was the first sight of the reality behind the news footage of destruction. This was the first group to arrive in East Timor to assess reconstruction needs, as part of the Joint Assessment Mission (JAM) of East Timorese and international specialists. In order to be able to look beyond immediate humanitarian needs, the group was tasked with identifying priority reconstruction programs and with assessing the cost of reconstruction.

The World Bank, which was responsible for co-ordinating the mission, had created a separate East Timor program in April 1999. This included contributing to an analysis on the East Timorese economy and poverty situation to a Columbia University study, and organising training on reconstruction planning and economic management for five East Timorese economists in Washington. As the ballot approached, the Bank discussed with the President

---

[1] Sarah Cliffe was Deputy Mission Leader of the Joint Assessment Mission and is now Chief of the World Bank Mission in East Timor. The views expressed in this chapter are solely those of the author and do not represent the official views of the World Bank.

of the CNRT, Xanana Gusmão, and with the United Nations Department of Political Affairs, facilitating a training seminar on reconstruction planning with both pro-independence and pro-integration sides of the then-to-be-formed consultative commission. This – it was planned – would lead to a meeting of donors in Washington at the end of September to discuss East Timor's reconstruction needs.

As jubilation after the ballot quickly turned into a concerted campaign of violence, all these plans disappeared in a puff of smoke. East Timor burnt. We went back to consult with both the UN and Timorese leadership. Should we continue with the Washington meeting in September? Yes, was the answer – now more than ever, international support and resources would be needed to repair the damage caused after the ballot. The donors' meeting of 29 September was addressed by Xanana Gusmão and José Ramos Horta, who sent a strong message that international support to reconstruction in East Timor, whilst desperately needed, should be well co-ordinated and should be identified in a joint process with East Timorese representatives. In response, the September meeting endorsed the idea of a Joint Assessment Mission on reconstruction in East Timor.

The Joint Assessment Mission was 'joint' in two senses. Firstly, every international member was paired with an East Timorese expert, including the mission co-ordinator and deputy. This was critical in ensuring the input of Timorese knowledge of conditions and priorities. More indirectly, the joint teams also ensured that the whole mission acted as a capacity-building exercise on reconstruction planning for the East Timorese mission members. Secondly, the international side of the mission came from a broad range of bilateral and multilateral donors and international organisations. Mission members were contributed by the Asian Development Bank, Australia, the European Union, Japan, Portugal, the United Kingdom, UNDP, UNHCR, UNICEF, USAID, WHO and the World Bank.[2] UNTAET assigned a deputy co-ordinator to the mission, who was responsible for ensuring compatibility with the United Nations Security Council resolution on East Timor. The

2   Other UN agencies, in particular OCHA and WFP, also provided a great deal of help on the ground.

mission was accompanied by a concurrent mission of the International Monetary Fund (IMF). The Bretton Woods institutions were involved unusually early on in East Timor, with a view to ensuring that economic perspectives entered right at the beginning of the debate on reconstruction priorities and costs.

The Joint Assessment Mission addressed eight sectors: community empowerment (dealing with local-level initiatives for social and economic reconstruction); macroeconomic management; civil service; judiciary; agriculture; education; health; and infrastructure. A fairly standard approach was used by each team. Teams spent one day in Darwin, discussing terms of reference and issues to be covered internally between team members. On arrival in Dili, teams in general spent the first one to two days in the capital, making contact with local specialists, ex-civil servants and international organisations in their areas. Each team then made field visits. Teams such as agriculture and infrastructure, for whom it is critical to get out and see the physical condition of buildings and crops, and talk with communities, spent almost all their time outside Dili. Input from communities was taken through meetings held in each sector team, and by a large town hall meeting in Dili which was addressed by Mario Carrascalão and Klaus Rohland, the joint mission leaders. Comments made at this meeting addressed not only urgent priorities for the population, but also strong feelings about respecting Timorese tradition and culture in the development of the aid program.

Working and living conditions were difficult during the assessment, reflecting the devastation which the population at large had experienced. All 50 team members lived in tents, sharing one big auditorium at the back of the governor's office. Water and electricity were intermittent, and team members on field visits ate military rations. Keeping this 'tent city' organised and reasonably sanitary was a full time job during the mission.[3] Critical assistance was given by UNTAET and AusAID, who provided most of the materials necessary for the mission. Everything from drinking water to military rations were flown in from Darwin with the assistance of UNTAET and AusAID: without this help the mission would have been impossible to conduct.

[3] Lisa Campeau, who organised the logistics for the JAM, achieved the impossible in this regard.

What were the main results of the assessment? Economically, the country has taken a major hit, in particular in the modern sectors. The mission estimated that GDP dropped by approximately 40 per cent in 1999 due to the disruption caused by the violence and population displacement. Buildings and equipment in the small modern sector were comprehensively destroyed or looted, including the complete destruction of the banking system infrastructure. Depositors lost access to savings held in the Indonesian banking system.[4] Power generation and distribution capacity was gravely damaged. Whilst road and transport infrastructure were not deliberately targeted, lack of maintenance and heavy use by military vehicles have caused a substantial deterioration. The return of Indonesians has caused a shortage of skilled personnel for the secondary and tertiary sectors, where Timorese were very often excluded from holding technical positions. However, there are reasons for cautious optimism. Production of staple foods, which constitutes the base of the Timorese economy, should revive substantially over the coming year to 65-70 per cent of 1998 levels. The coffee crop, a critical export earner, is estimated to come in during 2000 at levels consistent with the East Timor average.

Institutionally, the total collapse of the state is the critical area blocking rapid reconstruction. The civil service is not currently functioning at any level in East Timor. Over 70 per cent of administrative buildings have been partially or completely destroyed, and almost all office equipment and consumable materials have been destroyed. Government archives have been destroyed or removed. Accurate figures are not available on the number of civil servants remaining in the territory, but at least 20-25 per cent – those estimated to be of Indonesian origin – are likely to have left. Indonesian civil servants were concentrated in the higher grades and skilled technical positions, so this creates a serious skill deficit for the civil service. The Joint Assessment Mission concluded that institutional capacity at the local level had been less severely damaged than at the central level – whilst the Indonesian local governance arrangements have been rejected by the population, other traditional or resistance local structures are functioning.

In the social sectors, even prior to the post-ballot violence, East Timor under Indonesian occupation was characterised by very low

---

4   Unless they are able to travel to Indonesia to withdraw funds, an option which is not open to most families.

education and health outcomes: life expectancy was only 55 years and literacy rates were low. In health, this precarious situation has been further threatened by population displacement, pyscho-social stress, food insecurity, breakdown of water and sanitation and the collapse of almost all health services. The health system has lost all fixed equipment and consumables, and 130 out of 160 physicians. 75-80 per cent of primary schools were estimated during the mission to have been partially or completely destroyed, and the secondary school sector lost approximately 80 per cent of its teachers. Most textbooks and teaching materials were looted or destroyed.

The priorities identified during the mission covered a gamut of reconstruction initiatives, designed to take over as the humanitarian program wound down in around June 2000. Rehabilitation of physical infrastructure was of course a priority in all sectors, but was accompanied by identification of programs to restart agricultural activities and – over three years – improve productivity; to substitute teachers and doctors and train Timorese health and education workers; for local governance and community empowerment and support to Timorese culture; and for capacity-building in the civil service and judiciary. In total, the programs recommended by the Joint Assessment Mission reached a budget of $302 m over three years.

Some of the most sensitive recommendations were in the area of the civil service. The Joint Assessment Mission recommended that the civil service be reconstituted with only 12 200 civil servants, down from over 28 000 before the ballot. The mission noted that the Indonesian civil service had been characterised by:

- over-staffing, with 3.4 per cent of the population compared to an Asian average of 2.6 per cent;
- too many layers of bureaucracy for a small country, fostering inefficient decision-making and opportunities for graft;
- duplication of functions between line ministries and decentralised departments;
- a top-down organisational culture, with little community participation and marginalisation of traditional local decision-making structures; and
- exceptionally low pay levels, encouraging the establishment of legal and illegal fringe benefits.

A smaller leaner civil service was to allow for more professionalism, supported by higher wage levels than the Indonesian civil service. These recommendations were at all times strongly supported by the Timorese leadership.

How were relations between the Timorese and international team members? Press reports midway through the mission alleged criticisms from Xanana Gusmão, and unhappiness on the part of Timorese team members that their opinions were insufficiently respected by international counterparts. Most of this seems to have been misreporting by the press, and a survey of Timorese team members by their own co-ordinators showed that they wished the joint assessment model to be repeated in other aid programming missions. There were many heated debates between mission members as recommendations were developed, but this was, after all, a major objective of the exercise – to ensure that Timorese priorities and international aid perspectives were brought together to the table and a common path forward agreed upon.

The mission recommendations were taken to a donor meeting in Tokyo on 17 December, co-chaired by SRSG Sergio Vieira de Mello and World Bank Vice President Jean-Michel Severino. This meeting – the first ever donor meeting jointly chaired by the World Bank and the UN secretariat – was innovative in jointly presenting the humanitarian program, the recurrent budget together with reconstruction financing needs.

The Tokyo meeting was attended by over 25 donor countries and 15 UN agencies and NGOs. Discussions at the meeting focused on institutional mechanisms to ensure rapid disbursement of aid, and the need for Timorese leadership at all levels in planning and implementing the aid program. Pledges by donors at the meeting totalled US$522 m, of which US$149 m was dedicated to humanitarian needs, with the remainder split between the recurrent and development budgets. Donors gave an unprecedented level of support to the two trust fund mechanisms established during the meeting: over US$215 m was pledged to the World Bank trust fund for reconstruction and the UNTAET trust fund for recurrent budget and civil service capacity-building. The East Timorese leadership, UNTAET and the Bank agreed with donors that six-monthly meetings would be held to review progress on the reconstruction program and adjust cash flow and financing needs.

What seem to be the lessons of the donor co-ordination process which centred around the Joint Assessment Mission? We are still at the beginning of the reconstruction phase in East Timor, and it is difficult to identify all the strengths and weaknesses. My own – personal and preliminary – evaluation points to the following:

Economic reconstruction assessment missions, including involvement of the Bretton Woods organisations, need to occur early on after a conflict. At the time of the East Timor Joint Assessment Mission, several commentators conveyed the view that the assessment was premature: the humanitarian crisis was close to its peak, population movements made situation assessment difficult, counterparts were hard to identify. Yet there is a long lag time between such assessments, mobilisation of funds, programming of reconstruction projects and disbursement on the ground. Going in early meant that the reconstruction programs and projects will start before the humanitarian program winds down – any later, and there would have been a dangerous gap between humanitarian aid and reconstruction assistance. Furthermore, even if humanitarian agencies are taking on the burden of 'transitional' economic recovery projects, these are unlikely to be drawn up within the framework of a sustainable macroeconomic program unless a full economic reconstruction mission is launched.

To mitigate the problems of attempting an early assessment, missions need to:

• respect the need to focus most efforts on the immediate humanitarian disaster, by minimising demands of time from counterparts in humanitarian agencies, and supporting humanitarian agencies in mobilising financial resources;

• focus the assessment on arriving at aggregate cost estimates, with appropriate contingency for population movements and other unknowns, not on developing project outlines which may be subject to later change;

• stress to mission members that counterparts – in the usual sense of government officials who can provide data and programmatic direction, and undertake follow-up work – may not be available: mission members need to concretely assist the governing authorities to develop basic data, regulations or policy needed to restart economic activities and social services.

Ensure strong national leadership in the process of defining reconstruction needs, and a balance of local inputs to the process. At the time of the Joint Assessment Mission, CNRT was emerging from a banned movement under Indonesian occupation to being the dominant political force. Ensuring that the mission worked closely with CNRT leadership and technical officials was critical in gaining national ownership of recommendations.[5] However, it was still important that the Timorese mission members represented a variety of views within the country: whilst all members were nominated by CNRT, CNRT leadership therefore tried to ensure that roughly 50 per cent were not CNRT members. Failures of the mission in this regard were perhaps in two areas:

1. the balance of exiled and internal Timorese representatives on the mission tended rather heavily to the exiles, who represented roughly half of all mission members. Whilst mission members from the diaspora showed an exceptional level of commitment and expertise, this risked a failure to draw input from, and build capacity for, the critical internal cadres who will stay in the country on a permanent basis;
2. there was insufficient time or resources to build a really bottom-up process of defining reconstruction needs. Whilst several consultations were held in Dili during the mission, more time invested might have seen efforts to organise local groups in developing lists of reconstruction priorities.

The process of assessing reconstruction needs can in itself be a capacity-building exercise. One of the key benefits of the Joint Assessment Mission was the increase in knowledge and skills for mission members. On the Timorese side, some mission members had previously worked in the international development sector: for others, it was a first exposure to the approach and analytical tools used by international agencies. The intensive analysis performed during the JAM offered a good opportunity to Timorese mission members to learn new

---

[5] This is less simple in a post-conflict situation where a variety of political factions of roughly equal power compete for dominance: in this situation perhaps the only alternative is to attempt to identify, in consultation with all political groups, a group of more-or-less neutral technical experts who will be respected by all sides.

skills. At the same time, it transferred knowledge to international mission members on local conditions and culture, and on the systems operating before the ballot.

Closer co-ordination is needed between the international financial institutions (IFIs) and the UN. The JAM and the Tokyo donors' meeting marked an unusual degree of co-operation between the Bank and the United Nations Secretariat, first the Department of Political Affairs and later the Department of Peace-Keeping Operations (DPKO). However, the timing of the mission, right at the hand-over between the UN personnel who had staffed UNAMET and those who would lead UNTAET, interrupted continuity as the recommendations of the mission started to be implemented. This could perhaps have been avoided by a closer co-ordination between UNAMET/UNTAET personnel on the ground, DPKO in New York and the World Bank in Washington, together with faster placement of senior specialised staff both for UNTAET and for the IFI offices in Dili after the JAM.

The real impact of the JAM must be judged in the results it produces on the ground. If by the end of June 2000, as the humanitarian program winds down, reconstruction programs are up and running, are designed and implemented with Timorese leadership and communities, and are well-co-ordinated between donors, the JAM can be judged to have been a success.

17

Fiscal issues for a small war-torn Timor Loro Sa'e

João Mariano Saldanha

Introduction

The magnitude of the destruction in Timor Loro Sa'e after the post-referendum ballot has been amply documented.[1] As a consequence, Timor Loro Sa'e has been left with no civil service, no fiscal institutions, and little means to gather revenues, to make expenditures and to receive international aid. The United Nations Transitional Admin-istration in East Timor (UNTAET), which is administering the transition of Timor Loro Sa'e toward independence within two to three years, has created a Central Fiscal Agency (CFA) and a payment bureau as the embryos of a Ministry of Finance and a Bank of Timor, respectively. It is expected that the fiscal agency will move quickly to mobilise domestic revenue and to seek foreign aid to support the reconstruction needs and thus lay the foundations for long-term economic development. However, the payment bureau will only administer the payment system without conducting monetary policy because Timor Loro Sa'e has adopted the US dollar as legal tender.[2]

The role of fiscal policy is to correct market failure (its allocative

---

[1] See World Bank (1999a) for a complete assessment of the destruction of East Timor.

[2] For discussions on this issue see José Braz and João Mariano Saldanha (2000), 'Currency and exchange in East Timor: analysis and preliminary proposals'. Mimeo. OECD Development Centre, Paris.

role), to redistribute income (its distributive role), and to stabilise cyclical instability, unemployment, and inflation (its stability role).[3] The instruments of fiscal policy fall broadly into the three categories of taxation, expenditure and budget policy. Tanzi and Zee (1996) provide an exhaustive survey on how these instruments positively affect economic growth in the long run.

In countries devastated by destruction like Timor Loro Sa'e, fiscal policy plays an even more important role in recovery and transition toward sustained economic growth. Bevan and Pradhan (1994) argue that a post-war situation has profound budgetary consequences that can only be addressed through careful re-examination of expenditure patterns in conjunction with providing positive signals to the private sector in order to make investments possible. This poses enormous challenges to post-conflict governments in identifying priorities and establishing the basic conditions to encourage private sector participation in the reconstruction process. Haughton (1998) argues that introducing cash budgeting, setting up a payments system, seeking foreign aid for general budgetary purposes and revenue mobilisation are among the first generation issues of fiscal policy in post-conflict societies. Tax reform and decreasing the amount of foreign aid are among the second-generation issues of fiscal policy in reconstruction and recovery.

Howard (1992) argues that fiscal policy in small countries is constrained by economies of scale and limited possibilities of diversification. Therefore, a small economy needs foreign exchange and international aid for growth (de Vries 1975).

As a small war-torn economy, Timor Loro Sa'e needs to promote sustainable economic growth using fiscal instruments. It needs to set priorities of expenditure, mobilise revenue, and seek international aid in the short-term. In the medium-to-long-term perspective as international aid declines, Timor Loro Sa'e must develop like other small countries in the world. Therefore, Timor Loro Sa'e needs long-term fiscal sustainability. This is another critical area of fiscal policy that deserves closer analysis.

---

[3]   On the allocative, distributive, and stability roles of fiscal policy, see Musgrave (1959) who provides a conceptual framework of fiscal policy which remains useful to this day.

Internal revenue: short-term

Post-destruction conditions in Timor Loro Sa'e have reduced the capacity of the country to collect revenues. During the Indonesian occupation, 15 per cent of total revenues were raised internally.[4] Rough estimates by the IMF and the World Bank suggest that in fiscal year 2000, East Timor can raise $15 m from internal revenue sources.[5] This is an indication that there is potential for revenue mobilisation in Timor Loro Sa'e. Saldanha and da Costa (1999) identified six potential sources of internal revenue, namely from the exploitation of natural resources, particularly oil and gas; income and property taxes; exports of agricultural products (such as coffee, sugar, livestock and fish produce); tourism; remittances from abroad; and profits from state-owned enterprises. Additional sources of revenues could come from fishing rights, home industries, such as traditional clothing and craft products linked with the development of the tourism sector.

What kind of tax should UNTAET or the future Timor Loro Sa'e government collect? Easterly and Rebelo (1993) argue that developing countries tend to rely more on indirect taxes than on direct taxes because income levels are low. This is even more so in poor countries, especially those emerging from destruction like Timor Loro Sa'e. Governments are unlikely to collect both income and property taxes because politically these direct taxes are contentious and bureaucratically hard to collect. However, indirect taxes such as import duties, excise taxes and other levies can be collected as soon as the capacity to collect taxes is in place. Indirect taxes can often be the only source of revenue in post-conflict societies. However, even in peacetime, indirect taxes constitute a substantial proportion of total revenue, ranging from 40-60 per cent in small countries of the Caribbean (Howard 1992).

---

[4]   This number was underestimated because it only accounted for revenues collected by the provincial government such as levies and dues. East Timor Loro Sa'e only received a small percentage of tax and non-tax collected in the territory. See Pemerintahan Daerah TK I Timor Timur: *Anggaran Pendapatan dan Belanja Daerah 1999/2000.*
[5]   Unfortunately, data on how this figure was estimated is not available. This amount is cited in a footnote in a document prepared by UNTAET and the World Bank for the donors' meeting in Tokyo. See United Nations and World Bank, 'Overview of External Funding Requirements for East Timor', December 1999.

TABLE 1: *Timor Loro Sa'e: Projected revenues, 2000-2005 (US$m)*

Source of revenue	2000	2001	2002	2003	2004	2005
I. Internal revenue	14.90	17.33	20.09	23.02	41.13	47.20
1.1. Oil and gas[a]	3.60	3.96	4.36	5.00	20.00	23.00
1.2. Import duty (5 per cent)[b]	3.50	4.03	4.63	5.33	6.13	7.05
1.3. Export license fees (5 per cent)[c]	1.00	1.15	1.32	1.52	1.75	2.01
1.4. Sales tax (15 per cent)[b]	3.70	4.26	4.90	5.64	6.49	7.46
1.5. Excise tax[e]	2.80	3.64	4.73	6.15	6.77	7.45
1.6. Levies (15 per cent)[d]	0.26	0.29	0.32	0.35	0.39	0.43
1.7. Royalties of fishing rights	-	-	-	-	-	-
1.8. Remittance from abroad	-	-	-	-	-	-
II. International grants[f]	81.80	141.90	83.50	-	-	-
Total	96.70	159.23	103.79	23.44	41.33	47.51

Notes: Yet to be estimated. The projections are based on the following assumptions:

a. 10 per cent annual growth from 2000-2003 and jumps in 2003 before growing 15 per cent annually.

b. 10 per cent annual growth rate.

c. 15 per cent annual growth. Excise tax is comprised of liquor ($1.5/ltr), cigarettes ($15/kg), and fuel ($0.05/ltr).

d. Major components of these levies are port fees, landing fees, departure tax, and vehicle registration fees. It is expected they grow at 10 per cent annually.

e. 30 per cent growth from 2000-2003 and 10 per cent growth afterwards.

f. UNTAET and the World Bank (1999).

Source: Internal revenues are estimated by the author based on assumptions on breakdown of each category of revenues and the respective rates of taxes and levies.

For Timor Loro Sa'e, at least in the medium term (3-4 years), it would be advisable to avoid reliance on income and property taxes to allow people to rebuild their lives, find jobs, and rebuild their homes before starting to pay income or property taxes. In the short-run, Timor Loro Sa'e will have to rely on revenues from oil and gas, indirect taxation, and international transfers (grants). Expenditures from 2000 through 2002 have been secured at least on paper from the international community although there is no guarantee of full disbursements.

Table 1 presents some projections of revenues for 2000 through 2005. Aside from international grants, there are six categories of revenues, i.e. oil and gas, import and export duties, sales taxes (cars,

TABLE 2: *Timor Loro Sa'e: Share of oil in internal revenue, 2000-2005 (per cent)*

Year	Oil share	Non-oil share
2000	24.2	75.8
2001	23.1	76.9
2002	21.9	78.1
2003	21.7	78.3
2004	48.6	51.4
2005	48.7	51.3

Source: As for Table 1.

mobile phones, hotels and restaurants), excise taxes (fuel, liquor and cigarettes), and levies (port, airport and landing fees, departure tax and vehicle registration). In the year 2000, Timor Loro Sa'e can collect revenues of about $14.5 m, of which oil and gas, sales tax, import duties and excise taxes would be the major sources of revenue. From 2000 through 2003, their share in total domestic revenues is likely to be well over 90 per cent of revenue, and from 2004 to 2005, this share may even increase to around 97 per cent of revenue.

By spring 2000, revenue from oil and gas of $3.6 m in terms of royalties from the Timor Gap Joint-Exploration is guaranteed, if and when Timor – or more specifically UNTAET representing Timor Loro Sa'e – replaces Indonesia in the Treaty with Australia.[6] There have been different estimates on the potential revenues from Timor Gap exploitation. One estimate is that once it has been fully exploited, royalties for Timor Loro Sa'e could be around $88 m per year, which would amount to US$2.2 billion in 25 years.[7] Other sources mention A$800 m over the course of 20 years or around US$28 m per year.[8] Such figures need to be accepted with caution. There are no contending estimates to dismiss these optimistic estimates.

It is only by 2004 that commercial production will begin. So it is reasonable to assume that revenue from oil and gas from the Gap

[6] Australian Associated Press, 28 February 2000, 'New oil and gas pact agreed to by Australia and East Timor'. For an overview of Timor Gap issues, see Saldanha (1994) and East Timor Relief Association (1999).

[7] Williams (1999) and Australian Labor Party Press Release, 13 January 1999, available on Regeasttimor.

[8] 'East Timor, Australia eyes revenue from offshore developments', Dow Jones, 20 January 2000 and 'Woodside's Timor Sea oil field surprises on up side', Dow Jones, 20 January 2000.

will be around US$20 m to $23 m in 2004 and 2005, respectively (Table 1). If this is the case, then the share of oil and gas will constitute 50 per cent of the total revenue in those years (Table 2). This could have a significant impact on the local economy. On the positive side, Timor Loro Sa'e will be able to pay its bills, at least the recurrent budget which is estimated to be around $30 m in 2000 (UN and the World Bank 1999). The major component of this expenditure would be the wage bills and goods and services of the public sector. On the negative side, a dominant oil economy could have a 'Dutch disease' effect whereby increased spending in the non-tradeable sector, induced by the increase in oil revenues, would tend to reduce output in the importable sector. The negative effect of increased spending would not be sustained if revenue from oil decreases due to a decline in prices on the international market. Thus it is advisable that the expansion of revenue from the oil sector from 2004 onwards not be fully spent. Rather a substantial proportion of these revenues could constitute offshore reserves to smooth public expenditure in case there is a disruption in the oil industry.

In February 2000, the National Consultative Council (NCC), on the advice of the IMF, promulgated laws levying taxes. An import duty of five per cent was introduced across the board with additional sales tax of 15 per cent on items such as cars, mobile phones, and perfumes. Other components of sales tax would come from retail sales, hotels and restaurants. It is expected that sales tax will be extended as taxable items are identified and when the capacity of the Central Fiscal Agency to collect taxes improves. One positive indication of the potential for such taxes is the growing number of businesses, restaurants and hotels. By the end of February 2000, the UN had issued certificates of business registration for more than 2000 domestic, foreign or joint ventures.[9] Excise taxes of $1.5/litre on alcoholic beverages, of $15/kilogram on tobacco and cigarettes, and of 5 cents/litre for fuel have been levied. The estimates of sales and excise taxes in Table 1 employ these rates. It may be possible that when the UN leaves in 2-3 years, excise taxes may decrease but this seems unlikely because economic activity will increase, thus driving demand upward.

---

[9] See 'Open for business, but a while before good times roll', *Sydney Morning Herald*, 7 March 2000.

Revenues from levies would also increase as taxable items increased along with economic activity and the capacity of the Central Fiscal Agency improved.

The National Consultative Council (NCC), on the advice of the IMF, has agreed to levy taxes on exports, especially coffee. This decision was hotly debated within the NCC in the face of pressure from the IMF.[10] Some felt that it was premature to levy export fees on coffee because this might discourage attempts to expand production as well as diversification away from exporting only coffee beans. Assuming five per cent taxes on coffee exports, the revenue from exports is only $1.0 m or 6.6 per cent of the total internal revenue in 2000 (Table 1). It is premature to levy export fees on coffee exports because this levy may discourage attempts to expand production as well as diversification away from exporting only coffee beans. It is not too late to put on hold the implementation of this policy for coffee.

Two other important sources of revenues that need to be tapped in the short-term are remittances from abroad and fishing rights around the Timor Sea. Since the presence of the UNTAET in October 1999, only a few weeks after Interfet had landed, there has been a substantial inflow of remittances from Australia, Macau and Portugal. The amount of these remittances is not known but they could be a source of potential revenue for Timor Loro Sa'e. Royalties associated with fishing activities in the waters around Timor could also be another source of revenue. Japanese and Taiwanese fishermen have been reported to be operating illegal trawling in eastern Indonesian waters, including those of Timor Loro Sa'e, but they have never been required to contribute a share of their revenue. It may be all right to continue such fishing but the revenues associated with it ought to be shared with Timor Loro Sa'e as the owner of these resources. One of the immediate tasks of UNTAET is to initiate negotiations to share revenues of fishing activities in the Timor Sea.

Overall, collecting indirect taxes constitutes a great challenge for the Central Fiscal Agency. It is desirable that UNTAET develop guidelines for a collection system and the mechanisms for collections which are free of corruption. This mechanism must be enforced impartially. Such fiscal guidelines, mechanisms of enforcement, with impartiality of enforcement could be the great legacy of UNTAET for Timor Loro Sa'e.

---

10   See 'Timor ire at coffee tax', *Sydney Morning Herald*, 29 February 2000.

Internal revenue: medium-to-long-term

In the medium-to-long-term, there are a number of potential sources of revenues that the Timor Loro Sa'e government can collect. Three major sources of revenue could be telecommunications and the Internet, the leasing of the Baucau airport, and the development of either Atauro or Jaco islands as major resort areas.

Telecommunications and Internet: The role of telecommunications and Internet in economic development is yet to be fully understood. But there are ample indications that telecommunications, especially the Internet business, will become the engine of economic growth in developed countries, especially in the US electronic businesses based on e-trade (trade through the Internet) such as Amazon.com and eBay are flourishing in the United States. Small countries like Guyana, Moldavia and Netherlands Antilles now rent their telephone codes to major industries in developed countries. Guyana's revenue from telecommunications traffic is a startling 40 per cent of GDP.[11]

Timor Loro Sa'e could tap into this sector to raise revenue. Once a telecommunications system has been established, an aggressive move to lease phone codes for customer services (1-800-numbers) of major companies could be an important source of revenue. The potential market would be large or even medium-sized companies in the United States, Australia, New Zealand, Europe and Japan, where customer services and technical assistance for their customers can take hours, thus becoming a burden on their budget. This implies that the rates offered by Timor Loro Sa'e must be competitive. Guyana, Moldavia and Netherlands Antilles offer their services for sex chats but Timor Loro Sa'e does not need to take that road. There are plenty of companies around the world that provide post-sale services for their customers at low telephone costs. More research would need to be done to identify a market but these are the companies to which Timor Loro Sa'e could possibly offer its services.

Leasing the Baucau airport: Another potential source of revenue to consider would be to lease the airport at Baucau for international companies, like UPS, Federal Express or DHL as a hub for their

[11] See *The Economist*, 3 January 1998. 'Little countries: small but perfectly formed' for discussions on the advantages of small countries and the role of telecommunications in shaping their economic growth.

Asia-Pacific operations. The Philippines leased Clark Air Base to UPS for several years before it moved to the new Hong Kong airport. This kind of a lease could raise revenues of a couple million dollars annually for Timor Loro Sa'e. The period of the lease could be for five to ten years with a review at the end of the period. This would leave Timor Loro Sa'e with options in the future if other attractive offers emerged both commercially and strategically. Again the lease option would need to be studied carefully.

Timor Loro Sa'e has enough capacity to operate the airport of Dili for its public and commercial purposes. The Dili airport can accommodate medium-sized jets, such as Fokker-100s or an Airbus, which have the capacity to carry up to 200 passengers. Operating both the Dili and Baucau airports would be an enormous cost to the government and a drain on its budget. The government of Timor Loro Sa'e does not have the luxury to waste resources.

Politically, leasing the airport would provoke a heated debate but the reasons for doing so would be to mobilise revenues in order to provide decent livelihoods for its citizens. In other words, leasing the airport to raise revenues would help the people of Timor Loro Sa'e to realise their dreams. Although the revenue from leasing would not constitute a large proportion of the budget, it would help to put more children into schools and provide basic health cover to the poor.

Atauro as a tourism island: There has been much discussion about developing tourism as one of the major foreign exchange generators in Timor Loro Sa'e. Saldanha and da Costa (1999), da Costa (1999), Saldanha (forthcoming), and Pedersen and Arneberg (1999) discuss the possibility of tourism being a major source of foreign exchange for Timor Loro Sa'e. Whereas ideas for ecotourism (da Costa 1999) and backpacker accommodation (Saldanha and da Costa 1999) have been advanced, there are other options that need to be considered. One of them is designating either Atauro Island (north of Dili) or Jaco Island (at the eastern tip of Timor Loro Sa'e) as an exclusive tourist destination with resort hotels that might also offer the possibilities of gambling. These two islands, especially Jaco, are isolated from the mainland and therefore the negative effects that may arise from such tourism could be neutralised. Atauro Island has a population of less than 10 000 people while there is no settlement on Jaco. Atauro might be more attractive because of its closeness to Dili and the availability of basic infrastructure which would need to be further developed. Jaco, on the other hand, is isolated and would need an entire infrastructure to persuade people to live there. This might not be difficult once development started there. One of the positive issues of tourism development on these islands is that they would create jobs that will attract labour. Of course, these ideas need further study before proceeding with any serious attempt of implementation.

The competitor for either Atauro or Jaco is Christmas Island to the south of the island of Java where wealthy Indonesians with their private jets commute, especially at weekends to gamble. Another competitor is Darwin which has a casino and a far better infrastructure. Providing good incentives to build Atauro or Jaco as a modern tourist destination might make a difference. Going to Macau takes longer and is more expensive than flying to Dili and taking a helicopter or boat to Atauro.

This initiative would face strong resistance from the Catholic church but if approached properly, that resistance might soften over time. After all, Timor Loro Sa'e needs to develop all its potentials to create welfare and provide a decent life for its people who have suffered so much.

Expenditure: short-term

Bevan and Pradhan (1994) argue that the budgetary consequences of the transition from war to peace is a change in public expenditure patterns toward the civilian sector, and within the civilian sector, toward economic infrastructure and social spending. This implies that expenditures need to be shifted away from defence by giving priority to infrastructure, health, education, and to kick-start the economy through productive sectors such as agriculture and small scale trade activities.

An important element in the transition to peace in Timor Loro Sa'e, or in other transitions from war to peace economies, is the heavy presence of international agencies and international aid (Bevan and Pradhan 1994; Haughton 1998). Timor Loro Sa'e has both. Since October 1999, public expenditure in Timor Loro Sa'e has been funded by the international community. This expenditure is divided into four categories, namely the defence expenditure of Interfet and the UN peacekeeping force, humanitarian expenditure (appeal crisis), UN personnel expenditure, and expenditure on reconstruction and development, including governance and capacity-building. Since these expenditures have varying effects on Timor Loro Sa'e's economy, it is worth exploring each of them briefly with a focus on reconstruction and development.

Australia bore the bulk of the defence expenditure for the International Force in East Timor (Interfet). This budget was to restore order so it does not belong to the expenditure as described by Bevan and Pradhan. Although the expenditure had an effect on the local economy, this effect was relatively marginal because most consumption goods were imported. Interfet was replaced by the UN Peace-Keeping Force (UNPKF) in February. It is possible that the operation of the peace-keeping force will have a greater impact on the local economy because it is an operation that will last at least two years compared to Interfet's five months. The troops may hire some local staff for language translation and demand local products, especially agricultural produce.

The humanitarian budget, which runs from October 1999 through to June 2000 was allocated the task of supplying food and carrying out the resettlement of internally displaced people and of refugees returning from West Timor. About four per cent out of a budget of US$209.7 m was spent in West Timor where around 100 000 people are still stranded.

UN personnel's budget in terms of salaries, plus compensation for working in a dangerous country, is quite sizeable but contributes little directly to the economy because of a heavy reliance on imported goods and services with limited domestic supply. Large UN missions typically bring about a phenomenon called 'Dutch disease' in small countries. With the additional demand for urban services and other non-traded goods and services, labour costs increase, hampering the competitiveness of the economy and leaving it without a sector capable of earning or saving foreign exchange (World Bank 1999a:7). Timor Loro Sa'e may, however, only suffer limited effects of this 'Dutch disease' because most of the goods and services will be imported. This will mitigate against such effects (Bevan and Pradhan 1994). UN personnel do not even stay on land but instead they have been provided with two floating hotels (Olimpya and Amos W). Their economic activities are delinked from the local economy since many of their goods and services are imported, except low scale labour of the local Timorese. Most goods for infrastructure in the reconstruction programs are also imported.

TABLE 3: *Timor Loro Sa'e: Summary of external financing requirements 2000-2002 (US$m)*

Sector	2000	2001	2002	Total	Percentage
Community empowerment	9.2	10.9	9.8	30.9	10.5
Education	14.8	25.6	17.4	57.8	18.8
Health	7.5	17.0	15.7	40.2	13.1
Agriculture	7.1	14.3	3.0	24.4	7.9
Infrastructure	21.1	49.3	22.7	93.1	30.3
Economic management	4.3	6.5	5.4	16.2	5.3
Civil service	16.6	16.6	9.3	42.5	13.8
Judiciary	1.2	1.6	0.2	2.9	0.9
Total	81.8	141.9	83.5	307.2	100.6

Source: World Bank (1999b).

The negative effects of imported goods for consumption and infrastructure are distributional in nature. There are allegations that the UN presence and its reconstruction efforts do not favour the local economy because few local East Timorsese have been hired to work with UNTAET. Reconstruction in infrastructure and other sectors will rely on foreign contractors and even foreign labour. In addition, a high proportion of the budget is allocated to technical assistance, which may create resentment among the locals.

These are delicate issues that need to be addressed through compensatory policies, one of which would be to encourage companies to hire local people if they are capable and to use as much local materials as possible for construction and infrastructure. This would create some linkages that will stimulate the local economy on the one hand and lead to a more participatory reconstruction process on the other.

The budget for the civilian sector, which is one of the foci of this chapter, is presented in Table 3. The budget was estimated by the World Bank-led Joint Assessment Mission (JAM) and was subsequently submitted to the Donors Conference on Timor Loro Sa'e in Tokyo in December 1999. At that conference, the donors pledged to contribute US$261.7 m for reconstruction and development in infrastructure, agriculture, health, education and macroeconomics. An additional US$56.1 m was allocated for governance and capacity-building, which brings the total amount of funding allocated for reconstruction to US$317.8 m. This is a figure that is slightly higher than that in Table 3.

The budget allocated for the reconstruction and development is likely to get Timor Loro Sa'e moving because it will rebuild both shattered infrastructure and shattered institutions. There are three points, however, that I would like to discuss in relation with this reconstruction budget.

First, expenditure for the civil service, which targets the recruitment of 12 000 civil servants over the course of three years, raises the purchasing power of the economy, although only one small proportion of the population is involved. Almost 14 per cent of the budget in the transitional period has been allocated to the civil service. This will define the patterns of recurrent expenditure for Timor Loro Sa'e in the future. Timor Loro Sa'e has few options except to maintain this level of civil servants in the future since it is a more sustainable level than the 28 000 civil servants during the Indonesian occupation.

Second, expenditure for education, health and infrastructure sets the right direction for reconstruction. However, when one looks closely at the specific projects that have been designed, the education sector needs a review. Early childhood education, adult education and distance learning are luxuries that a country like Timor Loro Sa'e can hardly afford. Priority should be given to primary, secondary and university students in the country. In addition, a priority should be given to help those students of Timor Loro Sa'e who were studying in Indonesian universities to finish their studies.

Third, the budget for reconstruction also provides opportunities to kick-start the economy through the agricultural sector and micro-financing (micro-enterprise credit for start-up ventures and revolving credit for small and medium enterprises). Although this sector was not destroyed as was construction and trade, expenditure on cash crop production, especially rice and maize, will help reduce the food deficit. Directing more resources into the agricultural sector provides linkages to other sectors in terms of labour absorption, food sufficiency and balancing reconstruction programs that are heavily biased toward urban centres.[12] More spending in agriculture also restrain the urban sector tendency to draw limited productive labour force from rural areas to urban areas. Unfortunately, this sub-sector was not considered a priority. The agriculture budget only receives

---

[12]   For an extensive discussion of the agricultural sector in Timor Loro Sa'e, see Saldanha and da Costa (1999); also Pedersen and Arneberg (eds) (1999), especially the chapter on production.

eight per cent of the reconstruction budget. Therefore, it needs to be reviewed as far as implementation is concerned.

Expenditure: medium-to-long-term

Expenditure on education, health and infrastructure is important during the transition period (Bevan and Pradhan 1994) as well as in peacetime. Education and health are the two core sectors in human capital development that in the long-term contribute to economic growth (Tanzi and Zee 1996). Human capital development is even more important in small countries because they have a smaller reservoir of trained talent than larger countries, so they must depend more on technical assistance (de Vries 1975). Expenditure on infrastructure, especially transport and communications, also have a significant effect on economic growth (Easterly and Rebelo 1993). Therefore, the priorities of expenditure, in the medium-to-long-term, should continue to focus on developing infrastructure, education and health.

Timor Loro Sa'e may seem set to depend eternally on foreign aid, given its limited natural resources. However, the prospects are not that gloomy. At least as indicated in Table 1, Timor Loro Sa'e will have the capacity to finance its civil servants and provide the basic needs for its people. The government should concentrate on a few areas where it can perform well or where the private sector cannot afford to do so.

To avoid large budget deficits and debt, public expenditure in an independent Timor Loro Sa'e must achieve a trade-off between maintaining basic public services (civil servants and police) and infrastructure with the development of human capital (education and health), agriculture and tourism. Providing rural health clinics and access to schooling (up to high school) will possibly deter mass movements into urban areas, especially Dili. Control of growth in the public sector, especially the number of civil servants and their wages is equally important. Public expenditure also can be directed to stimulate the development of the agricultural sector from which almost 80 per cent of the people of Timor Loro Sa'e derive their income and livelihood. In addition, the tourism sector also deserves significant attention as one of the sectors that will generate foreign exchange in the future.

Although there is a great temptation for elected officials and their allies in the bureaucracy to provide perks for their constituents, government needs to be cautious of becoming too involved in the economy, thus crowding out the private sector. Therefore, the state needs to avoid creating state-owned enterprises, such as telecommunications, transport and communications because they may be the source of fiscal difficulties. Thus it may be more sensible to focus on water, postal and power management.

One question is whether the government will run budget deficits or borrow from abroad. Budget deficits can be financed in two ways. First, by selling government bonds to the public or asking the central bank to print more money. By adopting the US dollar as legal tender, Timor Loro Sa'e has given up its option to finance budget deficits through printing more money, at least during the transition process. One solution to the budget deficit problem would be to borrow from abroad. In any case, Timor Loro Sa'e will have to support a debt because international aid (grants) can not go on indefinitely. Therefore, the question is what kind of borrowing Timor Loro Sa'e needs to undertake and with what conditions attached to this borrowing?

International aid

After its destruction, Timor Loro Sa'e was left to the mercy of the international community for both its recurrent and reconstruction budget during the transition to independence. The initial reaction of the international community was positive. At the Tokyo Donors Conference on Timor Loro Sa'e in December 1999, the donor countries pledged $520 m for humanitarian, governance and reconstruction purposes to be given over a three-year period from 2000 to 2002. The question is whether these pledges will actually be translated into disbursements. Pledges do not automatically translate into disbursements (Haughton 1998; Heininger 1994; and Kadhr 1999). Disbursement can be as low as six per cent, as in Cambodia (Heininger 1994:59-61) or at best 40 per cent as in Palestine (Kadhr 1999:147). In Kosovo, the percentage of disbursement of pledged international aid is currently around 25 per cent. It is not clear whether Timor Loro Sa'e will have the same experience but precautionary measures need to be taken and the people of Timor Loro Sa'e should lower their expectations because there is a limit to international aid.

During the transitional period, the task of persuading the donors is supposedly entrusted to the Central Fiscal Agency working together with the World Bank and other multilateral agencies, such as the IMF and the Asia Development Bank. This task requires competence and a good working relationship with these institutions.

Although funds were pledged toward the end of 1999, it was not until the completion of the visit to East Timor by the president of the World Bank, James Wolfensohn, on 22 February 2000, that the first World Bank funds became available in the form of a US$7 m grant for an initial six-month period to support a community empowerment and local governance project, which will eventually receive US$21.5 m. Following election of local councils, communities are to receive US$15 000 each to support locally-determined projects. Additional funding will be provided by the Japanese government (US$1.5 m) and the Asian Development Bank (US$1 m).[13]

Conclusion

This chapter has discussed fiscal policy and its likely effect on the long-term development of Timor Loro Sa'e. Although internal revenue mobilisation is limited, Timor Loro Sa'e has the capacity to finance its recurrent budget. With carefully planned revenue mobilisation, which is not distortive, and implementation of a collection system, which is free of corruption, Timor Loro Sa'e may even be able to provide budgetary support for basic education and health.

Therefore, the fiscal strategy for the long-term will be to control the growth of both the number of civil servants and their wages and to limit government expenditures to education, health, agriculture and tourism, leaving other sectors to the private sector by creating the appropriate environment for the private sector to grow. Within this context, it may be a good idea to offer tax incentives in terms of tax holidays in certain industries or accelerated depreciation of capital that is attractive. In addition, it should be a priority to promulgate an investment law that can send the proper signals to long-term investors interested in Timor Loro Sa'e. The challenge for this purpose is land ownership, which is a delicate issue.

International aid will continue to be a substantial component of

[13] 'Rebuilding East Timor at the local level', The World Bank, 22 February 2000, available at east-timor.cig.apc.org.

Timor Loro Sa'e's budget. However, there is a limit to international aid and Timor Loro Sa'e will be better off mobilising its domestic revenues before contemplating whether to borrow or not. If Timor Loro Sa'e does borrow, it is imperative that the borrowing be limited to soft loans to complement internal revenue.

The idea would be to streamline expenditures and let the development and modernisation (or industrialisation) of Timor Loro Sa'e take its own course without overburdening future generations with debt because of the irresponsibility of their predecessors.

Acknowledgments

I have benefited from discussions with C. Peter Timmer. My thanks are due to James Fox for editorial work which has improved the presentation of this chapter. The usual disclaimer applies.

References

Aditjondro, George, 2000. 'Self-determination under globalisation: Timor Loro Sa'e's transformation from Jakarta's colony to a global capitalist outpost', Mimeo. Department of Sociology and Anthropology, University of Newcastle, Australia.

Agenor, Pierre-Richard and Peter J. Montiel, 1996. *Development Macroeconomics*. Princeton: Princeton University Press.

Australian Associated Press, February 28 2000. 'New oil and gas pact agreed to by Australia and East Timor'.

Bevan, David and Sanjay Pradhan, 1994. 'Fiscal aspects of the transition from war to peace: with illustration from Uganda and Ethiopia', in Jean Paul Azan *et al.* (eds), *Some Economic Consequences of the Transition from Civil War to Peace*. World Bank Policy Research Working Paper 1392.

Braz, José and João Mariano Saldanha, 2000. 'Currency and exchange in East Timor: analysis and preliminary proposals'. Mimeo. Paris: OECD Development Centre.

Cohen, Daniel, 1998. *The Wealth of the World and the Poverty of Nations*. Cambridge, MA: MIT Press.

da Costa, Helder, 1999. 'Economics of tourism in East Timor', Working Paper No. 5. East Timor Study Group. March.

de Vries, Barend A., 1975. 'Development aid to small countries' in Percy Selwyn (ed.), *Development Policy in Small Countries*. London: Croom Helm.

Dow Jones, January 20 2000. 'East Timor, Australia eyes revenue from offshore developments', and 'Woodside's Timor Sea oil field surprises on up side'.

Easterly, William and Sergio Rebelo, 1993. 'Fiscal policy and economic growth: an empirical investigation', *Journal of Monetary Economics* 32:417-458.

Economist, The, 1998. 'Little countries: small but perfectly formed', *The Economist Past Issues.* 3 January.

East Timor Relief Association, 1999. Collection on the Timor Gap. Newspaper Clippings. Australia: East Timor Relief Association.

Faber, Mike, 1992. 'Micro-states, increasing integration and awkward imperatives of adjustment: the case of the Republic of the Maldives', in Helen M. Hintjens and Malyn D.D. Newitt (eds), *The Political Economy of Small Tropical Islands: The Importance of Being Small.* Exeter, UK: University of Exeter Press.

Fairbairn, Te'o I.J., 1985. *Island Economies: Studies from the South Pacific.* Suva: IPS, University of the South Pacific.

Heininger, Janet, 1994. *Peace Keeping in Transition: The United Nations in Cambodia.* New York: Twentieth Century Fund Press.

Hope, Kempe R., 1987. *Development Finance and the Development Process: A Case Study of Selected Caribbean Countries.* New York: Greenwood Press.

Howard, Michael, 1992. *Public Finance in Small Open Economies: The Caribbean Experience.* Westport, CT: Praeger Publishers.

Haughton, Jonathan, 1998. 'The reconstruction of war-torn economies', CAER II Discussion Paper No. 23. HIID, Cambridge, MA.

Kadhr, Ali, 1999. 'Donor assistance', in Ishac Diwan and Radwan A. Shaban (eds), *Development Under Adversity: The Palestinian Economy in Transition.* Washington DC: The World Bank.

Katzenstein, Peter, 1985. *Small States and World Trade.* Ithaca, NY: Cornell University Press.

Musgrave, Richard A., 1959. *The Theory of Public Finance.* New York: McGraw-Hill, 1959.

Pedersen, Jon and Marie Arneberg (eds), 1999. *Social and Economic Conditions in East Timor.* Oslo: Fafo Institute of Applied Social Science.

Pemerintahan Daerah TK I Timor Timur. *Anggaran Pendapatan dan Belanja Daerah 1999/2000.*

Rosen, Harvey S., 1999. *Public Finance.* Fifth Edition. New York: Irwin-McGraw-Hill.

Saldanha, João M., 1994. *The Political Economy of East Timor Development.* Jakarta: Pustaka Sinar Harapan.

———, (forthcoming). 'The transition of a small war-torn economy into a new nation: economic reconstruction of East Timor', in Richard Tanter, Mark Zelden and Steven R. Shalom (eds), *East Timor, Indonesia and the World Community.*

——— and Helder da Costa, 1999. 'Economic viability of East Timor revisited', Working Paper No. 1, The East Timor Study Group (ETSG). San Diego, California.

Tanzi, Vito and Howel H. Zee, 1996. 'Fiscal policy and long run growth', IMF Working Paper, WP/96/119.

United Nations and The World Bank, 1999. 'Overview of external funding requirements for East Timor', Dili, East Timor.

Williams, Louise, 1999. 'New state will want a slice of Gap', *Sydney Morning Herald*, February 27 1999.

World Bank, 1991. *Pacific Island Economies. Toward Higher Growth in the 1990s.* Washington, DC.

———, 1999a. 'The Joint Assessment Mission: macroeconomics background paper', Washington, DC.

———, 1999b. 'A report of the Joint Assessment Mission to East Timor', Washington, DC.

18

Challenges for the future

Dionisio Babo Soares

Introduction

The new East Timor faces a number of social and political challenges particularly since differences among various factions within the resistance remain. Despite these factions' commitment to uphold a common ground – i.e., independence – they remain undecided over whether to advocate democracy first or build the country first and worry about democracy later.

East Timor must face other challenges which, if not resolved to the satisfaction of the various factions, could further heighten the divisions which have been left unresolved by past political conflicts. These challenges concern cultural values, the legal system, human rights, land rights, language and political differences. This chapter examines some of these critical challenges.

Conselho Nacional da Resistencia Timorense (CNRT) ideas for development

While frictions of the past may have little importance in future East Timor politics, issues such as reconciliation and national unity will be important once the country becomes independent.[1] On 25 August 1999,

[1] While writing this chapter, the Portuguese daily newspaper, *Diario de Noticias* (28/11/99), reported that the leaders of the East Timor pro-independence faction led by José Ramos Horta and pro-Indonesia faction led by former Indonesia's roving ambassador on East Timor, Francisco Lopes da Cruz had met in Singapore on 24-27 November 1999 to discuss ways to reconcile the East Timorese.

five days before the ballot day, José Alexandre 'Kay Rala Xanana' Gusmão, the leader of the CNRT, launched a 'blueprint' for the country's future development, outlining the fundamental issues involved in rebuilding East Timor. The six-page document containing 15 points called upon the East Timorese to forget the past and start a program of reconciliation, unity and national development for what he termed the 'transitional period' (*Diario de Noticias*, 20/10/99). The 15 points are:

- National reconciliation and unity
- The reconstruction of Timor Loro Sa'e
- The adoption of a market-oriented approach
- Social and economic development policies for the territory
- The adoption of a financial policy that upholds development
- Encouraging the inflow of capital (investment)
- Government apparatus
- Education and training
- Relations with ASEAN and Indonesia
- Relations with Portugal and CPLP (the Community of Portuguese-speaking Nations)
- Forging international and multilateral relations
- Recognition of Falintil (East Timor National Liberation Army)
- Granting general amnesty to Indonesian collaborators
- Maintaining sustainable development of the country
- Negotiations with Indonesia over political differences to forge new ties between the two countries.

There are two general objectives in this document: the need to develop a framework for national development and the need to forge relations with the international community. While the latter seems to face few problems given the support East Timor has enjoyed in the last five years, internal development will confront various challenges.

Challenges and potential conflicts

Political differences: The emergence of various political groups has coloured the contest among Timorese political parties. Reconciliation among the factions within the resistance, however, cannot be taken for granted. The rebuilding of a new 'democracy' for East Timor is still a long way ahead since the Timorese still remain divided over both ideological interests and national political orientation. Likewise, differences among various groups or within the resistance itself remain vast. Indeed, since the early days of East Timor's struggle against Indonesia, factions within the resistance have been divided over the issue of a national ideology.[2]

While the resistance successfully adopted the name CNRT in 1997 to refer to the only body that represented the resistance inside the territory and abroad, divergence among them remained. Interestingly, within Fretilin itself, differences among its members have been characteristic of the party since its inception. In the early 1980s, when Lobato died in a battle against the Indonesian army that lasted for almost three days, there was a dispute between Abilio Araujo, the leader of Fretilin in Portugal, and the other leaders within the resistance. Araujo was rejected by his companions who chose Xanana as their new leader.

In developments before the referendum, some members of Fretilin re-proclaimed the Democratic Republic of East Timor (*Republica Democratica de Timor Leste*: RDTL), claiming the party was unfaithful to its basic principles. Friction among its leaders, particularly those remaining inside East Timor, was so great that attempts to reconcile them failed. The RDTL faction refused to bow to Fretilin's leadership. Some Fretilin leaders turned their anger toward the CNRT leaders who were originally from other parties.[3] Despite current developments, particularly after the post-ballot violence which helped form a favourable atmosphere for advancing national interests first, much remains to be done.

On the other hand, the political situation on the ground has yet to calm down. Differences among groups such as the Organisation of Timorese Youth (*Organisacão de Juventude de Timor Leste*: OJETIL) and the East Timorese National Students Resistance (*Resistencia Nacional dos Estudantes de Timor Leste*: RENETIL) continue. A few months before the referendum, a street battle between the two groups took place in Baucau, leaving at least one person dead (*Kompas*, June 1999). Differences also continue to exist between various groups within the

---

[2] It should be understood that since Apodeti is pro-integration, much of this account regarding differences within the resistance excludes this political party.
[3] In my conversation with Leandro Isaac, a CNRT leader whose party was UDT, I was told that when attending the Algarve meeting in Portugal in October 1998, the friction among the resistance leaders remained intense and it would remain so should each political party refuse to uphold the national interest.

struggle. Some have come out and accused the Socialist Party of Timor (*Partido Socialista de Timor*: PST) of being another branch of the Timorese Nationalist Party (*Partido Nacionalista Timorense*: PNT), the party headed by the independence-turned integrationist leader, Abilio Araujo.[4] Some even alleged that it was Araujo who negotiated the release of Salar Kosi, the spokesperson of PST in Indonesia after Kosi was trapped within the Austrian embassy in Jakarta for more than a year while seeking political asylum there.

Divergence of opinion about the future may be widening. While most East Timorese remain faithful to CNRT as the only legitimate body that commands the resistance, some political parties have come out and disagreed openly with the leadership of CNRT, threatening to go 'their own way' and not listen to CNRT's leadership. Some have warned that they may quit their current post within the Political Commission, an organ within CNRT, and withdraw their support for this resistance body, emphasising the existing differences among the political elite. If such differences remain unreconciled, democracy and peace may still be a long way ahead.

Political feuds: Another possible threat to stability is a political dispute that has continued throughout the 24 years of conflict. During these years, the East Timorese were divided between two opposing views, pro- and anti-independence. It is certain that of these two groups, the former were always subject to repression by the Indonesian army in its campaign to quell the resistance. The estimated 200 000 people killed in the first 15 years of occupation by Indonesia may have been forgotten and, as time goes by, their relatives perhaps will not feel the need to retaliate or seek compensation. Nevertheless, since the Indonesian army has been withdrawn, retaliation, if it occurs, will certainly be focused against those considered collaborators with the army in the past.[5] Tension, therefore, will remain high.

[4] In my recollection, the debates surrounding the emergence of this party took place on the Internet between April and June 1999, where PST was accused of advocating autonomy and fighting only for its own survival instead of the national interest.

[5] During my visit to Darwin between 26 September and 5 October 1999, I had a chance to talk to several refugees about their experiences during Indonesia's occupation. While I did not conduct any statistical survey, it was clear that those affected by the events in the 1990s still show an eagerness for retaliation, should the opportunity present itself.

Political rivalries and wars among Timorese kingdoms were characteristic of pre-European colonisation. Likewise, the Portuguese government found it extremely hard to gain the 'hearts and minds' of the Timorese, from the time it arrived in the island in the sixteenth century up until approximately the end of the nineteenth century. In the first two centuries of European colonisation of Timor, rebellion and resistance against the colonial administration, especially in the enclave of Oecussi, cost thousands of lives including those of two governors and a Catholic bishop (Duarte 1930).[6] The colonial government gained effective political control over the eastern part of the island in 1912 when the Catholic church was asked to intervene and convince local traditional rulers to abandon their resistance.

Part of such rivalries and wars may be attributed to the injustices that prevailed at the time; people would choose to settle disputes according to their own ways. This can partly be attributed to the inability of the colonial government to reconcile differences within the society. Dissatisfactions, which then led to possible 'blood-feuds', created disputes that involved not only the main protagonists but also their offspring and future generations. However, memories of suffering, trauma and injustice that the East Timorese have endured during the past 24 years will not just fade away quickly. They could become the hidden basis which triggers further violence should those once 'colonised' decide to retaliate in the future.

Cultural challenges: One of the most challenging issues for the new country concerns that of cultural values, as for example, the preservation of traditional heritage. During the 450 years of Portuguese presence in Timor, the traditional system of organisation with its local leaders, despite being placed under the colonial administration system, was allowed to operate with a certain degree of autonomy. This was due to the fact that most of the population remained under the control of the traditional rulers (*liurai*). These traditional rulers, although subordinate to the colonial government, were given the power to direct and control local affairs. Not surprisingly,

---

[6]   Indeed, rebellions against both the Portuguese and the Dutch took place, especially in the western part of Timor, prior to the Contract of Paravicini in 1756 which contributed to the separation of the island into two halves: East and West Timor as it is known today (see de Castro 1943).

until the Portuguese departure from the island, this traditional system still played an important role in East Timorese social life.

During the 24 years of Indonesian administration, although the government recognised the existence of traditional institutions, traditional leaders were given no role to play as had been the case under the Portuguese colonial government. These 24 years were also characterised by a decline in the public credibility of state law. This prompted people to rely on traditional ways of solving disputes, rather than state courts. Although state courts were established in almost all regions in Timor (Babo Soares et al. 1996), the traditional legal system seems to have been the preferred means of settling non-criminal disputes. There are two further reasons for this:

1. During the first 20 years of military occupation, the credibility of state law failed in the eyes of the people due to the practise of bribery, which was commonly seen as a disease of the New Order government.[7] The degradation of the justice system has led the Timorese to invent the saying, *Se mak iha osan nia maka manan, se maka laiha osan nia leki let*: 'Only the rich are the winners, the poor are the losers'.

2. Many East Timorese cannot afford to settle their disputes in state courts simply because they cannot afford the cost of its procedures.[8] Rural people, who are mostly in the low-income group, prefer a judicial process that has less procedural bureaucracy and is therefore less costly and less time-consuming.

Although there is no quantitative data to distinguish accurately between those who prefer to resolve their disputes through customary courts and those who prefer to do the same through state courts, the fact that 70 per cent of the population still live in rural areas (Babo Soares et al. 1996) and have little access to the state legal system suggests that a majority of East Timorese will still be keen to settle their disputes through traditional

---

[7] The New Order refers to Soeharto's regime which came into being in 1967.
[8] Various statements regarding the poor performance of the state court have been reported by different independent organisations both inside and outside East Timor to the present day. This chapter points specifically to several independent investigations carried out by Yayasan HAK (Hukum, Hak Asasi dan Keadilan/Law, Human Rights and Justice), a local NGO which investigated various human rights abuses in the territory (1977-99).

institutions. Will the new government introduce a system that accommodates both cultural values and the need for change in social life? It is necessary to reintroduce the 'traditional legal system' and, if possible, integrate it into the national political system in the future. To be able to do this, re-institutionalisation of traditional organisations, provision of training and education to civil administrators and both codification and unification of 'customary law' are necessary. It seems imperative to establish a national task force whose responsibility would be to undertake research about local 'customary law' and integrate it into, or develop it as part of, a legal system. In addition, acknowledging the heterogeneous nature of Timorese society and the degree of cultural variation among different social groups is important, for a national legal and political system should not leave the interests of any group in the society unacknowledged.

Land rights: During the colonial period the social system was often defined by class and status dichotomies such as rural/urban, elite/ordinary or educated/illiterate, but this is not the case in the traditional social system. The standards for social and political identification were based on 'customary law'. These standards refer to the mechanisms applied to administer local social organisation such as rules regarding the status of 'houses', land rights and other rules used to regulate social life. Traube (1977) and Therik (1995) point to such mechanisms as rules to guide the people according to the *path set by the ancestors*, which can still be found in oral narratives. 'Standards' also refer to the legal system, a system employed to determine the organisation of society based on certain acceptable categories of seniority *(primus inter pares)*, place of dwelling, precedence (younger/elder), membership status in social groups (consanguinal/affinal) and so on. These principles govern the social system.

For example, in a society like that of the Tetun, a married man is entitled to a piece of land within the clan[9] by virtue of his membership in a lineage. His children, especially males, are full members of the clan and possess the right of access to land within the clan. The traditional land tenure system recognises no private ownership of land, for land belongs to the lineage (collective rights), i.e. it is indivisible and inalienable.

[9]   By 'clan', I refer to members of a lineage including their families and those who are categorically defined as 'outsiders' or men who marry into the lineage and their offspring. The term 'clan land' in this context refers to the land they occupy or claim as part of a clan's rights.

In the traditional land tenure system, tenure rights are based on collective rights. The system recognises the right to use but not to own.[10] Tenure of land in the traditional system grants every person in the lineage the right to use what is produced by the land, especially from land allocated to that person. Normally, land rights are granted exclusively to the descendants of a lineage. Land cannot be sold to people outside the clan. If a person dies or moves out of the community, his/her land will pass into the hands of the other members of the lineage.

Unmarried women, so long as they trace their origin through the male line and reside within the clan, also have access to land, although compared to their brothers, their portion is smaller. Regarding married women, different social groups or clans possess different ways of settling land rights, especially with regard to those who still want to reside on their natal land despite their marriage status. Generally, these women are given the rights to use of the land.

During the Portuguese period, despite being regulated by the state, societies were allowed to organise their land tenure under the traditional system. Disputes were mediated by the *lian nain* (lit., owner of words), *dato ua'in* (lit., high authority) and *macair fukun* (lit., holder of law). Nevertheless, 'customary law' was not independent of state law. Disputes were settled before state courts if one of the conflicting parties refused to accept a decision handed down at the 'traditional court'. Portuguese law regarding land only recognised 'property rights', not 'use rights'.

Under the Indonesian land tenure system, *Undang-Undang Pokok Agraria in 1965* (Law on Agrarian Reform 1965), two rights to land are recognised. These include *hak milik* (property rights) and *hak pakai* (use rights). Under this law, despite recognising the traditional land tenure system (*hak ulayat*), ownership and disputes were settled through state courts. 'Customary law' was given little room to operate. Ownership without the consent of the government (*laiha surat*, lit., 'without documentation') is not considered legal. People were obliged

---

[10] My own experience when conducting research on 'small-scale' industries in East Timor in 1996 under the auspices of the University of East Timor and the Department of Manpower of East Timor, provided me with valuable information about land ownership. Among various social groups, traditional land ownership is regarded as 'collective ownership' and claims 'to use' land within a group must be made with the approval of the 'clan' council.

to seek land registration in order to secure their land from 'strange' claims of ownership.[11] Thus, land disputes had to be settled through state tribunals, a situation that often gave rise to open hostilities should the victim refuse to honour a decision made in a state court.

Land remains a hereditary issue in most parts of East Timor and conflicts over land are best solved through traditional courts before state law is imposed upon such conflicts. It is therefore necessary that the establishment of the new political system should be followed by the re-institutionalisation of the traditional land tenure system or by the careful merging of both modern and traditional institutions. Preliminary studies and plans should be of a high priority, particularly during this transitional phase, pending the introduction of a new social, legal and political system.

Language problems: East Timor is a plural society with languages that belong to two major language families, Austronesian and non-Austronesian (Trans-New Guinea phylum). The former includes Tetun, the *lingua franca* spoken by half of the island, Uab Meto (spoken in the enclave of Oecussi), Mambai, Tokodede, Kemak, Galoli, Idate, Lakalei, Waima'a, Habu and Naueti. Trans-New Guinea phylum languages include Bunak, spoken in central Timor, Makassae and Fataluku (Dagada) spoken in the eastern part of the island. These three kindred idioms are related to each other and 'to the dialects of the nearby islands of Alor and Pantar' (Hull 1996).

Despite this mix of languages, an overwhelming majority of the younger generation of East Timorese speak *Bahasa Indonesia* (Jones, this volume) and more than 2000 university graduates are fluent in Indonesian. Between 500 and 1000 East Timorese, particularly among the youth, speak moderate English. Tetun came to be the *lingua franca* in the 1960s when the Catholic church adopted it to replace Portuguese as the liturgical medium in the diocese of Dili, which covered the whole territory of East Timor (Hull 1996). *Tetum praça* or *Tetun Dili* has wide acceptance through most of East Timor.

[11] The lack of recognition of the traditional land tenure system has had severe consequences for some East Timorese. Many people found their lands transferred into the hands of new owners who came and settled in East Timor after 1975 simply because these newcomers were able to produce 'chapters' which indicated their right of ownership to the land. Although there is no official record of this, the fact that a number of complaints have been addressed to NGOs and human rights groups in the territory provide evidence of this situation.

The question is, which language will be used as the national and official language of a new East Timor? Cox and Carey (1995) argued that perhaps only 0.25 per cent had received formal (Portuguese) education until late 1975. From 1975 onwards, the Indonesian educational curriculum was introduced throughout East Timor. Schools were built and under the government's program, illiteracy was to be eradicated. All Portuguese curricula and training schools were abolished, including those run by the church. As a consequence, during the 24 years of Indonesian occupation, the main language spoken in schools, government institutions and privately-owned institutions was Indonesian (*Bahasa Indonesia*). Now, in 1999, Portuguese-speakers in East Timor number only a few hundred and not all of them are fluent in writing and speaking. *Bahasa Indonesia* is the widest spoken language, second only to *Tetum praça*.

In April 1997, a decision was made at the first CNRT conference in Portugal to adopt Tetun as the national language and Portuguese as the official language in an independent East Timor. It is understood that this decision was partly made because of the historical and emotional ties between East Timor and the Portuguese people. In part, the decision was taken because of the desire to eradicate *Bahasa Indonesia* from East Timor and return to Portuguese.[12]

Nevertheless, questions have been raised as to the value of using Portuguese in the long-term. These questions are based largely on geographical and economic concerns and issues of national interest. Some politicians endorse the Portuguese language as a means of avoiding the 'cultural domination' of Indonesia over East Timor.[13] Others would argue from a cultural point of view that *Bahasa Indonesia*, which has its origin in the Malay language, was the language of traders and was spoken throughout eastern Indonesia prior to European colonialism of South-east Asia.[14] Malay had its influence in East Timor, which was located within a complex trading network. Not surprisingly, the word *malae* which in *Tetun* is used to refer to 'foreigners' is probably derived from the word for Malay.

12 Pers. comm., José Ramos Horta, 1998, Sydney.
13 Ibid.
14 A speech by Prof. James J. Fox at the Canberra Workshop of the East Timor Study Group, 27-28 April 1999, supported and sponsored by Centre for Democratic Institutions, the Research School of Pacific and Asian Studies, and the Faculty of Asian Studies, at the Australian National University.

Most East Timorese Indonesian-speaking graduates have reacted to the CNRT decision with caution. This does not necessarily imply that this group, which could constitute a strong pressure group in an independent East Timor, rejects the imposition of Portuguese as the official language. Cautious measures need to be taken and decisions on sensitive issues such as language need to be handled carefully because these could become a source of negative feelings in a still-traumatised society.

Human rights: In the lead-up to the ballot, certain sections within the East Timorese society, who were disappointed with President Habibie's decision, tried to derail the referendum through a well-orchestrated and systematic campaign of violence. The period between December 1998 and August 1999 saw the emergence of various militia groups in East Timor and the mass 'elimination' of pro-independence supporters by these groups. It is undeniable that the Indonesian military or some sections within the military worked together with the militia to undermine the referendum as well as to eliminate supporters of the independence movement.

Indeed, various reports of atrocities and first-hand accounts from eyewitnesses have been recorded. Different human rights organisations, non-governmental organisations, international observers[15] and UNAMET itself documented much of the violence which occurred in East Timor during the period before the 30 August ballot. Although the referendum was successful, the anti-independence group, who represented only 21 per cent of voters, still tried to reject the process. They argued that misconduct had occurred during the balloting and, instead of remaining neutral, the UN had cheated on the whole process. The anti-independence group spearheaded by figures such as Francisco Lopes da Cruz, Domingos Soares, Armindo Mariano, Basilio de Araujo, Tito Batista, João Tavarez and the notorious militia leader Eurico Guterres accused UNAMET of taking sides with the pro-independence group.

The UN decided to appoint a commission of inquiry into the killings and the forced evacuation of the civil population into West Timor. Such developments, however, did little to ameliorate the situation on the ground. In the meantime, former militia leaders such as Tomas

---

[15] Several international organisations accredited by the United Nations Assistance Mission in East Timor such as the IFET (International Federation for East Timor) and the Carter Center were among these international observers.

Aquino Goncalves and Rui Lopez, who defected to Macau, provided evidence on TNI-militia collusion. There were thus a number of significant indications suggesting that the TNI's scorched earth policy was well planned in advance.

Since the army-backed militia rampage, none of the militia leaders has been brought before any court. Many of the militia leaders predicted in advance that there would be a flood of blood and a situation worse than 1975 if the pro-autonomy supporters lost the referendum. This, too, indicates that they knew in advance what was going to happen. A lot of home-made weapons were in the hands of these militia and there are indications that they had received some training in making weapons. While the militia killed with impunity, the military stayed motionless. That the relatives of the militia were brought to West Timor before or soon after the ballot also suggests that they knew in advance the consequence of a pro-autonomy loss.

Other developments that suggest that the violence had been planned in advance are as follows: All pro-autonomy leaders were flown to Jakarta by special planes arranged within hours after the result of the ballot was announced. The subsequent militia rampage around Dili involving the killing of pro-independence leaders, forced evacuation and looting with impunity were not dealt with by the security forces, despite the fact that martial law had been declared. UNAMET officials and foreign journalists were forced to leave East Timor at gunpoint (*Canberra Times*, 5 September 1999). In addition, burning of property and transportation of goods looted from burned houses accompanied the withdrawal of TNI, soon after the arrival of the Multinational Force in East Timor.

It is necessary for the United Nations to initiate immediate measures to bring all the parties to this conflict together to solve the issue once and for all. Despite current developments indicating that the militia threat will fade as democratic changes occur within Indonesia and that Indonesia will seek to establish good relations with the government of East Timor, steps need to be taken to prevent further violence and the loss of lives from taking place again in the territory. For this purpose, in addition to addressing economic and cultural issues, there is a need for the new government:

• To establish a South African-style 'Truth and Reconciliation Commission' in order to initiate a reconciliation process and to consider the evidence on the violation of human rights committed in the past.

- To set up a judicial system, a police and a court system to enable the government to investigate atrocities and killings in the past.
- To grant amnesty, pardon and abolition from prosecution based on legal, moral and humanitarian grounds for certain individuals. This, for example, could be based on the type of political crimes committed and on the circumstances in which these crimes were committed.
- To restart the relationship with any future Indonesian government and resolve past disputes in a peaceful manner. It is hoped that this relationship would allow the East Timorese and Indonesian governments to work on the basis of an understanding for their mutual benefit.
- To apply for UN membership as well as to become an active player in both the South Pacific Forum and ASEAN. Given its geographical location, East Timor will surely benefit from joining both the UN and these two regional organisations so as to strengthen its links with the international community.

Closing remarks

East Timor needs internal stability if it is to develop. However, the challenges raised in this chapter are a warning that continuing conflict could recur unless attention is paid to healing the 'hearts and minds' of the people. The introduction of 'democracy' in its first years will be a challenge to both the new government and the East Timorese people. Arguably, apart from reconciliation among the East Timorese, efforts need to be made to redress moral and material disadvantages, which the East Timorese have suffered during the years of political turmoil. Thus, alongside the points made in Xanana's development blueprint, the following concepts need to be considered as well:

- Emotional recovery needs to proceed along with material development among the people.
- Counselling and trauma healing are necessary in the short-term in order to avoid vengeance, blood-feuds or reoccurrence of long-standing disputes among the East Timorese. Negotiation and conflict management are both of considerable importance to this process.
- The establishment of a South African-style Truth and Reconciliation Commission seems imperative to heal past wounds.

- Selective amnesty by the government is necessary, while 'criminals' should be given a chance to experience justice.
- Economic development should be based on egalitarian principles to avoid widening the gap between the poor and the rich.
- Checks and balances should be put in place on all government activities.
- Combating corruption, collusion and nepotism among the elite should be of high priority in order to keep the economy going and to keep people satisfied with their expectations and the political system.
- Adopting a legal system that upholds the *rule of law* must be a priority.
- Most importantly, attention should be given to traditional East Timorese leaders and to customary practice. Ways of integrating local traditions into the nation's political and legal/practice system should be explored.

A nation will survive not because of forces from outside; its survival will depend on how its people endeavour to sort out problems within their own society.

References

Babo Soares, D.D.C. *et al.*, 1996. *Pola Penyusunan Kesempatan Kerja Repelita VII Timor Timur 1997-2003* (A Framework for Employment in the Seventh Five Year Program for East Timor, 1997-2003), Kerjasama Unversitas Timor Timur dan Kantor Wilayah Tenaga Kerja Timor Timur.

Cox, S. and P. Carey, 1995. *Generations of Resistance*. London: Cassell.

de Castro, G.P., 1943. *Timor: Subsídios Para A Sua História*. Agencia Geral das Colonias. Lisboa – MCMXLIV.

Diario de Notícias, 28/10/1999 (Portuguese daily newspaper).

Duarte, T., 1930. *Timor: Ante-Câmara do Inferno?* Tip. 'Minerva' de Gaspar Pinto de Sousa & Irmão.

Dunn, James, 1996. *Timor: A People Betrayed*. Sydney: ABC Books.

Fox, James J., 1999. 'Language History in Eastern Indonesia and East Timor'. Paper at the Canberra Workshop of the East Timor Study Group, 27-28 April 1999, supported and sponsored by Centre for Democratic Institutions, the Research School of Pacific and Asian Studies, and the Faculty of Asian Studies, at the Australian National University.

Hull, G.S., 1996. *Mai kolia Tetun: A Course in Tetum-Praca, the Lingua Franca of East Timor*. North Sydney: Australian Catholic Relief, Australian Catholic Social Justice Council (rev. ed.).

Kompas, June 1999 (Indonesian daily newspaper).

Ó Publico 19/11/1999. *Nova Força Política Apresenta e Princípios: Abílio Araújo à Frente de Xanana* (Portuguese daily newspaper).

Therik, Gerzon Tom, 1995. Wehali: the four corner land: the cosmology and traditions of a Timorese ritual centre. Unpublished PhD thesis, Department of Anthropology, Research School of Pacific and Asian Studies, The Australian National University.

Traube, Elizabeth G., 1986. *Cosmology and Social Life: Ritual Exchange Among the Mambai of East Timor.* Chicago: University of Chicago Press.